GENERAL SIR RICHARD MEADE

GENERAL SIR RICHARD MEADE

AND THE

FEUDATORY STATES OF CENTRAL AND SOUTHERN INDIA

A RECORD OF

FORTY- THREE YEARS' SERVICE

AS

SOLDIER, POLITICAL OFFICER AND ADMINISTRATOR

THOMAS HENRY THORNTON, C.S.I., D.C.L.

GYAN

Published by

GYAN

Gyan Publishing House
5, Ansari Road
Daryaganj, New Delhi-110002
Phone: 011-47034999, 9811692060
E-mail: books@gyanbooks.com

Distribution Network
gyanbooks.com
India, USA, Canada, UK, Australia, France

ISBN: 978-81-212-9284-9 (PB)
First Published, 1898

2nd Impression 2023

Printed at: Gyan Press, Delhi.

GENERAL SIR RICHARD MEADE

AUTHOR: THOMAS HENRY THORNTON

GENERAL SIR RICHARD MEADE

AND THE

FEUDATORY STATES OF CENTRAL AND SOUTHERN INDIA

A RECORD OF

FORTY-THREE YEARS' SERVICE

AS

SOLDIER, POLITICAL OFFICER AND ADMINISTRATOR

BY

THOMAS HENRY THORNTON, C.S.I., D.C.L.

SOMETIME FOREIGN SECRETARY TO THE GOVERNMENT OF INDIA
AUTHOR OF "THE LIFE AND WORK OF COLONEL
SIR ROBERT SANDEMAN"

WITH PORTRAIT, MAP AND ILLUSTRATIONS

LONGMANS, GREEN, AND CO.
39 PATERNOSTER ROW, LONDON
NEW YORK AND BOMBAY
1898

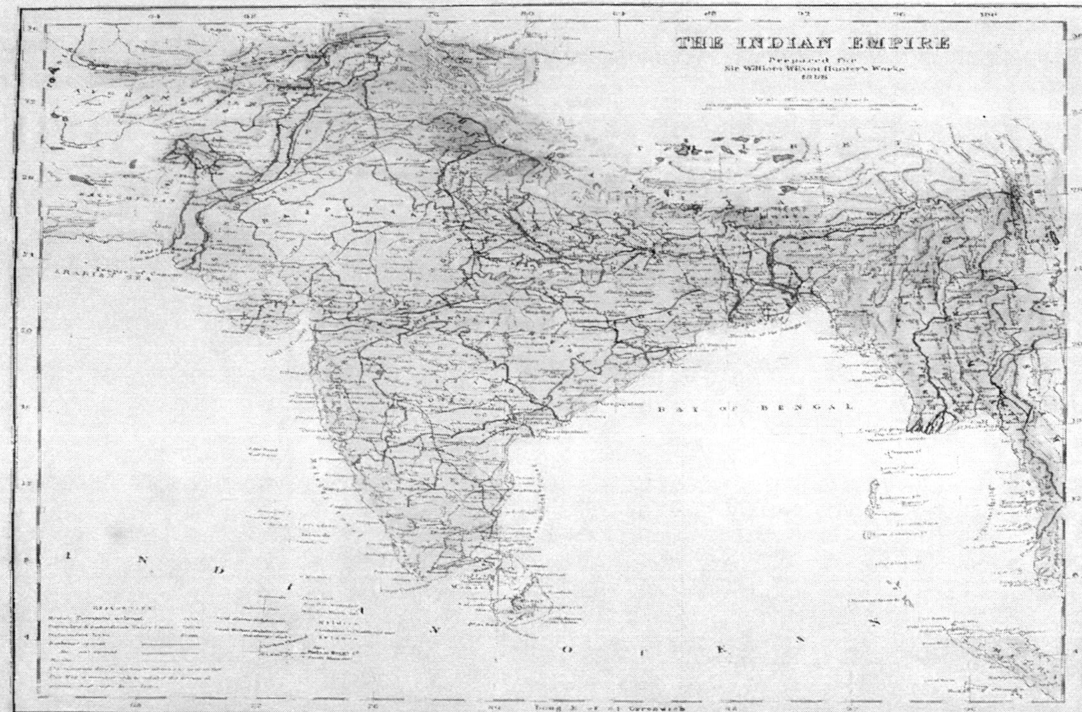

NOTE.—*In this Map Dependent States and Territories which came under Sir R. Meade's political or administrative control are coloured dark yellow.*

INTRODUCTORY.

THE Indian career of the late GENERAL SIR RICHARD MEADE, K.C.S.I., C.I.E., who died at Hyères in March, 1894, though little known in England, has some claim to be remembered.

For it was the career of one who, besides performing valuable military services, conducted, for upwards of twenty years, the relations of the British Government with some of the principal Native States of India, and, as confidential adviser and Agent to seven successive Viceroys, played a more or less important part in influencing and carrying out their policy.

And it was a career in some respects unique. Born in 1821, Meade proceeded to India so long ago as 1838. For nearly twenty years he passed an uneventful life as regimental or staff officer in the Bengal Army, without a chance of military distinction. His social qualities made him a general favourite, and he was recognised as a very promising officer, but there was little scope for his abilities, and none could have predicted that the genial infantry captain of those days was to become known to fame as a dashing leader of cavalry, and as having filled with credit four of the highest political appointments under the Crown in India.

But so it was. On the outbreak of the great Mutiny of 1857, he held the office of Brigade-Major of the Gwalior Contingent—a force maintained at the expense of SINDHIA, the Maráatha chief, but officered by Englishmen and composed largely of sepoys from Hindústán. The force mutinied; several officers and other Europeans—men, women and children—were shot down, and Captain Meade and his young wife, the present LADY MEADE (whose calmness and courage during these trying times were specially noticed by the Government of India), with difficulty escaped to Agra.

At Agra he took part in the engagements with the mutineers, and raised a regiment of cavalry, which, under the name of "Meade's Horse," did admirable service for four years.

In June, 1858, when Sindhia's own army deserted to the rebels, and Sindhia himself fled for his life to Agra, Meade was selected to escort him to the camp of SIR HUGH ROSE (afterwards LORD STRATHNAIRN), who, after a brilliant campaign in Central India, had marched from Kálpi to recapture Gwalior and reinstate the Mahárája in his capital.

By dint of a forced march of sixty-five miles in twenty-four hours Meade reached the General's head-quarters at Morár (the old cantonment of the Contingent) on the morning of the 18th June. Leaving the Mahárája in camp he accompanied Sir Hugh Rose as A.D.C. during the action on the following day, and, after the defeat of the enemy, conducted the British troops through the narrow streets of the town to the palace, still in possession of the rebels.

At great personal risk he entered the palace, full at the time of armed and excited soldiery, parleyed with the occupants and induced them to surrender without firing a shot; thus saving many lives and much destruction of property, and winning the lasting gratitude of the Marátha Chief.

After the recapture of Gwalior he was employed on a commission for trying and punishing the rebel soldiers, then scoured the country with his cavalry and, thanks to his influence with local chiefs, accurate intelligence and rapid movement, had the good fortune to capture and bring to justice the rebel leader TANTIA TOPI—believed to have been one of the NÁNA's chief agents in perpetrating the Cawnpore massacres.

His firmness, tact and justice in dealing with the chiefs and people with whom he was brought in contact attracted the notice of the Governor-General, LORD CANNING, who appointed him in 1859, first temporarily then permanently, POLITICAL AGENT AT GWALIOR.

Two years afterwards he was advanced to the post of GOVERNOR-GENERAL'S AGENT FOR THE STATES OF CENTRAL INDIA; a most important charge, including, besides the great Marátha States of Gwalior and Indore and their subordinate chiefs, the Afghán principality of Bhopál (next to Hyderabad the most powerful Mussulman State in India) and the Rájput States in Bundelkhand and Rewah—all in a condition more or less disturbed, and some of them but recently the seat of war.

Here he completely re-established the *pax Britannica*, and maintained it successfully for eight years, without once calling out the regular troops; settled numberless disputes and several political questions of great delicacy; opened up the country with new roads; established rest-houses and dispensaries; laid the foundations of forest conservancy; advanced education and administrative reforms; working, at the same time, with judgment and caution; taking care to have the Chiefs with him in all he did and enjoining the same course on his subordinates.

For his success he was decorated with the C.S.I., on the recommendation of SIR JOHN LAWRENCE, and it led to his being selected by LORD MAYO, in 1870, to succeed Mr. LEWIN BOWRING in the CHIEF COMMISSIONERSHIP of MYSORE, as an officer specially qualified to prepare the province for restoration to native rule.

In 1873, while closely engaged in the work entrusted to him, he was appointed by LORD NORTHBROOK President of a Commission to inquire into serious charges of maladministration made against MALHAR

RAO, Gaekwar of Baroda—the first in rank, if not in power, of all the Marátha Ruling Chiefs; and in 1875 took part in the Chief's trial for an alleged attempt to poison COLONEL PHAYRE, the British Resident.

After the conclusion of the trial, but before the decision was announced, he was appointed to succeed SIR LEWIS PELLY (whose health had broken down) as SPECIAL COMMISSIONER FOR THE AFFAIRS OF BARODA.

In this capacity he carried out the sentence of deposition passed against Malhar Rao, put down a rising at Baroda in his favour, took part in selecting his successor, and reorganised the administration on principles which have been followed ever since, to the great benefit of all classes in the State.

In recognition of his services on the first Baroda Commission he was created K.C.S.I.; his services as Special Commissioner were publicly acknowledged in the *Gazette*, and, in November, 1875, he was selected by Lord Northbrook for the office of RESIDENT AT HYDERABAD—the blue ribbon of the political service and then regarded as the "most important and difficult position in India".

Here for five years he ably represented the British Government during a critical period.

While firmly maintaining, as in duty bound, the supremacy of the Suzerain Power, and withstanding the assumption of uncontrolled authority by the late Chief's minister, he strenuously upheld the interests of the Hyderabad State and of its Ruler (then a minor), for whom he persisted in securing the benefit of a proper education.

Surrounded by intrigue on every side he identified himself with no party in the State, but earned the respect and esteem even of those whose policy and projects it was his duty to oppose.

During the excitement of the Afghán war he aided Sir Sálár Jang in maintaining order in the Nizám's territories, and heartily seconded his efforts in effecting administrative reforms; and, at length, all serious difficulties in Hyderabad being over, and the administration of the Berár districts well in hand, he was able to retire from the service with the satisfaction of feeling that he had fully accomplished the work he was specially appointed to perform.

Accordingly, in March, 1881 (at the close of an extended term of office), he returned to England, after forty-three years of Indian service, during which he paid only one brief visit to his native country.

After retirement Sir Richard Meade was the subject of a series of malignant newspaper attacks; but, for reasons of State, he was debarred from either prosecuting his assailant or publishing the despatches in which his conduct was completely vindicated. Extracts from those despatches are now published for the first time, not indeed for the vindication of his memory (no such vindication is required), but for the satisfaction of his family.

The libels are forgotten, and throughout the States of Central and Southern India—territories as populous as Italy and little less extensive than the German Empire—the memory of RICHARD MEADE is still held in reverence and affectionate regard as a firm and friendly representative of the protecting Power and the impersonation of justice, courtesy and honour.

* * * * * * * * * * *

Such is a brief sketch of the career and services which it is the object of the following pages more fully to describe.

The task, besides being most congenial, has been rendered comparatively easy by the never-failing help of one whose name the writer hopes to be forgiven for mentioning—Sir Richard's eldest daughter, Mrs. W. H. CAINE, whose careful cataloguing, indexing and analysis of her late father's voluminous papers would do credit to a highly trained official. And MAJOR (now LIEUTENANT-COLONEL) MALCOLM MEADE, the eldest son, at present British Resident at Bushire, furnished an excellent sketch of his father's career, which has formed the basis of the present narrative.

The chief difficulty has lain, not in want of well-arranged material, but in the confidential character of the work in which the subject of the memoir was engaged. Much that is deeply interesting, much that is important, much that is due to the memory of the deceased has had, perforce, to be omitted, but sufficient remains to show (it is hoped) how much England and her great Dependency are indebted to the energy, courage and wisdom of the late *doyen* of the political service of India.

The writer has also to acknowledge the valuable assistance he has received from—

SIR LEPEL HENRY GRIFFIN, K.C.S.I. (late Agent to the Governor-General for the States of Central India).

MR. LEWIN BOWRING, C.S.I. (formerly Chief Commissioner of Mysore).

MR. P. S. MELVILL, C.S.I. (late Agent to the Governor-General for Baroda).

THE RT. HON. SIR RICHARD COUCH (formerly Chief Justice of Bengal, and President of the Commission to inquire into the charges against Malhar Rao).

COLONEL G. H. TREVOR, C.S.I. (late Governor-General's Agent for Rájputána, and formerly First Assistant to the Resident at Hyderabad).

And is much indebted to—

THE RT. HON. THE EARL OF NORTHBROOK,

THE RT. HON. THE EARL OF CRANBROOK,

THE RT. HON. THE COUNTESS OF LYTTON,

for having kindly placed important letters at his disposal; and to SIR WILLIAM HUNTER, K.C.S.I., for the map of India attached.

In the spelling of Oriental names the system employed in the *Imperial Gazetteer of India* has been generally followed. Under that system the vowels are ordinarily sounded as in Italian, and the consonants transliterated from the Úrdú by fixed equivalents; but an exception is made in the case of names of places of which the spelling is fixed by usage. Thus *Cawnpore* is written, not *Káhnpúr; Mysore*, not *Maisúr; Meerut*, not *Mírath*. In one case the *Gazetteer* spelling has not been followed. The name of the Nizám's capital is written *Hyderabad*, not *Haidarábád*. The latter is, of course, more accurate, but the former is the spelling officially employed by the Calcutta Foreign Office, and has the sanction of long usage.

CONTENTS.

CHAPTER IX.

CHAPTER X.

CHAPTER XI.

CHAPTER XV.

CHAPTER XVI.

CHAPTER XVII.

CHAPTER XVIII.

CHAPTER XXII.

CHAPTER XXIII.

CHAPTER XXIV.

CHAPTER XXV.

LIST OF ILLUSTRATIONS, ETC.

CHAPTER I.

BIRTH, PARENTAGE, AND EARLY YEARS.

Birth and parentage—Account of the Meade family—Their attitude in the Irish rebellions of 1568-1601—Execution of Patrick Meed —Conduct in the Civil War—Meade's father and mother—Innishannon and its surroundings—Meade's education and early life —Appointed cadet in the East India Company's service.

General Sir Richard John Meade, K.C.S.I., C.I.E., the subject of this memoir, was born on the 25th September, 1821, at Innishannon, a picturesque village on the river Bandon, about seven miles (by road) from Kinsale, County Cork; and was the eldest son of Captain John Meade, R.N., and Elizabeth, daughter of Thomas Quin, Esq., K.C., of Fir Grove, Innishannon.

His father's family, variously designated in earlier writings *Le Med*, *Miagh*, *Meagh* and *Meed*, is one of the oldest in the county.

Settled, from a remote period, in the valley of the Bandon, it held, in the sixteenth century, a high position among the burghers of Kinsale, a quaint old town on a steep hill-side, overlooking the land-locked estuary which forms the harbour; a town full of historic memories,—of Danish raids and settlements in days gone by, of fights with Spanish fleets in later times, of Rupert, of Cromwell, of James II., of Marlborough, and giving a name to the great headland, which, towering high above the waves of the Atlantic, serves as a beacon to the liners from the West.

To return to the family:—

There is a deed still in existence executed by Adam Meagh of County Cork in the year A.D. 1341, making grants of nineteen manors to certain persons specified, to which his seal is appended, comprising a coat-of-arms almost identical with that now borne by the Meade family.

A stone tablet, on the north side of the altar in the old church of Kinsale, states in Latin that "Patrick Meed, often sovereign [*i.e.* mayor] of Kinsale, rebuilt this sanctuary in A.D. 1558, for the good of his own soul and the souls of his parents". In his will, preserved in the British Museum, he leaves Tysassany[1] (Tissasson)—two miles from Kinsale—and Knocknacorry to his son Robert, a third part of his land to his wife, and the remainder to his son Richard.

Patrick Meed (or Meagh) perished on the scaffold in 1577 during the troubles in Elizabeth's reign, when the Meaghs were, according to Smith, the historian of Cork, "among the chief lords and gentles of the county".

What was the particular offence with which Patrick Meed was charged is not stated, but it is probable enough that, as a staunch Roman Catholic and leading citizen, he was implicated in the great Desmond rebellion, which, for fifteen years,—from A.D. 1568 to A.D. 1583—desolated the province of Munster.

Queen Elizabeth's policy of forcing Protestantism upon an unwilling population and the high-handed proceedings of her Lords Deputies had caused wide-

[1] Tysassany means "place of the Saxons," and refers, doubtless, to some old Saxon settlement in that locality.

spread disaffection,[1] and when, with the Pope's blessing, James Fitzmaurice of Desmond raised the standard of revolt he was joined, we are told, "by all the English and Irish of Munster from the Barrow to Cape Clear". Each British triumph was followed by wholesale executions; and it was, doubtless, on one of these occasions that Patrick Meed fell victim.

But executions failed to stem the tide of disaffection. Then wholesale forfeiture was tried, and attempts made to "plant" the confiscated lands with British settlers. But all in vain. The Munster confiscations were followed in 1589 by a general insurrection of the Irish clans, until in 1601 a Spanish fleet of fifty sail, under Don Juan del Aguila, entered the harbour of Kinsale and, with the connivance of the leading men, including presumably the Meaghs, occupied the town. On this occasion, we are told, "the sovereign [or mayor] opened the gates to the invaders, with his white wand in his hand, going to billet and cess them in several houses, more ready than if they had been the Queen's forces". And when the Queen's forces, under Mountjoy, advanced for the recapture of the town and fort, they found the entire population hostile; and when the clans which had flocked to the assistance of the invaders were defeated and driven off, they reassembled—it may be noted—at Innishannon, afterwards the home of the Meade family.

[1] Holinshed informs us that a deputation was sent from Ireland to remonstrate. The Queen in Council, however, instead of redressing grievances, imprisoned the members of the deputation, but, at the same time, observed to her Lord Deputy that, "though her Irish subjects had behaved badly, they should be *pulled*, not *flayed*".

But whatever may have been the attitude of the Meaghs towards their Sovereign in 1577 and 1601, it was, in after times, extremely loyal.

During the Civil War, Robert Meagh of Tissasson (grandson of the Robert Meagh above named, and great-grandson of Patrick Meed) was a staunch Royalist. Prince Rupert is said to have obtained shelter in the mansion, and, in acknowledgment of the service rendered, to have left a picture of himself and a chain which were long kept as heirlooms in the family. A ditch once surrounding the mansion (which has disappeared) is still locally known as "Rupert's Trench".

But Robert Meagh suffered severely for his loyalty. Eighteen properties are mentioned in Cromwell's "Book of Forfeitures" as having been confiscated from him and others of his name, and it is said that the family mansion was, for a time, occupied by Cromwell's son-in-law Ireton.

After the Restoration Robert Meagh regained all he had lost, but was again deprived of his estates at the Revolution of 1689. The estates were then granted to his nephew Richard Meade, a Protestant, and ultimately passed to Richard's nephew Martin, from whom the subject of this memoir was a direct descendant.

The land on which the old house of Tissasson stood is in the possession of De Courcy Meade, Esq., (Sir Richard's cousin), but the original estate has been divided, and a large portion has passed into other hands.

Sir Richard's grandfather, Richard Meade, took holy orders, and became Rector of Innishannon (about eight miles from Tissasson), and married Mary, eldest daughter of the twenty-fifth Lord Kingsale, whose family, De Courcy, claims descent from Charlemagne, and whose peerage is the oldest in the United Kingdom.

Captain John Meade, Sir Richard's father, was the second son of this marriage. He joined the navy in 1798, and was present, as midshipman on board the *Magnanime*, at the action off Lough Swilly, when the French line-of-battle ship *Hoche*, with Wolfe Tone on board, was taken. He was on active service in American waters until 1808, when he joined the *Tonnant* under his uncle, Admiral de Courcy, off the coast of Portugal, and witnessed the battle of Corunna —afterwards doing his best to alleviate the sufferings of the troops. After a few more years' service on the Brazil station he retired and married in 1814,—devoting the remaining years of his life, thirty-seven in number, to the education of his family of five daughters and four sons, and to the kindly treatment of those around him. Besides possessing the generous instincts and practical training of a tried naval officer, he was blessed with a specially happy temperament, was a universal favourite and general peacemaker, and was one of the few naval officers of the period who was never known to use an oath.

Sir Richard's mother was, as we have stated, Elizabeth, daughter of Thomas Quin. Her father was a lawyer of considerable repute and good family. She was a lady of strong convictions and much religious earnestness; but her religious opinions being of a somewhat severe and gloomy character, her views of life and happiness presented a marked contrast to those of her eminently blithesome husband.

Their son Richard, whose earnestness of purpose was as remarkable as the geniality of his disposition, seems to have combined in these respects the virtues of both parents.

However this may be, the subject of our memoir was connected (it will be perceived), both on the father's and the mother's side, with the old landed gentry of the South of Ireland—a class not favourably known, perhaps, for thrift, but which has long been distinguished for pluck, courtesy, and cheeriness; and has produced many distinguished members of the civil, military and naval services of the Crown,—including, with many others, the present Marquis of Lansdowne, Admiral Lord Clanwilliam (a Meade), and his brother, Sir Robert Meade, the late Under Secretary at the Colonial Office, F. M. Lord Roberts, Lord Charles and Lord William Beresford.

Meade's father was, as we have seen, in the navy; one uncle, Lieutenant Michael de Courcy Meade, of the 39th Regiment, fell at the battle of Vittoria; another, General Frederick Meade, of the Connaught Rangers, served through the Peninsular War, and was badly wounded at the battle of Salamanca; he then proceeded to India on the staff of Sir Thomas Reynell and took part in the second siege and capture of Bhartpur, under Sir Stapleton Cotton, afterwards Lord Combermere, and was the proximate cause of his nephew's adopting an Indian career. Sir Richard's two younger brothers (one still living) were in the Royal Marines.

Innishannon, the birthplace of Sir Richard Meade,

is a pretty village in one of the loveliest portions of the valley of the Bandon River:—

"The pleasant Bandon crowned with many a wood,"[1]

a blending of hill and dale, forest and running water, with glimpses of ruined castles, offering a succession of views of romantic interest and beauty.

"Among such scenes," says Major Meade, "my father and his brothers were brought up.

"Here," continues Major Meade, "they mixed with the country people, the frank Irish peasantry, who formed the back-bone of the battalions who fought in the Peninsula and were to fight in India. Here my father must have acquired his taste for riding,[2] fishing and boating which he retained through life; and received an early training which left its impress on his character.

"My father's school studies were, at first, conducted by the village schoolmaster—a personage of the name of Horgan, who is said to have scrupulously obeyed the injunction against 'sparing the rod'. He succeeded, however, in spite of—or, perhaps, in consequence of—his somewhat Spartan system, in grounding his pupils well; and when my father went, at the age of ten, to the Royal Naval School at New Cross, he took a high position among his fellows. The training received at the school was excellent, and, although my father often regretted that his education was cut short early, he was probably more thoroughly trained and

[1] Spenser's *Faery Queene* (book iv., canto xi., stanza 44), part of which is said to have been written in a castle near Innishannon.

[2] He was long remembered at Innishannon as a "red-haired lad, who scoured the country on a white pony called Chevalier".

better equipped with general knowledge than many who now-a-days pass competitive examinations after long and expensive cramming. 'Your father,' said an old friend of his to me, 'was one of the best men all round I ever met with. Some men are good at one thing, and some at another, but your father could do everything well. He was a good rider and shot, and was, besides, an accomplished musician, good draughtsman and billiard player.'

"In after years my father became vice-president of the council of his old school, and it was a curious coincidence that a namesake, Admiral Lord Clanwilliam, who is also a Richard Meade, head of the Meades of Ballintober, another branch of the family, was president of the council at the same time.

"It was originally intended that my father should go into the navy, and, when he was ten, a naval cadetship was offered for him by Lord Lauderdale, my grandmother's cousin; but my grandfather, upon consideration, decided to save his son 'from the miseries he had himself endured'. Ultimately, through the influence of his uncle, my father and his two brothers entered the army. Before the age of seventeen my father obtained, through my grandfather's cousin, Sir A. Agnew, a cadetship in the East India Company's service, and started for India *viâ* the Cape of Good Hope in March, 1838."

CHAPTER II.

INDIA—FIRST NINETEEN YEARS.

Proceeds to Arracan—After holding various temporary appointments joins the Gwalior Contingent in 1845—Origin and history of Contingents explained—Advancement in the service—Marriage in 1853—Proceeds to Burmah and serves for a year as Assistant Adjutant-General of the Pegu Division—Returns to Gwalior, 1855, until the outbreak of the Mutiny of 1857.

YOUNG Meade reached Calcutta in July, 1838, and was at once posted as ensign to the 58th N.I., but was transferred in the following November to the 65th N.I.—on the *cadre* of which he remained until he elected to join the Bengal Staff Corps. The 65th N.I. was stationed in Assam, and consequently took no part in the campaigns on the North-West frontier, but was engaged in garrison duty in our recently acquired province of Arracan and Tenasserim.

This monotonous duty gave little scope for his abilities, but he took the opportunity of mastering Persian and the vernacular languages of the Presidency, and while his social qualities rendered him a general favourite, he was soon recognised as a very promising officer.

He became a lieutenant in March, 1840, and was appointed in February, 1841, to officiate as interpreter and quartermaster of his regiment.

During the next two years he was employed in the

Commissariat Department in Dinapur and Cawnpore: in 1844 he returned to his regiment as interpreter and quartermaster; in October, 1845, he became station staff officer at Nowgong in Bundelkhand, and two months later was appointed second in command of the 6th Infantry Battalion of the Gwalior Contingent.

And here it may be well to explain, for the benefit of the general reader, that a "Contingent" *was* a special force, maintained in some of the principal native States at the expense of the ruling chiefs, to enable them, in accordance with the terms of their engagement, to co-operate effectively with the British Government in time of war, and to maintain order in their territories in time of peace.

The organisation of such special forces was the outcome of a policy, greatly extended and developed (if not invented) by Lord Mornington, afterwards Marquis of Wellesley, between 1798 and 1805, and continued, after an interval of disastrous reaction, by Lord Moira, afterwards Marquis of Hastings, between 1813 and 1822, and by Lord Dalhousie and most of his successors—the policy of welding together the principal States of India with the British Government, as Paramount Power, for joint defence against external danger and the maintenance of internal peace: a policy long accepted as the only true one for England in India, though the degree and method of its enforcement have varied and will vary from time to time.

It was effected in the days of Lord Hastings and his great predecessor by a system of treaty-engagements, known as Subsidiary Alliances, most of them still subsisting, their main object being, to quote Lord Hastings' words, "to render the British Government paramount in effect, if not declaredly so, to hold the other states as vassals, though not in name, and to oblige them in return for our guarantee and protection to perform the two great feudatory duties of supporting our rule with all their forces, and submitting their mutual differences to our arbitration".

In furtherance of this policy a detachment of the British army, technically known as the Subsidiary Force, was located within or near the boundaries of the State concerned, for its protection from aggression and the maintenance of the ruler's legitimate authority.

But this force, it should be explained, was not to be employed on ordinary duties of civil administration, or collection of the revenues; indeed, the British Government generally agreed not to interfere in such matters, but only on occasions of importance.

Per contra a subsidy, sufficient for the charges of the force, was furnished by the protected State, either in periodical money payments or by territorial cession, more frequently the latter; and at the same time, a force of native troops—known as the Contingent—of a strength and character defined in the engagement, was to be maintained in readiness to act with the British troops, and for its efficiency the protected State was answerable.

Many important consequences followed from the relation thus established between the Paramount Power and its subordinate allies, but they need not be referred to here. Suffice it to say that, under the provisions of the several engagements, Contingents of various strength were arranged for in all the principal States of Central and Southern India.

But it was found in practice that, while the British Government's part in the transaction—*viz.*, the furnishing of an efficient Subsidiary Force,—was faithfully performed, the native Contingent was often unready when called for, and when furnished, inefficient and unreliable.

In these circumstances some of the principal States were induced to place their Contingents under the command and control of British officers; and in this way "anglicised" Contingents were formed in Hyderabad, Bhopál, Málwa, Gwalior, and elsewhere.

The services of some of the reformed Contingents, notably that of Hyderabad, were very valuable; but the conduct of several in the great Mutiny gave the system, as then practised, a bad name, and many were disbanded; but the system still survives, under another name and altered conditions, in the Imperial Service Corps, which many of our Feudatories are now maintaining; a special force, not "anglicised," like the old reformed Contingents, but subject to the *inspection* of selected British officers. Some of these Imperial Service Corps, especially those of Kashmír and Hunza, have already done brilliant service in campaigns, and nine have taken part with the Imperial forces in the recent military operations against the tribes of the North-West frontier and earned the hearty thanks of the British Government.[1]

[1] During the late campaign on the North-West frontier, Imperial Service Corps from the following States were employed:—

But we are greatly anticipating events and must return to the Gwalior Contingent as it was in 1845. This force was originally formed in 1817 by the Maráthа chief, Daulat Rao Sindhia, with a view of effectually co-operating with the British Government in the suppression of the Pindári hordes. It was, at first, far from efficient, but was afterwards reorganised by his successor and placed in charge of British officers.

After the mutiny of the Gwalior army in 1843 and its destruction at the battles of Mahárájpur and Panniar the Contingent (which had behaved excellently) was enlarged, and consisted, when Meade joined it, of seven infantry and two cavalry regiments and five batteries of artillery; it had a full complement of English officers and was recruited (unfortunately as it happened) from the same sources as the British sepoy army.

With this corps he served continuously (except for a short time in 1853-4) until he joined the Political Department in 1859.

In October, 1850, he was made officiating Commandant of his regiment, and in 1851, Brigade-major of the entire force; Paymaster in 1852, Commissariat officer

Patiála (Sikh), cavalry and infantry.
Jhínd (Sikh), infantry.
Nábha (Sikh), infantry.
Kapúrthala (Sikh), infantry.
Maler Kotla (Muhammadan), sappers.
Jodhpur (Rájput), lancers.
Sirmor (Hill Rájput), sappers.
Jaipur (Rájput), transport.
Gwalior (Marátha), transport.

H.H. the Mahárája of Patiála, Mahárája Sir Partáb Singh of Jodhpur and the Mahárája of Kúch Behár acted as extra aides-de-camp to the General commanding; and General Elles, in his despatch on the operations of the Mohmand Field Force, reports that "the Imperial Service Corps under his command had proved their fitness to fight in the first rank".

in 1853, holding the three appointments conjointly. His work, therefore, must have been constant and engrossing, but he found time during this period to pass with credit a departmental examination in civil engineering.

Early in 1853 an event of great importance for his future happiness occurred. Captain Meade was united in marriage with Emily, second daughter of Colonel Duncan Malcolm, then Resident at Gwalior, a very promising member of the political service,[1] and nephew of the great soldier, statesman and historian, General Sir John Malcolm—a distinguished member of the "galaxy of talent" which gave "solidity and splendour to the Company's government during the first quarter of the present century".

Mrs. Meade's sister was in the following year married to Captain, now General Sir John Murray, who raised the cavalry regiment, well known during the Mutiny under the name of "Murray's Ját Horse" and now as the 14th Bengal Lancers.

In 1852 war broke out with Burmah, and Meade hoped for active service, but his old regiment, the 65th N.I., though not far from the scene of operations, was required for garrison duty in Arracan and was not moved to Rangoon until the close of the war. Meade at once rejoined his regiment, but by the time it

[1] He had been for many years assistant to the Resident at Hyderabad, where Lady Meade was born, and was afterwards Resident at Jodhpur in Rájputána. He left Gwalior and became Resident at Baroda in 1854, where he died at the early age of forty-seven, one month after the death of his wife.

arrived in Rangoon the war was practically over and the annexation of Pegu proclaimed. He was appointed Assistant-Adjutant General for the Pegu Division, but saw no opening for military distinction, and, accordingly, after an uneventful year of service in Burmah, returned early in 1855 to his old post in Gwalior.

He was again appointed Brigade-major of the Contingent, and for two years carried on the ordinary duties of his office without the slightest anticipation of the event which was the turning-point of his career—the great Mutiny—which, after smouldering for a considerable period, burst into flame at Meerut on the 10th May, 1857, then rapidly extended from one military station to another, and lost us temporarily all the central portion of Northern India.

As to its cause or causes—whether they were religious, or political, or social, or all combined—opinions are endless, but there can be no doubt that the revolt was primarily a military one, the result of growing disaffection in the native army, and especially that portion of it recruited from the recently annexed territories of Oude; the rebellious movement consequently extended not only to troops forming part of the British native army, but to the Contingents of our native allies which had been recruited from the same localities.

What happened at Gwalior will be narrated in the next chapter.

CHAPTER III.

GWALIOR.

Account of Gwalior—Its extent, population, and political condition in 1857—Sindhia—His antecedents—Invested with full powers of sovereignty in 1852—Appoints as his Minister Dinkar Rao—Dinkar Rao's reforms—Major Malcolm, the political agent, transferred to another appointment—Dinkar Rao dismissed from office, and affairs fall into confusion—Is reinstated on the representation of Major Malcolm's successor, Major Charters Macpherson—Visit of Sindhia to Lord Canning in 1857—Its effect—Description of the town, fortress and cantonments of Gwalior.

GWALIOR is the most important of the group of Feudatory States [1] which occupy the table-land of Central India, between the Bombay Presidency on the South-West, and the Valley of the Jamna on the North-East.

It comprises the remnant of the territory of Sindhia left after the Maráṭha wars of 1803, 1817, and 1843;

[1] The term *feudatory*, as applied to the Protected Chiefs and States of India, has been objected to. From a purely legal point of view the term is, of course, inaccurate; but there is much to be said in its favour, and it has, *inter alia*, the sanction of long usage. *Vassal*, the proper correlative of *Suzerain*, offends susceptibilities; and *Dependent* is open to the same objection. *Subordinate Ally*, a term sometimes employed, is apt to be misleading and is often cumbrous. *Native Prince* is not sufficiently distinctive, as it includes titular as well as territorial chiefs, and, for this and other reasons, is not favoured by the latter. Upon the whole the term *feudatory* seems at once the most descriptive and least open to serious objection.

but even now has an area of more than 30,000 square miles—an area, that is to say, larger than Scotland —and a population of about 3,000,000.

The population is extremely mixed, comprising, besides Maráthas (the ruling race), Rájputs, Játs, Ahírs, Gújars, Brahmans, Bundelas and other Hindu races, with a sprinkling of Muhammadans; but the various races are not, as is generally the case in British India, blended into one organised community, but form a collection of local and tribal chiefships. Eight of these chiefships are "mediatised"—that is, held on conditions guaranteed by the British Government; but most of them are at the mercy of the Marátha chief; and one of the functions of the Contingent was to aid him in keeping these petty chiefs, whether "mediatised" or not, in order.

This state of affairs, it may be observed in passing, however objectionable from the point of view of civilised administration, was not without its advantages in the dark days of 1857.

Sindhia is the family name of a series of Marátha chieftains who rose to importance on the decadence of the great Marátha power established by Sívaji and his successor. At the close of the last century, Mahdoji Sindhia, the second of the series, exercised dominion, not only in his hereditary fief in Málwa, but in Broch (on the Gulf of Cambay), in the fairest portions of the Deccan, in Dehli and Agra, in Rájputána and the Sikh States south of the river Satlaj. With the help of a sepoy force, 26,000 strong, organised by Count de Boigne, on the model of British battalions, he became the most formidable member of the Marátha Confederation, and though nominally servant of the *Peshwa*,[1] was in reality the ruler of Hindústán.

The name of his successor, Daulat Rao Sindhia, figures largely in the Marátha wars of 1803 and 1817, and his northern army, commanded and officered by Frenchmen, constituted the most formidable force we had to deal with in the early years of the present century.

But his power was completely broken by Wellington (then Sir A. Wellesley) at Assay and Argaum, and by Lake at Aligarh, Dehli and Laswári; he was stripped of all his outlying dominions, and by the treaties of 1803-4-5, and subsequently those of 1817-8, he accepted the position of a Protected Feudatory.

The representative of the family, who held the chiefship at the time of the Mutiny, was Ali Jah Jáya Ji Rao Sindhia, a son adopted by the widow of Daulat Rao's successor, who had died childless in 1843. He was recognised by the British Government, but, under the influence of intriguers, the army rose in mutiny and tried to usurp supreme power in the State; whereupon the British Government, in accordance with its treaty obligation, intervened to protect the dynasty; defeated and destroyed the rebellious army at Mahárájpur and Panniar and placed the young chief, then ten years old, upon the throne; and, by a treaty executed in 1844, the Contingent, which had done good service in the war, was increased, and the extra cost provided for by territorial cession; while the rest

[1] *Peshwa* was the title given to the hereditary prime minister, and director of the Marátha Confederacy under the nominal headship of the *fainéant* representative of Sívaji, the founder.

H.H. JÁYA JI RAO SINDHIA,
Mahárája of Gwalior.

of the chief's army was reduced to moderate dimensions.

The Gwalior Chief thus owed his position, and probably his life, to the British Government, and he was not ungrateful. During his minority his conduct was said to be "exemplary," and in 1852, on the death of the President of the Council of Regency, it was decided to invest him with the full powers of the chiefship, ten months before the time appointed in the treaty. At the same time he was induced to appoint as his minister a young Maráthа Brahman, of Gwalior, by name Dinkar Rao, afterwards Rája Sir Dinkar Rao, whose character and rare ability had been discerned by the Political Agent, Major Malcolm.

The minister soon justified his choice, and threw himself energetically into the work of administrative reform. Within less than two years, law and order were established to an extent previously unknown; fiscal oppression was put a stop to; taxation reduced; the subordinate races fairly dealt with; roads constructed; transit duties abolished, and the foundations of an educational system laid, while, thanks to diminished peculation, and a large increase of the cultivated area, the revenues of the State expanded.

But Major Malcolm obtained promotion and proceeded to Baroda, and Gwalior for a time was left to itself, and the result was somewhat disastrous. During the interval which elapsed between Major Malcolm's departure and the advent of his successor, the young Chief, who chafed under the tutelage of the Paramount Power, rashly took the reins into his own hands. The minister, whose reforms had made him a host of enemies, was virtually dismissed from office, and affairs soon drifted into dire confusion.

Fortunately Major Malcolm's successor was an officer of ripe experience and earnestness—Major Charters Macpherson, who had spent the best part of a noble life in humanising the wild races of the Khonds in the malarious hill-tracts of Southern India. Under his influence Sindhia soon saw his error and restored his minister to office, if not to favour, and the administrative reforms were again pushed on.

Early in 1857 Sindhia was taken to Calcutta to pay his respects to the new Viceroy, Lord Canning. He was much pleased at the graciousness of his reception and the assurances conveyed to him that his dynasty would be maintained. He was also greatly impressed with the power and the resources of the British Government; but at the same time he regarded with far more anxiety than British statesmen the signs of disaffection which had manifested themselves in our native army. What his attitude would be towards the Paramount Power in times of difficulty was then far from certain, but it was matter of supreme importance to the British Government.

The territories of the State are scattered; but the northern and most important portion abuts on the valley of the Ganges and its tributaries, and its capital Gwalior is only sixty miles from Agra. The ancient fortress and citadel crowns a precipitous ridge of ochreous sandstone, running from south to north; well under the north end of the ridge (its highest part) lies the old

DINKAR RAO
(afterwards Rája Sir Dinkar Rao, K.C.S.I.),
Minister, Gwalior.

town, close-packed and irregularly built; on the south-west stretches the Lashkar, or military quarter, formerly the standing camp of the Marátha army—now "a filthy collection of mud buildings"—bisected by the bed of a small river flowing round the east side of the town and fortress, towards the river Chambal; in the midst of the Lashkar is the palace of the Mahárája.

Morár, the site of the cantonments of the Contingent force, is three and a half miles east of the town, and five miles north-east of the Lashkar,—on the far side of a deep torrent-bed, spanned by a handsome bridge.[1] Until the preceding rainy season the torrent (known as the *Morár Naddi*), held up by an embankment, flowed by the cantonments in a deep stream; but, providentially, a flood during the last July had carried away the embankment, so that, at the time of the Mutiny, the water was spread out and shallow and thus easily fordable by fugitives. On the west side of the river runs the road to Agra. On the road to Agra, seven miles from the town, was the British Residency.

The Political Agent, as we have stated, was Major Charters Macpherson; his immediate superior, the Governor-General's Agent at Indore, was Lt.-Col. (afterwards Sir Henry) Durand, C.B., R.E., who was acting for Sir Robert Hamilton; the Commander of the Contingent was Brigadier Ramsay, and his Brigade-major was Captain Meade.

[1] This somewhat inconvenient situation was probably selected on military grounds to protect the Contingent from possible attack by Sindhia's army in the event of a repetition of the occurrences of 1843. The possibility of the Contingent mutinying was not thought of.

The force at Gwalior consisted of three infantry, two cavalry regiments and two batteries of the Contingent (stationed at Morár)—the remainder being at Nímach, Ágar, Lalitpur and elsewhere—and Sindhia's army (nearly 10,000 strong) located in the Lashkar. There were no European troops nearer than Agra, and only a single regiment and battery there.

Such was the situation in Gwalior when the tidings came of the outbreak at Meerut, and the occupation of Dehli by the mutineers.

CHAPTER IV.

THE MUTINY AT GWALIOR.

Effects of outbreak at Meerut—Attitude of the Brigadier—Action of Political Agent—Loyal conduct of Sindhia—Ladies and children sent to the Residency and then to the palace for protection—Proceeding disapproved of by the Brigadier—Mrs. Meade and her sister return to cantonments and are followed next day by the other ladies—Action of Brigadier approved by Government of India, and Mrs. Meade and Mrs. Murray's conduct officially eulogised—Anxiety—Outbreak on the 14th June—Conduct of sepoys—Mrs. Murray's narrative of the escape of Captain Meade and those with him from cantonments to the Phulbágh Palace—Political Agent and fugitives leave for Agra on following morning—Sindhia promises to do his best to detain the mutineers at Gwalior—Perils of the journey—Difficulties at the river Chambal—A band of fanatics—Baldeo Singh, a Brahman chief, comes to the rescue and passes them over the river into the Dholpur State—Loyal conduct of its chief—The party reach Agra on the 17th—Rewards to Baldeo Singh and the Rána.

THE news of the events at Meerut and Dehli naturally caused serious alarm at Gwalior,[1] but the Brigadier

[1] Of the events in Gwalior following the Meerut outbreak the best general account is to be found in the despatches of Major Macpherson, the Political Agent, which have been embodied in chap. xxiii. of the memoir of that distinguished officer's services published by his brother in 1865.

Of the outbreak in the cantonments of the Contingent force and the escape of the fugitives to Agra the most graphic narrative yet published is that of Mrs. Coopland, wife of the chaplain (who was one of the victims), in a volume entitled *A Lady's Escape* and his officers generously clung to the belief that their own men at any rate were faithful.

The Brigadier was pressed to send the women and children from cantonments to the Residency, where Sindhia promised to have them protected by a Marátha guard; but the Brigadier, still believing in his sepoys and unwilling to show distrust of them, declined the offer.

And here we must pause to say a word in praise of the service rendered in this crisis of affairs by the Political Agent at Gwalior. Without derogating from the credit due to the Marátha Chief and to his minister, whose conduct deserves the highest recognition, it is only due to the memory of a deserving officer to mention that the Government was at this juncture most faithfully served by its representative at the Court of Sindhia, "who"—to quote the words of Lord Canning's minute—"holding a post of great importance, far removed from his immediate superior at Indore, and often struggling against sickness, discharged his difficult duties with complete success". He was in constant—almost hourly--communication, personally or by letter, with the minister and his chief, and by patient argument and, what is more, by the powerful influence of an earnest and upright character, made the latter at length to feel that loyalty to the British Government was not only his duty but the best policy;

from Gwalior, extracts from which are given in Colonel Malleson's work.

These form the basis of the present narrative, but it has been supplemented by information and letters placed at the writer's disposal by Sir Richard Meade's family.

for it was pointed out with irresistible force that the destruction of British rule would mean, in his case, the simultaneous rising of the Játs, the Rájputs, and other warlike tribes within his territory, at present kept in order by the prestige and power of his great Ally and Suzerain.

Thus influenced Sindhia did his utmost in this anxious time to co-operate with the British Government.

On the 11th of May he placed at the disposal of the Lieutenant-Governor of the North-West Provinces one and a half regiments of infantry, 100 horse and a battery—one half of the Contingent force at Gwalior; on the 13th he agreed to the despatch of a regiment of cavalry; on the 14th he despatched half his own body-guard and a horsed battery to Agra; on the 22nd of May he sent the 1st Infantry Regiment of the Contingent together with his personal Marátha troop of cavalry to assist the local authorities of Etáwah, and on the 27th of May he gave warning that "the Contingent sepoys had entirely ceased to be servants of the British Government".

This warning was duly communicated to the Brigadier; but, while admitting that there were mutinously disposed men amongst his troops, he refused to believe that, as a body, they were unfaithful.

At length, however, the Brigadier became alarmed. On the 28th of May, having received intelligence that the sepoys of the Contingent were to mutiny that night, he issued directions that, when the ladies were out for their usual evening drive, they should take their children with them to the Residency.

This was done, and the ladies of the station, with their families, proceeded in melancholy procession to the place indicated, firmly believing that their husbands, who were to be left in cantonments, would all be murdered. But outside cantonments the outlook was not promising, for on the road they met a body of Marátha horsemen, who galloped wildly round the carriages, calling out, "These people's hearts are broken". They began to fear for their own lives too, and entered the Residency with very sad forebodings.

As no warning of their advent had been given, there had been no time to prepare for their reception; so, in spite of the kind exertions of the Agent's sister, a night of great discomfort followed. But the minister was there and instantly rode off to inform his chief. Sindhia promptly came in person, with a strong body of horse, and posted parties in and near the Residency for its protection. At the same time he strongly recommended that the ladies and their families should be brought next morning to a large English mansion in the palace precincts, as he would be better able to protect them there, while he would thus publicly demonstrate his determination to support the British Government.

The arrangement was gratefully accepted by the Political Agent, and next morning it was carried into effect. The sad *cortège* was headed by a carriage containing the Agent and his sister, Mrs. McLeod Innes, who had anxieties of her own—for her husband, Lieutenant (now General) McLeod Innes, V.C., R.E., was one of the Lucknow garrison—and was preceded and followed by detachments of Sindhia's body-guard. It had to pass through the crowded streets of the native town, and the roof of every house was covered, it is said, with "jeering and insulting spectators,"—a proof that, in electing to "support the British Government," Sindhia was risking the allegiance of his own people; a fact creditable to His Highness's loyalty, but not encouraging to the fugitives.

But the party reached the precincts of the palace without mishap. There had been no time to get the mansion ready for so large a party, so a good deal of discomfort was inevitable; but discomfort was not all that had to be complained of, for the reception was in other respects far from friendly. In the case of the Political Agent, indeed, and those with him, the Maharáni and the chief's adoptive mother, the Baiza Bai, sent kindly messages and dishes from their own table, but the rest of the fugitives (owing probably to the hostile feeling of the chief's *entourage* and servants) were treated with marked neglect and scant courtesy; while the two gentlemen of their party—the chaplain and the young son of a colonel (Hennessey)—were made to deliver up their arms, a circumstance which naturally caused much uneasiness.

That night the General and staff and artillery officers slept in front of the loaded guns, and all passed off quietly. The Brigadier began to think the alarm was false, to trust the sepoys more and Sindhia less. He strongly disapproved of the removal of the ladies and children to the palace and requested their return.

The minister, the Political Agent and others deprecated this course; but Mrs. Meade, whose husband, believing the position of the palace (in the heart of the Lashkar) to be dangerous, desired her return, determined to rejoin him at all risks; and her sister Mrs. Murray decided to accompany her. They returned accordingly and on reaching the cantonments received an ovation from the sepoys, who expressed the greatest delight that the ladies should have shown this mark of confidence in them.

The Brigadier was more than ever convinced that the alarm had been a false one, insisted upon all the other ladies and children returning to cantonments, and reported his proceedings, through the Agent at Indore, to the Government of India. The Government, in concurrence with the officiating Agent—Lieut.-Colonel Durand, no mean authority—entirely approved of the proceedings of the Brigadier, and paid the following handsome tribute to the conduct of the ladies :—

"The Governor-General in Council [so runs the despatch] has viewed with the warmest admiration the calm confidence and decision, and the noble indifference to personal danger exhibited by Mrs. Meade and Mrs. Murray in disregarding the threatened outbreak, and returning to cantonments when they were informed by the Brigadier that their remaining at the palace was fraught with mischief".

The ladies and children returned to cantonments, but there was still anxiety. Day after day brought fresh tidings. There had been mutiny at Ajmír and Nasírábád and Rohilkhand, and there was ominous absence of news from Cawnpore and Allahábad. On 4th June the 7th Regiment of the Contingent, which was stationed at Nímach, revolted and marched to Agra, and other detachments of the force at Sípri and Lalitpur were more or less disaffected.

On the 12th a sanguinary outbreak occurred at Jhánsi, seventy miles distant to the S.S.E., and help was sought from Gwalior. The 4th Infantry Regiment volunteered for the service, and a wing was sent with a battery of artillery under the command of Captain (now General Sir John) Murray. But at Deborah, thirty miles from their destination, the terrible news was brought that every European in Jhánsi had been brutally massacred, so the party had to return. From this moment the men evinced a restless spirit, the artillery were in almost open mutiny, and the officers had the greatest difficulty in restraining the men from breaking out on the march.

The next morning, the 14th, was Sunday. There was service as usual and the Holy Communion was administered. He who administered it and several of those receiving it, did so, alas! for the last time. In the afternoon the mess-house and a bungalow in cantonments were burned down. But on this occasion the sepoys of the 4th Regiment worked with good-humoured alacrity to extinguish the flames; and it was fondly hoped that it was the work of a few incendiaries. Soon after 8 P.M., it was reported that the artillery had loaded their guns without orders. On the officers proceeding to the spot the men explained that they had been alarmed by a report that a European regiment was about to attack them. The officers assured them to the contrary and returned to their homes satisfied in their own minds that their men were all right.

But when the nine o'clock gun fired there was a commotion, then bugling, then shots, and then a volley. The end had come.

We will not attempt to give full details of the murderous scenes that followed, which have been vividly described in the pages of Malleson and elsewhere. Suffice it to say that six officers and the chaplain, six sergeants and pensioners, three women and three children, nineteen in all, were killed, chiefly by volleys of musketry directed against all those attempting to reach the regimental lines or cross the main road of the cantonments. Major Blake, commanding the 2nd Regiment, was shot as he reached the lines; but some of his men (by whom he was much beloved) placed him under a guard and sent for the regimental doctor, whom they brought safely to his side. Major Blake soon expired; whereupon the doctor was called upon to leave, and escorted to the river-side. One lady (Mrs. Stewart) fell while tending a wounded officer; her little boy was killed at the same time; her daughter was saved. Her husband (Captain Stewart of the artillery), attempting to reach his battery, fell, severely wounded, was nursed through the night by two of his men, but deliberately shot next day; whether by the same two men or others does not appear.

But it is fair to mention, that, though officers were pursued and shot down without mercy, the lives of women and children were generally spared; and even in regard to the treatment of their officers the sepoys of the Contingent generally were by no means of one mind. Four out of the seven infantry regiments, two out of the four batteries of artillery, and the two regiments of cavalry, excepting a party at Gwalior, allowed their officers to escape unharmed. Three men of the 2nd Regiment escorted a lieutenant—carrying his wife in a litter—seven miles to the Residency. The guard of the 1st Regiment, in charge of the family of its absent commandant, behaved admirably, and both Captain Meade and Captain Murray and their families were, as will be seen, well served by a portion of the 4th Regiment.

Captain Meade's house was by the river—close to the bridge, and divided from the second of the two rows of bungalows and the regimental lines in rear of them by a broad road. At one corner of the garden was the cantonment treasury with a guard of fifty sepoys. At another corner, overlooking the river bed, was a circular guard-house, occupied by a non-commissioned native officer and ten men. In front of the house was another guard of the same regiment. So the garden swarmed with sepoys and was, in fact, the most dangerous centre in cantonments, and if the three guards had been like-minded, or the river in flood, none could have escaped. But the water was low, and it so happened that, while the guard in front of the house was mutinous and bloodthirsty, that in the guard-house by the river, was, for the time being, faithful, and saved the lives of Mrs. Meade, her sister, and their children.

The circumstances are thus described by Mrs. (now Lady) Murray[1] in a letter (written a few days after the occurrences):—

"We had tea as usual at 8 P.M. Richard[2] then

[1] A few additional details have been inserted from a letter by Mrs. Meade, written about the same time.

[2] Captain Meade.

went out and spoke to the havildár[1] in charge of the night watch and told him to take great care not to allow any suspicious-looking person to enter the compound.[2] The man replied: 'Yes, sahib, I will shoot all who go into the house and all who leave it'. Richard returned looking grave. Soon after this a sergeant reported that the artillery had loaded their guns. Captains Stewart and Hawkins went to their batteries and found their men, as they pretended, had been alarmed by some reports that a European regiment was on them. The officers assured them to the contrary and returned to their homes satisfied that their men were all right.

"After this the gentlemen went to lie down. Emily[3] and I were just beginning to undress, when the nine o'clock gun fired. Immediately after this we heard a great noise in the direction of the lines. The bugling commenced, shots were heard, then a volley was fired. We ran and called the gentlemen, who were on the other side of the house. Richard told us to put out all lights, as the sepoys could see through the venetians into the rooms. A Chaprassie[4] was immediately sent to warn some ladies who were at a distance that there was danger. The man was stopped at the gate by the guard of the treasury. An orderly was also sent off to the lines to find out the cause of the alarm, whilst the horses were being saddled to take the gentlemen to the lines; but these the sepoys would not allow to leave the stables.

"The orderly returned saying that some men of the 2nd had rushed into the lines of the 4th Regiment call-

[1] Native sergeant. [2] Garden. [3] Mrs. Meade. [4] Messenger.

ing out that the Europeans were upon them (this seemed the watchword in many places), but, he added, all would soon be right. Scarcely a minute elapsed ere the noise recommenced and another bungalow was in flames.

"Richard and John[1] made up their minds to put us in some place of safety. We snatched the poor sleeping children from their beds, and all went out into the garden by the side-door of the bedroom, Richard going first, with his sword in his hand, as we did not know if the sepoy who guarded the door could be depended on. He however allowed Richard to lead him round the corner of the house whilst we all slipped past. It was all the work of a minute.

"We hastened to a building in the rear of the compound, where there was a guard composed of a havildár and ten sepoys. Providentially these men (at least for the time) were with us. The gentlemen asked the havildár to protect us, whilst they went to the Brigadier, who lived in the next compound.

"The havildár made us follow him up the stairs to the roof of the building. It was a small round tower about seven feet in height; he then told us to lie down; no sooner had he left us and returned to his men than the guard, who had been posted in front of our house, came to them, and we heard them ask him where the 'mem-sahibs and babas' had gone, as they wanted them. The man replied he had not seen us. If one of the babies had cried we should have been betrayed; but all were quiet. As soon as these traitors had turned their backs, the havildár made

[1] Captain Murray.

signs to us that we could be seen from below, as E. and I, in our suspense and anxiety, were bending over the little parapet of the tower.

"Shortly after, to our great joy, John and Richard returned. We had been full of anxiety on their account, as the firing had been constant. They brought us down from our hiding-place, and told us that the Brigadier had ordered them not to go to the lines, as it was evident the men were beyond control; indeed whilst they were at the Brigadier's they had to retire from the front verandah to the back of the house as bullets were falling all around them.

"The havildár urged us to cross the river without delay, as the guards were already firing at other fugitives who were attempting to escape farther up the stream. He and three men actually escorted us over. Our bungalow was on the banks of the Morár River, but as the bridge was strongly guarded, we could not attempt to cross by it but were obliged to scramble down the steep banks and wade through the water, which fortunately was shallow. Just after crossing, E. and I fell into a ditch; she sprained her foot severely and had great difficulty in proceeding, carrying her heavy child in her arms.

"Here the havildár and his men said they must leave us and return to Morár."[1]

[1] Captain Meade, after his return to Gwalior, tried to trace the havildár to whose fidelity he and his family owed their lives; but for some time without success. Several men claimed a reward; but, on examination, their claims were proved to be without foundation. At last, after a lapse of two years, Captain Meade received a letter from the superintendent of a jail in Oude, who informed him that one of the prisoners in his charge asserted that he had saved the lives of the families of Captains Meade and

THE MORÁR RIVER,
with the Gwalior Fortress in the distance.
(From a Sketch by Mrs. Daly.)

At length the sound of musketry, which had been more or less continuous, ceased, and Captain Murray, who had his charger with him, tried to return to cantonments by the bridge and see if anything could be done to restore order and bring the troops to reason; but it was held in force by the mutineers, his life was threatened, and he was compelled to retreat.

After wandering for some time amidst thorny fields (Mrs. Meade with a sprained foot), crouching down from time to time at every sound of footsteps, they saw another bungalow in flames, and, believing return to cantonments hopeless, and that there was no chance of safety at the Residency, decided to throw themselves on the protection of the Mahárája.

At one o'clock on the morning of the 15th June, they reached the garden of Sindhia's country mansion (situate outside the Lashkar), known as the Phúlbágh Palace, and were delighted to hear from the Brigadier, who met them on the road, that Sindhia was willing to receive them.

"We were escorted," says Mrs. Murray, "through the palace gardens and taken up a steep flight of steps to a small turret, where His Highness, with a number of his sirdárs, was sitting on the ground by the light of a tall native lamp. It was a strange sight; the gardens full of His Highness's cavalry and artillery; the alarmed looks of the people, including the Mahárája, who, when he heard the Political Agent was on his way to the palace, wrung his hands in despair. We rested

Murray during the mutiny at Gwalior. The man was sent to Gwalior and identified; and Captain Meade was thus enabled to make some return for the great service he had rendered in the hour of danger.

ourselves on some cushions, but, after some time, begged for some place to lie down in. They took us to another part of the palace, gave us some tea and some bedding; but who could rest? At two o'clock A.M., to our great joy, more fugitives arrived; they told us every one else was murdered."

On hearing of the outbreak, Major Macpherson, the Political Agent, proceeded with his sister and an officer who had escaped from cantonments, to join the Mahárája, escorted by a party of Marátha horsemen —some of Sindhia's body-guard. His carriage was stopped by a party of *gházis* or Muhammadan fanatics, who demanded the lives of the Agent and those with him; but the Marátha captain of the guard averred that he was taking the Agent as prisoner to Sindhia, so they were allowed to pass.

On arrival at the palace he was informed by the Mahárája that the attitude of the mutineers and the feeling of his own troops had become so hostile that it would be impossible for him to protect the fugitives for any length of time. He urged, therefore, that the Political Agent and all who had escaped should leave as soon as possible for Agra, and undertook to provide carriages, palanquins, and an escort as far as the Chambal River. This was agreed to.

But, before leaving, Major Macpherson took occasion earnestly to impress upon the Mahárája the importance of doing his best to detain the mutinous troops at Gwalior until the British Government was in a position to crush the rebels at Dehli.

The Mahárája and his minister promised to do their best, and they kept their word.

At daybreak on the 15th a start was made, and as they passed the Residency, which lay on the road to Agra, more fugitives joined the party, which now included Major Macpherson (the Resident) and his sister, Brigadier-General Ramsay, Captain Meade (Brigade Major) and Mrs. Meade, Captain Murray (commanding the 4th Infantry Regiment of the Contingent) and Mrs. Murray (sister of Mrs. Meade), who had just buried one of their infant children, and others. At Hingona, twelve miles from the river Chambal, which separates Gwalior territory from the petty State of Dholpur, they were met by a party of religious fanatics headed by one Jahángír Khan, formerly a native officer of the Contingent, then a favourite captain of Sindhia's army, but now a *gházi* leader. "He appeared," says Major Macpherson, "arrayed in green, with beads fingered in ceaseless prayer," protesting that "he had no desire to injure them," but at the same time had a band of plunderers in the ravines fringing the river ready to attack them.

The Marátha escort refused to proceed beyond Hingona, and the party had to spend a night of discomfort in the carriages or on the grass, with far from pleasant anticipations for the morrow.

But deliverance was at hand. Soon after midnight the glitter of torches was seen in the distance, and a growing murmur of voices and the measured tread of an advancing force were heard. The hearts of many of the fugitives sank within them. But to their intense relief the advancing force proved to be the following of a friendly chief. It was the following of Thakor Baldeo Singh, chief of the Dandautia

Brahmans, a robust and warlike tribe, who had come with a strong body of his clansmen to defend them.

It appears that the minister, Dinkar Rao, anticipating difficulties at the river Chambal, had thoughtfully summoned the loyal Thakor to go to the rescue of the fugitives, and he promptly obeyed. The minister's policy of "dealing fairly with the subordinate races" had thus borne fruit.

On the farther bank of the Chambal elephants and an escort sent by the Rána (chief) of Dholpur, a small Ját State, also loyal to the British Government, awaited the fugitives. But in the ravines leading to the river a party of Jahángír's band had been posted and meant mischief. However Baldeo Singh got information of their presence, and, after placing some of his own men to watch the *gházi* leader, took the party to the river by another route and passed them safely over.

The Rána of Dholpur loaded the fugitives with kindness, and despatched them in carts, with a strong escort, a distance of six and thirty miles to Agra, where they arrived safely on the forenoon of the 17th.

Similar kindness was shown by both of the chiefs to two other parties of fugitives from Gwalior who came a few days later.

The services of Baldeo Singh and those of the Dholpur chief were not forgotten. The former received a grant of land in British territory; and a *jágír* or assignment of the revenues of certain villages from Sindhia; and 100 of his tribesmen, under the command of Gopál Singh,[1] the chief's brother, were selected to form a troop in a cavalry regiment, subsequently raised by Captain Meade, and known during the mutiny as "Meade's Horse".

The latter received the honour of K.C.S.I.

[1] Gopál Singh had a distinguished career. He became Ressaldar Major (principal native commissioned officer) of the Central India Horse, and did good service in Afghanistan in 1879-80, and, when he died, about three years ago, he was native A.D.C. to the Viceroy. "He was more than six feet high," says Major Meade, "and the most soldier-like man I ever saw."

CHAPTER V.

EVENTS AT AGRA AND GWALIOR.

Situation at Agra—Advance of the rebel force from Nímach and Nasírábád—Defection of the troops of friendly States—Disastrous fight at Sassiah—Part taken by Meade—Rising at Agra—Fall of Dehli—Greathed's column—Advance of rebels from Mhau and Indore—Greathed's column reaches Agra—Attacked by rebels—Rebels defeated with loss—Meade raises a regiment of native cavalry—Its services—Rebel forces driven from Kalpi approach Gwalior—Sindhia attacks them—His troops join the enemy—Sindhia flies to Agra—Gwalior occupied by rebels.

WHEN the fugitives reached Agra, as described in the last chapter, their troubles were over for the time. The native regiments of the garrison had been disarmed and disbanded; the cavalry regiment and battery of the Gwalior Contingent, which had been despatched by Sindhia to Agra on the Lieut.-Governor's requisition—a force from which danger might have been apprehended—had been sent away from the capital to keep order in the district of Aligarh,[1] while, thanks to the efforts of the Mahárája and his minister, who were in daily communication with Major Macpherson at Agra, the mutinous regiments of Gwalior were detained there for the present. The old Mughal fort of Agra was held by an English

[1] The regiment soon afterwards mutinied but the men did not shoot down their officers, who escaped to Agra.

regiment and battery, and the station was further protected by a force of English and Eurasian volunteers, a portion of the Contingent of the Rája of Kotah (a friendly Rájput State)—a force officered by Englishmen—some cavalry furnished by the State of Bhartpur, and 600 matchlock men from Karauli (another Rájput State), commanded by Saifullah Khan, a Muhammadan gentleman of influence.

But the surrounding country was in a very disturbed condition. The police sympathised with the mutineers; law and order had disappeared and there were rumours of an advance by a strong body of rebels from Nímach and Nasírábád.

The truth of these rumours was soon confirmed, and, at the end of June, the Christian residents of the city and station, with a few exceptions, took refuge in the fort.

On the 4th July, the Kotah Contingent mutinied and joined the enemy; the Karauli levies refused to fight and were sent home; the Bhartpur cavalry deserted.

On the 5th July, the enemy now amounting to 4000 infantry, 1500 cavalry, with eleven guns, reached Sassiah, a village five miles off, and Brigadier Polwhele, commanding at Agra, decided to attack them with the small force at his disposal,—namely, one English regiment and battery and about fifty volunteers, in all a force of about 700 men and six guns.

After a long artillery engagement, during which the British force expended an enormous amount of ammunition, but suffered more than the enemy, an attack was delivered and the village of Sassiah carried;

but by this time the ammunition was exhausted and our troops had to retire, harassed by the enemy and suffering considerable loss.

Captain Meade took part in the action as a volunteer, and during the retreat was in considerable danger, as he remained behind with some others vainly endeavouring to extricate and remove a gun which had become embedded in mud. The gun had to be left on the field, but was not carried off by the enemy.

The enemy did not follow up their success by an attack on Agra and moved on to Dehli; but the ruffians of the city and the adjoining villages, joined by many of the police and the prisoners from the jail, rose *en masse*, and for two days the station was given up to pillage; bungalows were burnt, property carried off, and upwards of twenty Christians, European and native, lost their lives.

Order was at length restored at Agra and measures taken for relieving Aligarh, but the surrounding population was still far from friendly.

However on the 15th of September Dehli was successfully assaulted, and, after a struggle of some days, entirely recaptured—an event which had, of course, an important effect in pacifying the surrounding country and allaying the growing excitement in the Punjab as well as the North-Western Provinces.

A few days after the recapture of Dehli a column under the command of Lieut.-Colonel Greathed was despatched to clear the road between Dehli and Cawnpore.

While Greathed's force is on the march let us

glance for a moment at the affairs of Gwalior. We have seen how the Mahárája, by the advice of his minister Dinkar Rao, and in communication with the Political Agent, had succeeded in restraining the mutinous Contingent regiments from proceeding to attack Agra, or joining their brethren at Dehli.

But soon a new danger appeared. On the 31st July there arrived at Gwalior a formidable rebel force from Mhau and Indore, comprising not only the mutinous regiments of those stations, but 600 men of Holkar's army, with seven guns and 1000 fanatics led by a person styling himself Firoz Shah, Prince of Dehli, and also the 5th Contingent Infantry Regiment which joined it *en route*. After vainly endeavouring to detain this force at Gwalior the Mahárája was constrained to allow it to proceed to Agra, and, accordingly, between the 5th and 7th September they crossed the Chambal.

On hearing of the approach of this rebel force the Agra authorities applied for assistance to Greathed's column, which, accordingly, turned aside from the direct route to Cawnpore, and marched into Agra early on the morning of the 10th October.

Of what followed we have a graphic narrative from the pen of F.M. Lord Roberts. While the wayworn British troops were settling down in camp they were suddenly attacked by the rebel force and a desperate conflict ensued. But after much hand-to-hand fighting, grand practice by the artillery, and splendid charges from the cavalry, English and Indian, the enemy were beaten off and promptly pursued and dispersed, and their camp taken with thirteen guns and a great quantity of ammunition.

The Agra garrison seeing the attack hastened from the fort to assist the Dehli column and arrived just as the enemy had been defeated; but they were in time to take part in the pursuit of the retreating foe. Captain Meade was with the Agra force, but has left no detailed account of his services on the occasion.

To return to Gwalior: after the departure of the Mhau and Indore rebels for Agra the Contingent became more and more unmanageable, and at length the bulk of the force, seduced by emissaries from the Nána Sáhib, marched from Gwalior, under the command of Tantia Topi, now the Nána's chief agent,—not however for Agra, but for Bundelkhand and Cawnpore. Before leaving they destroyed the cantonments at Morár and, as they proceeded, laid waste Sindhia's territory, declaring that he was the enemy of their cause. The Contingent left on the 15th October, and between that date and the following May, with the exception of some local disturbances, the peace of Gwalior was fairly maintained by the Mahárája and his officials.

Meanwhile we have to record the proceedings of Captain Meade at Agra. After having remained five months in the unsatisfactory position of "doing duty officer," that is an officer available for any kind of service required, but with no definite military duty assigned to him, he had the gratification of receiving, at the end of November, instructions from the Government of India to raise a regiment of native cavalry for general service.

He set to work at once *con amore*, but the task was somewhat arduous, for trustworthy recruits were not to be had in the vicinity, while those whose loyalty was satisfactory were, as a rule, entirely innocent of the art of riding. However by dint of incessant labour and his personal popularity with native races he was able, in a little more than two months' time, to get together and prepare for service a cavalry regiment nearly 600 strong. It was what is technically known as a "class" regiment, that is a regiment in which each troop is composed of men of distinctive castes or nationalities. Thus of the six troops composing Meade's regiment one troop consisted of Sikhs, another of Punjábi Muhammadans, another of Játs, another of native Christians; the fifth was a troop of Gwalior men under the command of Gopál Singh, brother of the loyal Thakor Baldeo Singh, who had befriended the fugitives at the river Chambal, and the sixth a troop of mixed races. The regiment was under the command of Captain Meade with six English officers selected by himself, and when inspected by Brigadier-General Showers in March, 1858, was declared to be "as fine a body of native cavalry as he had ever seen".

Between January and June, 1858, Meade's Horse, as the regiment was designated, was constantly employed in maintaining order in the Agra district. In June it took part in the actions near Gwalior, including the brilliant attack on the retreating rebel force on 21st June, 1858, then joined Sir Robert Napier's Field Force and was engaged in the operations against Rája Mán Singh; the capture of Pauri, and the action at Bíjapur, earning for its services the special acknowledgments of the Government of India.[1] It was unceasingly employed in 1858-59 on the west and south of Gwalior, and shared in the operations resulting in the surrender of Rája Mán Singh and the capture of Tantia Topi. A portion of the regiment was in the fight at Garroya, which closed the rebellion in Gwalior, and the entire regiment was more or less actively employed in Málwa until 1861, when it was incorporated with the Central India Horse.

But we are somewhat anticipating events and must again return to Gwalior.

The Mhau and Indore rebels had, as we have seen, passed through Gwalior and been disposed of, and the Contingent had left for Cawnpore; but now Sindhia's own army, 10,000 strong, and composed of races more or less in sympathy with our own sepoys and corrupted by Marátha emissaries, began to get out of hand. At this juncture Kálpi, on the Jamna, the last stronghold of the rebel forces in Central India, was taken by Sir Hugh Rose, and the occupants fled in disorder across the river Chambal. Informed, however, of the state of Sindhia's army they suddenly rallied, recrossed the river and advanced on Gwalior. Their leaders were the Rao Sáhib, connected by adoption with the

[1] "His Lordship [Lord Canning] is well aware of the indefatigable manner in which you and your men have performed your duties in the neighbourhood of Agra, and of the good services which you have rendered, and for which the Governor-General feels desirous now to offer you his acknowledgments." —From Secretary to the Government of India to Captain Meade, 28th September, 1858.

Nána, Tantia Topi, "the soul of the Nána's cause," and believed to be one of his chief agents in the massacres of Cawnpore, the once friendly, but now rebellious, Nawáb of Bánda, who had just been defeated by General Whitelock, but had still a force of serviceable cavalry; and lastly the brave, but bloodthirsty, Ráni of Jhánsi, a determined foe of the British Government, and authoress of a massacre of men, women and children as revolting and deliberate as that of Cawnpore; she is described by some as the "Joan of Arc" of India, but by Major Macpherson "as an ardent, daring, licentious woman, under thirty, who rode in male military attire with sword and pistols, and had as her A.D.C. a Brahminee concubine of her late husband".[1]

On the 29th May, the invading force arrived within eight miles of Gwalior. On the morning of the 31st, Sindhia moved to Bahádurpur to attack them with 8000 men and twenty-four guns. After a brief show of fighting, on the morning of the 1st June Sindhia's troops fraternised with the rebels, and the Mahárája, attended only by his minister and a very few adherents, fled to Agra, where he was received with the greatest honour and sympathy. Gwalior was occupied by the rebels, who looted the treasury and jewels; the palace, the fort and arsenal

[1] The Ráni of Jhánsi was widow of the chief of a petty *ráj* or principality in Bundelkhand, which had been created by the British Government in 1832, but resumed in default of heirs in 1854 in accordance with the views of Sir W. Metcalfe and Colonel (afterwards Sir) R. Low—both warm supporters of native dynasties—and the practice of the East India Company in previous cases of similar character.

came into their hands. "And thus," says Sir Owen Burne, "the rebels who had fled a disorderly and helpless mob from Kálpi now found themselves provided with abundance of money, with material of war and with Sindhia's army as their allies." Their leader, the Rao Sáhib, appointed Tantia Topi commander-in-chief of the rebel forces, and, anxious to secure the sympathy of the inhabitants, peremptorily forbade all indiscriminate plundering, and confirmed nearly all Sindhia's officers in their posts. The Residency and the palace in the Phúlbágh, where the fugitives had obtained shelter, were destroyed, and the Ránis with the chief nobles of the State, including Sindhia's queen and his adoptive mother the Baiza Bai, and a small Marátha guard, fled to the fort of Narwar thirty miles off. The Baiza Bai, who had the reputation of being hostile to the British Government, received from the Rao Sáhib an offer to be placed in charge of affairs at Gwalior, but she rejected his overtures, sent on his letters to the Governor-General's Agent for Central India, and, on the arrival of Sir H. Rose before Gwalior, joined his camp at Morár.

But the success of the rebels was shortlived, as will be seen in the next chapter.

CHAPTER VI.

THE RECAPTURE OF GWALIOR.

Sir H. Rose moves from Kálpi on 5th June—His force—Morár occupied—Advance of Smith's brigade from Sípri—Sweeps the hills and captures the Phúlbágh batteries, but has to retire—Death of the Ráni of Jhánsi—Sindhia summoned to the camp—Meade appointed to escort him—Reaches Morár on the 18th—Sir H. Rose decides to join his force with Smith's and takes Meade with him—Fighting on the 19th; Meade having reconnoitred enemy's position, Sir H. Rose storms the heights—Enemy driven off and all its guns (26) captured, and rebel force in the plain driven into the Lashkar—General decides to advance at once through the Lashkar to the palace—Meade acts as guide, and, on arrival at the palace, enters the courtyard alone and induces the holders to surrender without bloodshed—On the 20th Sindhia received by Sir H. Rose at the head of his troops, and conducted to his palace—Meade leaves to join the pursuing column—Just too late for the victory of the 21st—No mention of Meade's special service in procuring surrender of the palace contained in Sir H. Rose's despatch—Meade vainly attempts to get the omission rectified—Remarkable speech by Sindhia.

After the flight of the rebel forces from Kálpi a pursuing column was organised, but the General, sorely requiring rest, obtained leave to return to Bombay, and the command was given to Brigadier-General Sir R. Napier (afterwards Lord Napier of Magdala). But on the news of the occupation of Gwalior and the flight of Sindhia reaching him, Sir Hugh Rose at once offered to cancel his leave and take command of the avenging force. His offer was accepted, and at the same time General Napier generously agreed to act as his second in command.

The force consisted of a portion of the garrison of Kálpi, a column under Brigadier Stuart, the Hyderabad Contingent, and the Rajputána Field Force under Brigadier Smith.

At six in the morning of the 16th June the force from Kálpi reached Bahádurpur, the scene of Sindhia's defeat, and then pushed on to Morár (the cantonment of the Contingent), which was held by the enemy. After a sharp action, in which the 71st Highlanders greatly distinguished themselves, the enemy was driven out with loss, closely pursued by a wing of the 14th Light Dragoons.

Brigadier Smith, whose force was at Kotha-ki-Sarai, was then directed to advance on Gwalior from the east. He did so on the 17th, and the operations are thus described by Major Macpherson :—

"Between Kotha-ki-Sarai and Gwalior lies a chain of low hills a mile broad ; and through a defile in these runs the Jhánsi Road, flanked on the westward by a canal impassable for guns or horses except by a bridge just burnt by the rebels. To oppose Smith, the rebels had planted guns at six points upon the summits of the hills on either side of the defile, supporting them by a numerous infantry. Beyond the hills towards Gwalior, in the plain which spreads between it and Morár, were two batteries of six and five guns, near the Phúlbágh Palace, under Tantia Topi, while two eighteen pounders were placed in the plain to the left, and many guns at other points.

"Smith swept the hills with the 95th Foot and 10th Bombay N.I., while his guns and a wing of the

8th Hussars and Bombay Lancers advanced by the defile. The hills passed, the cavalry charged straight into the plain, which was held by some 1500 horse, and immediately carried the two Phúlbágh batteries. But it was evening, and the troops had not breakfasted. Of the 95th alone, from hunger and extreme fatigue and exposure in sweeping the hills, four officers and eighty-five men were disabled by sunstroke. The force, therefore, necessarily retired within the defile, securing four of the captured guns."

This action is memorable for the death of the Ráni of Jhánsi, who was mortally wounded in a gallant charge by a squadron of the 8th Hussars. "She was seated near the Phúlbágh batteries drinking sherbet, when the alarm was given that the Hussars approached." The Ráni—clad in a red jacket and trousers and white turban, and wearing a pearl necklace just looted from Sindhia's treasury—mounted her horse, and, attended by her ever-faithful A.D.C., tried to avoid the charge by leaping the canal. But her horse refused. Meanwhile the Hussars, led by Captain Heneage, swept by. The Ráni received a shot in the side and a sabre cut on the head, but rode off. Soon afterwards she fell, was moved into a tent and died, and her remains were burnt with much ceremony in a garden close by.[1] The

[1] Her faithful A.D.C. (the Brahminee concubine of her late husband) received a sabre wound at the same time, but was able to ride into the city. Here she was tended by a fakír and a Muhammadan official, and dying in their hands was treated as a convert to Islám and *buried!* It is said that the Ráni, when dying, begged that the ornaments on her person, which were very valuable, might be distributed among her troops, for whose services she expressed the deepest gratitude.

Ráni's death greatly dispirited the rebel army. She was undoubtedly the bravest and best military leader they had.

Meanwhile Sindhia had been summoned from Agra, and his consort (the Maharáni) and his adoptive mother (the Baiza Bai) from the fort of Narwar (where they had taken refuge), to make it evident that our advance from Gwalior was undertaken with a view of reinstating the dynasty in accordance with treaty engagements, and not for purposes of annexation.

The duty of escorting Sindhia back to his capital was entrusted to Captain Meade. They left Agra on the 13th of June, accompanied by two squadrons of Meade's Horse, and by forced marches reached Sir Hugh Rose's camp at Morár, on the 18th. The Ránis reached the camp next day.

At 5 P.M. on the 18th the General proceeded to join his force with that of Brigadier Smith, who held a portion of the heights commanding Gwalior, but was hard pressed by the enemy, who occupied the remaining portion. He was accompanied (as acting A.D.C.) by Captain Meade, whose knowledge of the locality rendered him of the greatest use during the ensuing operations.

After a particularly harassing march Sir Hugh Rose reached his destination early in the morning of the 19th and placed his guns in position, but the enemy's fire was heavy and the General was anxious to dislodge them. He therefore sent Captain Meade to reconnoitre and ascertain the best point of attack. Captain Meade performed the duty, and at midday the troops crossed the canal (which had been temporarily bridged) and advanced to storm the heights. This was done successfully, after four hours' hard work; all the enemy's guns, twenty-six in number, and magazines were taken, and the rebels were in full retreat. Meanwhile the horse artillery opened fire upon a mass of the enemy (some 10,000 strong, with numerous cavalry) drawn up on the parade ground. They fled into the Lashkar or military quarter of the town, in the direction of the Mahárája's palace, while the British cavalry swept the plain.

Sir Hugh Rose had, at first, intended to bivouac for the night upon the plain, and attack the town next morning, in conjunction with Sir Robert Napier's force from Morár, and that of Brigadier Smith, who had been directed meanwhile to attack and capture the Phúlbágh batteries. But encouraged by his success he determined, in consultation with Meade, who volunteered to act as guide, to push forward at once through the Lashkar to the palace, which it was proposed, if necessary, to storm.

This was a particularly hazardous proceeding, as the Lashkar was presumably full of armed men with not a few fanatical Mewattis, while the streets were long and narrow, but Sir Hugh Rose was bold to rashness, and placed himself at the head of the column with Captain Meade at his side, and advanced—each officer having his pistol at full-cock in his hand. Some twenty or thirty of the enemy were killed *en route*, but the column threaded its way through the interminable streets, and at length arrived without a casualty at the open space in front of the palace, which seemed full of armed men and ruffians in a state of wild excitement.

We have now to describe an act of service performed by Captain Meade which, owing to various circumstances, has obtained little official recognition; though it was one which, besides involving great personal risk, had the effect of saving much life and property and earning the lasting gratitude of the Mahárája. It can best be described in Captain Meade's own words:—

"On the head of the column reaching the end of the street which debouches on the open space around the palace enclosure, and coming within sight of the latter, we found that the courtyard and building were occupied by a large number of armed men, whose intentions we, of course, had at the moment no means of knowing.

"The approach to the palace block was entirely commanded by its upper storeyed buildings, which are of substantial masonry with terraced roofs screened by a parapet, and under the feeling that any attempt to storm these buildings must be attended with heavy loss—especially if the occupants included, as I thought probable, some of the Mewattis and other desperadoes of the Lashkar—and that, if possible, Sindhia's palace ought to be preserved from such a fate, I volunteered to ride forward alone, and to endeavour to obtain the surrender of the place to the British force.

"The general assented, and by his orders the column halted while I rode up to the gateway which formed the entrance to the courtyard. There was no gate, but I found all ingress through the gateway barred to a horseman by a beam of wood which was fixed in a socket in the wall on either side, and for some minutes, while I was detained by this barrier, my life was certainly in the most imminent peril, for several muskets were levelled at me, and a single shot from the Europeans in the rear would have ensured my destruction. The people inside were in the wildest confusion, and I gathered that some of them were determined to resist our troops.

"The delay in getting inside the courtyard was most embarrassing, for I felt that every moment was precious; but such was the confusion that I could not for some time get any one's attention, beyond menaces of the nature already stated. At length, to my great relief, a little wizened Mussulman, who was close to the gateway, recognised me, and shouted out three or four times, 'This is Meade Sahib,' and hearing this, three or four men at last complied with my repeated demand to remove the barrier, and I dashed into the courtyard, up to a group of some five or six men whom I had previously noticed as being evidently the leaders of the party. Taking one of these—a tall powerful man, who appeared to be the chief, and who I afterwards learnt was one of the palace ***hujras*** (or attendants), who, with his companions generally, had joined the rebels—by the shoulder, I told them I would save their lives if they would obey my orders, but that there must be no delay, as the British force outside was prepared and eager to attack them. After a moment's consultation, they said they would hold the palace for the Mahárája and would give it up to him on his coming to it, but that they would not surrender it to the English. I replied that this was impossible, that the Chief was away at Morár, and that the palace must be at once given up, or it would be stormed forthwith, in which event not a man of them would escape. They again spoke together, and the tall man at last said: 'We will do what you order'.

"There were a large number of men at the time in the courtyard, and also inside and on the roofs of the building, and as it struck me that the great object at the moment was to get them out of sight, so as to avoid the chance of any firing between them and our troops, which might have led to a serious struggle, I directed every man to get at once inside the building, and to remain there perfectly quiet till they had permission to leave, or orders were issued for their disposal. This was effected, after a little difficulty, by the urgent efforts of the leaders and those who seemed amenable to their authority, and in a short time I was left alone in the courtyard with only three or four of these men with me.

"I then told the tall man that he and his fellow-leaders would be held responsible for the conduct of the men who were with them, and for the preservation of the interior of the palace buildings, so long as they remained in the latter; and then, after a few words of earnest warning to them, I rode back to report the result to the General, and begged that I might have a party of Europeans and sepoys to post for the due security of the place. A company each of the 95th Foot and 25th Bombay N.I. were ordered forward with me for this purpose, and I placed the sepoys inside the courtyard, posting sentries from them over the treasury entrance and at some other points, and the Europeans in and outside the gateway.

"In the meantime the column was moved up into the open space outside the enclosure, and there piled arms; and I then, at Sir Hugh Rose's request, went a short distance down the main street, and told some of the bankers, who had up to that moment been trembling in their houses, that the Lashkar had been cleared of the enemy, and that the palace was in the occupation of the British force, and I called on them to come and pay their respects to the General.

"Numbers of them at once repaired to the gateway, where Sir Hugh Rose was seated, and in a short time the street was full of well-dressed men of this class, all vociferating their gratitude for the expulsion of the rebels and their release from the terror under which they had been labouring during the period (nearly three weeks) of their occupation of the city. Some champagne and brandy were produced from one of the palace storehouses, and those who had the fortune to get a share of the same thoroughly enjoyed the grateful liquids.

"After a halt of about an hour, during which arrangements were made for the security of the palace, and also of the main streets, the force moved back to the camp, and I proceeded by the General's order to the Phúlbágh to ascertain the state of affairs there."

Captain Meade found that the Phúlbágh had been gallantly captured by the force under Brigadier Smith, with trifling loss to ourselves and great loss to the enemy; and during the night the fortress of Gwalior was evacuated.

Next morning Sindhia, accompanied by Sir Robert Hamilton, Agent to the Governor-General for Central India, proceeded from the Morár cantonments and was received by Sir Hugh Rose at the head of his troops on the parade ground[1] near the Phúlbágh and conducted in triumph to his palace in the Lashkar amid the rejoicings of the townspeople. A reception was held in the Durbar-hall of the palace, at which the Mahárája expressed, with deep emotion, his gratitude to the British Government for having restored him to his throne.[2] And he insisted upon giving the General and his staff a banquet that evening in the palace.

At this banquet Captain Meade was unable to be present, for he had other work to do. His corps was with Sir Robert Napier, who had been instructed to pursue the enemy who were moving in force from

[1] The ceremony was unexpectedly disturbed by a remarkable manifestation of fanaticism. After the surrender of the fortress thirteen men (nine of them Patáns), with two women and a child, after proceeding some miles towards Agra, resolved deliberately to return and die in it. They fired from the guns on the ramparts four or five shots at the troops drawn out to receive Sindhia, and as he and the Agent advanced with their *cortège* one struck the ground immediately in front of them. Lieutenant Rose, the general's nephew, with a company of the 25th Bombay N.I. and some police proceeded to attack them. They had flung over the walls into the city all their gold and silver coins and other property, and took post upon a bastion, a gun of which commanded the line of approach. The gun burst at the third discharge and Rose and his men advanced. The fanatics slew their women and child. Collecting his skirmishers into line Rose successfully stormed the position, but was himself mortally wounded and nine of the men with him killed, before the desperadoes could be destroyed.—Major Macpherson's Report.

[2] He was afterwards anxious to present a medal with his device (a serpent) to all the officers and men of the Central Indian Field Force together with six months' *batta*. Lord Canning approved of the presentation of the medal, but permission was refused by the Home Government.—Sir O. Burne.

Gwalior, and he was of course anxious to be with it. He did his best to join the pursuing column, but unfortunately arrived just too late to take part in the brilliant engagement of the 21st, when Sir Robert Napier with one troop of Horse Artillery and 500 cavalry, including two squadrons of Meade's Horse, attacked and completely routed the enemy, 10,000 strong, with twenty-six guns, all of which were captured.

Thus Gwalior was reoccupied—to the unbounded gratitude of the people and high credit of the troops engaged—with marvellous rapidity and comparatively trifling loss to us.

Its speedy recapture and the prompt reinstatement of our ally as Ruling Chief caused a profound sensation throughout India. A royal salute was fired in every large town, and in recognition of his brilliant services, worthily crowned by this last exploit, the General received the honour of G.C.B., the colonelcy of the 45th Regiment and a vote of thanks from both Houses of Parliament.

But it will be generally admitted that for the last success, and especially for the occupation of the palace without bloodshed or destruction of property, no small share of credit was due to the subject of this memoir; for, without his local knowledge, it would have been impossible to follow up the victory of the 19th by the immediate capture of the palace; and it would not have been possible to occupy the palace without bloodshed but for the bold and judicious action of Captain Meade, and the friendly feelings entertained towards him by some of its armed occupants.

His services were warmly acknowledged at the time by the General commanding, who spoke in similar terms regarding them to the Political Officers present,—Sir Robert Hamilton and Major Macpherson. Captain Meade was heartily congratulated by those present, and was the hero of the hour.

In these circumstances he not unnaturally expected that some mention of the special service he had thus rendered would be made in the official despatch. But he was disappointed. No despatch appeared for nine months, and when it did appear there was no reference made to his action in obtaining possession of the palace. He was thanked, indeed, in general terms, for his "zeal and knowledge of the locality," but his cool daring in entering the palace when full of excited soldiery and arranging for its peaceable surrender was totally ignored;[1] while the only military reward conferred upon him was a brevet majority which antedated his promotion for a few months only.

Meade was surprised and disappointed, but though strongly urged by his friends to make a respectful representation of his claims, he thought such action would be indecorous and remained silent.

But in the year 1867, when the Viceroy—then Sir John Lawrence—was visiting Sindhia at Gwalior,

[1] The words of the despatch are: "Captain Meade volunteered to accompany me as acting A.D.C. His zeal and knowledge of the country rendered him of great use to me during the operations." In the list of meritorious officers appended to the despatch his name is entered thus: "Captain Meade, commanding Meade's Horse (special mention), good service, acting on my staff and giving me important local information".

the story of Meade's having saved the palace was recounted to His Excellency by the Chief himself. His Excellency was much interested and expressed the opinion that so signal a service should be placed upon official record.

Thus encouraged, Lieut.-Colonel Meade (he had obtained this rank in 1866) at length yielded to his friends' advice, and, while on furlough in 1869, placed himself in communication personally and by letter with Lord Strathnairn (formerly Sir Hugh Rose), recalled the occasion to his lordship's memory, and prayed his assistance in securing the official record desired by the Viceroy. But his lordship, whose recollection of these events was imperfect and inaccurate, did not see his way to comply with Meade's request.[1]

Meade then applied to the Commander-in-Chief in India (Lord Sandhurst) for permission to include a statement of the Gwalior palace incident in the official record of his services. His application was supported (it is said) by the Commander-in-Chief, and the papers were sent on to the Government of India; but these

[1] That his Lordship's recollection of these events should be imperfect is no matter for surprise. Eleven years had elapsed since they occurred, and when they occurred he was suffering from the effects of repeated sunstrokes,—a condition not favourable to retentiveness of memory. But Major-General Sir Owen Burne in his memoir of Lord Strathnairn (last edition) has added the following footnote regarding the capture of the Gwalior palace: "This was effected without bloodshed through the useful interposition of Captain (now Sir Richard) Meade. He happened to be well known to the Gwalior men, and gallantly volunteered to go forward alone to the palace courtyard, which was full of armed and excited soldiery, to persuade them to submit peaceably, and to give up the palace. They fortunately recognised him, and after some delay, acted on his advice."

were unfortunately mislaid or lost, and no order was passed on his application.

But Sindhia's gratitude was pronounced and lasting, and in 1872, at a public banquet given by the Mahárája when Lord Northbrook visited Bombay, His Highness, in returning thanks after his health had been proposed, used the following remarkable words, which will fitly close the present chapter:—

"There were three things," His Highness said, "for which he would ever be grateful to the British Government. The first was that the British Government had re-established his power in 1844, after the battles of Maharájpur and Panniar; the second was that the British Government had saved him and his State in the Mutiny; and the third was that Meade Sahib had saved his palace when occupied by rebels who were being driven before our troops."

CHAPTER VII.

RESTORATION OF ORDER IN GWALIOR—SURRENDER OF MÁN SINGH—CAPTURE AND EXECUTION OF TANTIA TOPI.

State of Gwalior—Measures taken to restore order—Major Meade appointed on a commission to inquire into the conduct of the troops—Carries it out with justice and efficiency and earns the thanks of the Government of India and Secretary of State—Brigadier-General Napier takes in hand the disaffected portion of Gwalior territory, where Rája Mán Singh had influence—Mán Singh seizes the fort of Pauri, which is promptly attacked and taken by Napier, but Mán Singh escapes and is joined by Tantia Topi—Meade, having completed his inquiry, joins Napier's force, and is placed in command of a detachment—Captures and executes Tantia Topi—Statement by the latter before trial—His conduct and bearing after sentence—Tantia's prompt execution has a most salutary effect—Congratulations by Sir R. Hamilton, General Napier, Sir Hugh Rose and the Government of India—Verses in honour of the occasion by an English sergeant—Meade successfully attacks and disperses a rebel gathering at Garroya, thus ending the campaign in this part of India, and receives the thanks of Government.

THOUGH Sindhia had been triumphantly reinstated by the British Government, in the manner described in the preceding chapter, a good deal more remained to be done before his authority could be said to be completely re-established.

The capital itself was still crowded with rebels and a centre of disaffection and intrigue.

Of the army (regular and irregular) located at the capital and numbering nearly 13,000 men, only about

1200 had remained faithful; of the rest, some 1500 had left with Tantia Topi's force, and about 9000 were either in hiding in the city or Lashkar, or harboured in the surrounding villages.

In the territory outside the capital, the local chiefs, thanks to their generous treatment by Dinkar Rao, had, for the most part, continued loyal, but there was a tract of country to the south of Gwalior, west of the main road from Gwalior to Indore, where the population was still hostile. The territory included the old domains of two Rájput chiefships, that of Narwar, an ancient town and fortress on the Sindh River, and Sheopur, on the western border, which had been conquered and, in part, confiscated by Daulat Rao Sindhia some fifty years previously; but the representatives of the conquered chiefs, namely, Rája Mán Singh, descendant of the chiefs of Narwar, and Rája Balwant Singh of Sheopur, still possessed much influence in the locality and seized the opportunity of attempting to recover their lost possessions. The territories remaining to the latter were considerable, covering about 158 square miles. Rája Mán Singh resided at Paron, not far from Gúnah, where he held a *jágír* which had been assigned to his uncle in 1818 on the mediation of the British Government. The *jágír* was small in extent, but the character of the country, a hilly plateau intersected with ravines, with valleys difficult of access and covered in parts with patches of dense jungle, made it a convenient rendezvous and hiding-place for rebels and their followers.

In these circumstances three important measures called for immediate attention :—

1. To restore and maintain order in Gwalior.

2. To deal with the rebellious army; disarming and discharging the untrustworthy, and punishing ringleaders and murderers.

3. To bring under control the disaffected tract above described.

With regard to the first and second of the three measures Sindhia was disposed at first to purchase present peace by compromising with the rebel soldiery in a manner not uncommon in Asiatic States, for he shrank from the trouble and also the unpopularity of an investigation in which many of his former boon companions would be involved. But it was pointed out to him that, while indiscriminate severity should be avoided, mutiny and rebellion were crimes too dangerous to be passed over with impunity. Sindhia at length yielded, and, on the suggestion of the Political Agent and the advice of the minister, he agreed to entrust Major Meade with the duty of maintaining order in the capital, and to appoint him, in conjunction with Bulwant Rao, the late Commander-in-Chief, on a commission of inquiry into the conduct of the troops.

Both these measures were most efficiently performed, and the latter was of a specially onerous character; for the cases of upwards of 12,000 soldiers had to be inquired into, of whom between 5000 and 6000 actually appeared before the commission.

The inquiry, which lasted until the end of the year, was conducted by Major Meade with patience and impartiality, and the punishments awarded were moderate and discriminating. Of the delinquents, four only were executed; some 120 were awarded terms of imprisonment; a few were released on security. The rest of the faithless portion of the army were disbanded, and 4732 stand of arms and 1000 cavalry horses were recovered for the State. Meanwhile, in spite of the hostile movements of Tantia Topi in the vicinity of Gwalior territory, the soldiery, having confidence in the fairness of the commission, remained quiescent.

"From first to last," wrote Sir Richmond Shakespear, "throughout all the details of this difficult and delicate duty, Major Meade has not only carried the Mahárája with him, but has so arranged that His Highness should openly appear as superintending every step in the proceeding.

"The turbulent populace of the city of Gwalior has seen this considerable band of mutineers disarmed by the Mahárája with all the order and formality which characterised our disarming operations in 1844, after the battle of Maharájpur. The moral effect has been immense; there is not an enemy of ours who does not feel that had rebellion not received its death-blow this body of mutineers would never have marched here to be disarmed; if a hope of successful rebellion still lingered in the minds of the disaffected it must have been obliterated by this notable triumph of order and assertion of authority.

"Major Meade gives the credit to the Mahárája, but it is my pleasing duty to point out that, admirable as His Highness's conduct has been, it has been mainly caused by Major Meade's tact and judgment."

The Governor-General in Council highly commended the "tact and judgment" displayed by "Major

Meade in this difficult matter," and the Secretary of State endorsed the commendation.

The third measure—that of bringing under control the disaffected portion of Sindhia's territory—was taken in hand by the British General commanding in Gwalior, Sir Robert Napier; and in its execution he had in Meade's Horse a most serviceable corps.

On 2nd August, 1858, while Meade was closely engaged on the work of the commission, Mán Singh summoning his followers—12,000 strong, including the men of Sheopur—seized Sindhia's strong fort of Pauri, eighteen miles north-west of Sípri.

It was promptly attacked by forces from Sípri and Gwalior under Sir Robert Napier, and, after a brief bombardment, evacuated. Part of the retreating garrison, under Mán Singh's uncle, Ajít Singh, was caught and severely cut up; but both Mán Singh and Ajít Singh escaped. The chief of Sheopur surrendered to the Political Agent, but Mán Singh and his uncle remained at large in the difficult country surrounding the Rája's *jágír;* and the former was there joined by no less a personage than the arch-rebel and reputed murderer, Tantia Topi, who, notwithstanding his crushing defeat on the 21st June, had resumed active operations as a guerilla leader, and, after harassing Central India for well-nigh a year, was fairly run to earth in the jungle of Paron.

Tantia's adventurous career has been fully described in Colonel Malleson's pages and need not be detailed here. Suffice it to say that, though no less than five columns were on his track, he was able for a period of nine months successfully to evade capture; while he kept all the territory surrounding Gwalior on the west and south and east in a state of terror and unrest.

His troops had numerous collisions with detachments of British troops and were invariably defeated. But he was undismayed by defeat, and turned up in some fresh locality, keeping up the spirit of his followers by plundering some petty chief *en route*. Thus after his defeat at Jaura Alipur on the 21st June he proceeded rapidly to Tonk, defeated the Nawáb, and carried off spoil and guns. After being defeated by General Roberts at Bhílwára and on the Banás River in Jaipur territory he crossed the Chambal and moved to Jhálra Patan, where he levied a heavy contribution. Having possessed himself of the Rája's guns—thirty in number—he conceived the bold idea of marching on Indore in hopes of inducing Holkar's disaffected troops to join him. On the road he was attacked by General Michel's column at Rájgarh and utterly defeated, again losing all his guns.

But he obtained four fresh guns at Saronj and proceeded against Isagarh, a small fort in Sindhia's territory, which he stormed and plundered, obtaining seven fresh guns. He was again found and defeated by Michel. Again defeated at Mangrauli, he was joined by the Rao Sáhib's force at Lalitpur, then retreated southwards towards the Narbadda River. On the road he was attacked by Michel at Kurai and lost half his following; but he succeeded in crossing the Narbadda into the recently annexed territory of Nágpur, in the expectation of raising the country in his favour.

But six years' experience of British rule had produced a marked change in the feelings of the Marátha peasantry. They received Tantia and his followers not merely without enthusiasm, but with antipathy; not only declining to join his standard, but refusing him supplies.

Foiled in his hopes of aid in Nágpur, he recrossed the river, close pressed by British troops, and moved rapidly, in a westerly direction, towards Baroda, the seat of a Marátha dynasty where he had many sympathisers and hoped to obtain a more favourable reception. But he was caught by a force under Colonel Parke at Chota Udaipur, and again completely routed.

His position was now well-nigh desperate. His pursuers closed around him and the end seemed near; but he rallied his followers and rapidly moving to the north escaped their clutches, and was joined by a force under the pseudo-prince, Firoz Shah; he then tried to break through the pursuing columns on the north-west, but was caught by Brigadier Showers at Dewása in Rajputána, and his force routed and dispersed. Tantia fled through Márwár, but was again fallen upon by Holmes.

At length, to use his own words, Tantia became "tired of running away"; Firoz Shah separated from him, and, having quarrelled with his chief the Rao Sáhib, Tantia left the remnant of his force at Saronji and took refuge in the jungle near Paron, under the protection of Rája Mán Singh, whose clansmen, faithful as Highlanders, never revealed the hiding-place of their chief's guest, though he was for upwards of five weeks within a few miles of Sir Robert Napier's force of 2500 men.

Such was the situation in the beginning of 1859, when Major Meade, having completed his inquiry, joined the force of Sir Robert Napier, then moving from Nahnaghar, near Sheopur, to Saronji, fifty or sixty miles south-east of Gúna.

He was placed in charge of a field detachment of 260 Europeans, 500 native infantry and 250 cavalry (Meade's Horse), and directed to move on to Sirsi Mhau and open out roads and endeavour to capture or destroy Rája Mán Singh or Tantia Topi.

His proceedings and their results are thus described in a memorandum found amongst Sir Richard Meade's papers:—

"I reached Sirsi Mhau on the morning of the 3rd of March, and found it wholly deserted. The village, containing probably some 2000 to 3000 inhabitants, belonged to Thakor Naranjan Singh, an old man of sixty-five years of age, formerly a Pindári leader, who was connected with Rája Mán Singh and possessed much influence in the neighbourhood.

"It was known that Mán Singh had resided for some time at Sirsi Mhau, and that Naranjan Singh and his people had all been more or less concerned in his depredations, and retaliation for this was feared by the Thakor and his people.

"On the afternoon of the 3rd March I pushed a strong patrol through the Sirsi *ghát*, a difficult ascent of 400 or 500 feet to the higher plateau of the Jaláwar tableland, and opened communications with Major Little's column the same evening. During the 5th I was joined by his force and every exertion was made to clear a road up the *ghát*, which was rugged and densely wooded. This work was continued during the 6th, 7th and 8th, up to which dates I could get no tidings of Naranjan Singh.

"On the morning of the 8th I received information that Naranjan Singh with many of his people was at a village four or five miles distant. All the accounts that had reached me satisfied me that it was of the utmost importance to get him in, both for the local settlement of the immediate district and for the purpose of opening a communication with Mán Singh through him. I therefore determined at once to go and see him, and, taking two sowars (native horsemen), I galloped off to the village where I heard he was. On arriving there his son came out and I told him to tell his father that I was going some distance farther to examine the country, but that I expected he would be ready to see me on my return. On my return I found him with some fifty or sixty people waiting for me. He appeared nervous and alarmed, but I addressed him kindly and endeavoured to reassure him. Before I left him he promised to return to Sirsi Mhau that afternoon. This promise he fulfilled and the same evening I had a long conversation with him, which ended in his engaging to bring Mán Singh's confidential man to me in two or three days, and to do all in his power to induce Mán Singh himself to surrender.

"On the 11th March his son brought in Mán Singh's confidential man. I had a long conversation with him and communicated to him the conditions I was authorised to offer Mán Singh, *viz.:* a guarantee of life and subsistence; and I dismissed him the following morning with instructions to find out the Rája's family and household, and to invite them in my name to come in to me, in which case I promised to do everything in my power for their comfort. I sent with him a confidential orderly, with a communication addressed to the Ránis to the above effect, and another to Mán Singh himself, inviting his surrender; I however particularly instructed both the messengers that their first efforts were to be directed to get in the ladies and their followers, as if this were effected I felt sure that Mán Singh would follow them.

"I continued moving about till the 25th March, but could get no intelligence of Mán Singh or his people. The entire country was hostile to us and no one would give us information.

"But early on the 25th I received notice of the advent of the ladies and household. They arrived, in number about seventy people, that afternoon. I received them kindly and sent them the next day to one of the Rája's villages. . . .

"After some further communication with Mán Singh I had the satisfaction of receiving him in my camp on the morning of the 2nd April. During that and the following day I had many conversations with the Rája, and urged him to perform some service to entitle him to the consideration of the Government.

"At 11 P.M. on the 3rd I received intelligence that the Rája's uncle, Ajít Singh, with a band of rebels, was some fifteen miles off in the jungle, and at once started off with a party of 150 men to attack him, Mán Singh himself accompanying me. We reached the place where he had been marked down the previous night before daybreak, but found that he and his band had moved off during the night. We pushed on some seven miles farther to a place where the jungle was so dense that cavalry was useless and at which the rebels still were. It was now broad daylight, and, though we got close to them unobserved, they became aware of our approach before we could close on or surround them and to our great mortification all got away.

"We returned to camp at 1 P.M. that day, the 4th, utterly worn out and disappointed, having marched forty-five miles since 11 P.M. the previous night. Mán Singh was also in great despair at the result of the attempt to catch his uncle, who had threatened to take his life for coming in. All, however, was ordered for the best; Tantia Topi was then in the same jungle, and, had we attacked Ajít Singh, he would doubtless have taken the alarm and got out of the way. During the next three days I became fully satisfied that Tantia Topi was in the neighbourhood, and at length I got Mán Singh to acknowledge that he could point out where he was. I had the utmost difficulty in bringing him to the point of consenting to betray him and to enable us to catch him; at length, on the afternoon of the 7th April, he agreed to put him in my hands.[1]

"Much caution was necessary, as Tantia Topi had spies in my camp, and I could not therefore send an officer or European troops upon this duty; I selected therefore a party of the 9th Bombay N.I. under an intelligent native officer, and despatched them into the

[1] Great indignation has been expressed at the conduct of Mán Singh in betraying his guest; but it must be remembered that as a *mediatised* chief he owed a great deal of gratitude to the British Government, which had protected his family for forty years. He died in 1882, and has been succeeded by his son Gajendar Singh.

jungle that evening, and, under Mán Singh's direction, they captured Tantia Topi and brought him a prisoner into my camp by sunrise the following morning.

"It appeared that he had already started to join the rebels near Saronj, and that he had been in full communication with the Contingent troops (1000 strong) at Sheopur, whom he endeavoured to induce to join him.

"He stated, after his capture, that he was quite set up by the rest he had enjoyed, and that he intended recommencing his movements about the country, doing all the mischief he could.

"I took him to Sípri and tried him there by court martial, by which he was sentenced to death. He was hanged at Sípri on the 18th April, 1859."

Nothing was found upon him but a sword, a *kúkri* (a formidable knife[1]), and a purse containing 118 gold pieces. His two attendants, who may have had his papers, unfortunately escaped.

Tantia Topi was a Brahman by caste, and described himself as a native of the district of Púna (which has been British territory since 1818) and a resident of Bithúr, near Cawnpore (also in British territory), where he was in the service of the Nána as *musáhib* or A.D.C. He is said to have served for a time in the East India Company's army, and, at a later period, to have exercised the calling of money-lender; he entered the Nána's service in the capacity of *karáni*, *i.e.*, writer or accountant, but rose to the posi-

[1] Shaped something like a cob of maize (*kúkri*), whence, probably, its name.

tion of confidential agent. He spoke Urdú as well as Gujaráthi and Maráthi. His knowledge of English was very limited, but he could write his name in English characters.

In appearance he was a man of forty-five to fifty years of age, about five feet six inches in height, stout and well made; he had a particularly large head, of great breadth from ear to ear, covered plentifully with strong grey hair, with beard, moustaches and whiskers to match. His cheek-bones were slightly elevated, and his black eyes, under sharply arched eyebrows, were clear and piercing. Altogether his features are described as intelligent and expressive, denoting decision, energy, and ability. He answered questions put to him in Hindustáni curtly and apparently straightforwardly.

Before his trial Tantia Topi dictated a statement (which he carefully corrected) giving a concise account of his career from the date of the mutiny at Cawnpore to the time of his capture.

This statement, a translation of which is given *in extenso* in vol. vi. of Colonel Malleson's *History*, is a remarkable one. It is so terse and business-like as to be wearisome; but, so far as it can be tested, the narrative is, for the most part, singularly accurate. It nowhere minimises defeats or exaggerates successes, and gives the impression, at any rate, of being strictly true.

On two important points, however, Tantia's statements are quite at variance with general belief.

He asserts that the Nána Sáhib, usually believed to be a main-spring of disaffection, joined the mutineers in the first instance under compulsion and was in fact a mere puppet in their hands.

Some colour is given to this statement in the report of Lieut.-Colonel Williams, Commissioner of Military Police, who, during 1858-9, made elaborate inquiry into the circumstances of the Cawnpore defence, surrender, and massacres; for he states "that the Nána and his court possessed little or no authority over the rebel troops, who, it is evident, did just as they pleased".

However this may be it is clear, from Tantia Topi's own admission, that the Nána afterwards identified his cause with that of the rebel troops; and (so Colonel Williams tells us) in counsel with his brother Bála Sáhib and Azímullah, his *vakeel*, induced the rebels, when on their way to Dehli, to return to Cawnpore and carry on the siege.

With regard to the massacre at the *ghát*, Tantia Topi asserts in his statement and asserted verbally before execution that, under the direction of the Nána, he prepared the boats in good faith for the despatch of the fugitives, and placed provisions in them and started them; and that the massacre which followed was entirely the work of the infuriated sepoys, the Nána himself being innocent of all participation in it.

In the case of the Nána there is some evidence that, on news being brought to him in cantonments that women and children were being massacred at the *ghát*, he sent orders to the sepoys to cease firing; but as he had, as we have seen, "little or no authority over the troops," this was of little use.

But as regards Tantia Topi the truth of the statement has been emphatically denied by Mr. G. Lance, formerly magistrate of Cawnpore, who avers that there is ample evidence to show that Tantia, if he did not first plan the massacre, assisted in it by posting his men in ambush at the *ghát*, or by giving orders to that effect to Jawála Parshád, the Nána's brigadier-general of the mutinous regiments.

In regard to the question, who gave the signal for the massacre to commence? the evidence is conflicting. Two witnesses distinctly state that it was Tantia Topi. But other witnesses state that it was the Nána's brother, Bála Sáhib, or Azímullah, his *vakeel.* Colonel Williams seems to consider that it was the two latter and not Tantia Topi. The fact that the firing commenced on the Oude side of the river seems to indicate that in *carrying out* the massacre the Sepoys may have acted independently of the Nána's people. But this, if true, does not absolve the latter from the charge of *planning*, or, at least, *permitting* it.

And all agree that Tantia Topi was present in the Fisherman's Temple and that neither he nor any member of the Nána's party took any visible steps to prevent the massacre.

There is no evidence directly connecting Tantia Topi with the second massacre (in the *Bibighar*), but it was committed within 100 yards of the Nána's head-quarters and was not disavowed at the time either by the Nána or his staff.

From a general review of the evidence the probability appears to be that the Nána, under the influence of his more determined brother, and his unscrupulous *vakeel*, of Jawála Parshád (his brigadier), and one

Tíkam, an officer of one of the rebel regiments whom he had promoted, passively assented to atrocities he was too inert to plan and too irresolute to stay, and that Tantia Topi acted as his henchman.

The Government of India was very anxious that the question of Tantia Topi's complicity in the massacres should be dealt with at the trial, and on the 14th April, 1859, telegraphed to Colonel Williams, then at Allahabad, to send all available information to Meade's superior, General Sir R. Napier. But the information, if sent, arrived too late.

Accordingly Tantia Topi was not charged at his trial (which took place on the 15th) with complicity in the Cawnpore massacres or with murder, but with "having been in rebellion and having waged war against the British Government between January, 1857, and December, 1858, especially at Jhánsi and Gwalior".

In answer to the charge he said (in Urdú) :—

"I only obeyed in all things that I did my master's orders, that is to say the Nána's orders, up to the capture of Kálpi, and afterwards those of the Rao Sáhib. I have nothing to state except that I have had nothing to do with the murder of any Europeans, men, women, or children; neither did I at any time give orders for any one to be hanged."

He declined to ask the witnesses any questions.

He was found guilty of the offence charged, and very properly sentenced to death.

After sentence he comported himself with dignity and bravery, replying briefly and clearly to pertinent inquiries courteously made, but dismissing unnecessary or flippant questioning by a curt *Mâlum nahîn* (I don't know). "A glance of great contempt is observed on his countenance," says the *Times* correspondent, "when following the departure from his presence of some mediocre superior; but for Major Meade Tantia appears to have considerable respect."

He evinced no craving for life, and, even before his trial, he begged that he might be put out of his misery as soon as possible. "Blow me from a gun or hang me, but deliver me from these!" he said, holding up his irons.

He expressed no wish to see his family, but spoke tenderly of his *babalog* (children), and prayed that the Government would not allow them to suffer for any offence he had committed. He maintained to the last his innocence of murder.

He was executed at 4 P.M. on the 18th April, on the parade ground near the fort, in a square formed by the troops of the garrison, and surrounded by a large concourse of native spectators.

On his irons being removed he ascended the gallows with a firm step and placed his neck in the noose with the greatest *sang-froid*.

The propriety of the sentence has been called in question, and the *Friend of India*, commenting on the event, observed: "Among the horde of princelings, zemindars and adventurers, who rose to command among the mutineers, Tantia Topi is the only one whose fate will elicit in India a solitary expression of regret".

But his execution can be fully justified. It is true that his complicity in massacre, though generally believed, was never judicially established; but, irrespective of such complicity, it was proved at the trial that he was an important leader of rebellion; and, as such, the author of incalculable mischief and misery and much loss of life. At the time of his capture he was engaged in planning fresh enterprises; his escape from custody was by no means an impossibility; and in the circumstances of the time clemency would have been misplaced. His prompt execution, therefore, besides being in accordance with the law (Act xiv. of 1857), was urgently called for in the interests of peace; it tranquillised forthwith vast tracts of country and saved, there can be little doubt, a multitude of lives.

But his complicity in massacre, though never judicially investigated, is sufficiently proved for the purposes of history. The exact degree or extent of his complicity may, indeed, be open to dispute, but that he was *particeps criminis*—whether as prime mover, subordinate agent, or accessory, matters little—can admit of no reasonable doubt.

The value of the service rendered by Major Meade was at once recognised by public opinion throughout India. He was warmly congratulated by his political and military superiors, Sir Robert Hamilton, the Governor-General's Agent for Central India, then on his way to England, and Brigadier-General Sir Robert Napier, commanding in Gwalior; and by the General (Sir Hugh Rose) whose splendid recapture of the town and fortress was described in the last chapter. In reporting the capture Sir R. Napier described it as a

" national service," and a few months later the Government of India thus recognised the good work done :—

" From the Secretary to the Government of India to the officiating Adjutant-General of the Army.

"*Dated 26th August*, 1859.

" SIR,—With reference to the letter . . . forwarding for the information of Government documents relating to the capture of Tantia Topeh, and the surrender of Mán Singh, I am now desired to acquaint you, for the information of the Rt. Hon. the Commander-in-Chief, that His Excellency the Governor-General in Council considers the proceedings of Brigadier-General Sir R. Napier, K.C.B., and Major Meade to deserve the best thanks of Government.

" The admirable judgment exercised by the latter officer is especially to be commended. The value of his service has been thoroughly tested by the four months which have passed since it was rendered, and it may safely be said that few incidents in the contest which we have been waging in India have had a more direct effect in facilitating a return to peace and order than the surrender of Mán Singh and the capture of Tantia Topeh, both the work of Major Meade.

" I have, etc.,

" R. J. H. BIRCH, Major-General,

"*Secretary to the Government of India.*"

The Secretary of State for India endorsed the recognition of Meade's service, and in an autograph letter to Major Meade Lord Canning speaks of it as a "service for which the State is deeply indebted to you".

Sir Hugh Rose wrote as follows, and his letter is specially interesting, as it expresses his opinion of the military abilities of Tantia Topi :—

"POONAH, 14*th January*, 1860.

"MY DEAR MAJOR MEADE,—I am *extremely obliged* to you for your kind letter and Tantia Topee's confession, both of which I received to-day. . . .

"I have always thought that you rendered a most important service in effecting the capture of Tantia Topee, and I think that his success in escaping his pursuers, of every kind, is the best proof of the tact, ability and knowledge of the country and its inhabitants with which you effected the capture.

"There can be no doubt that of all the rebel chiefs who acted a part in the rebellion Tantia possessed the greatest enterprise, as regards initiation, and the most enduring resolution in character. His talents for organisation were also remarkable. You have no idea how much talent he displayed in this way in the preparation of the so-called Peishwa's army (which I see he estimates at 600 men); he had a little siege train, with the requisites in a rough way, and had not forgotten material for Jhánsi, which he intended to relieve.

"I hope you have been well rewarded for the service you did. . . .

"Yours sincerely,

"HUGH ROSE."

But perhaps the best testimony to the importance of the service rendered is to be found in the number of those who claimed a share in it. These are humorously described in the following doggerel lines by a sergeant of the 3rd Bengal Europeans:—

"Who caught Tantia Topee?
'Twas I, said the Digger,[1]
With spade, sword, and trigger,
I caught Tantia Topee.

[1] Brigadier-General Sir R. Napier, R.E., who sought to find Tantia by driving a number of cross-roads through the jungle, where he was known to be hidden.

"Who caught Tantia Topee?
'Twas I, said Pat Meade,
By palaver and speed,
Who else did the deed?

"Who caught Tantia Topee?
'Twas I, said "our Showers,"[1]
By hot haste and dours,
He funked me, he did, "by the Powers"!

"Who caught Tantia Topee?
'Twas I, said Durbár,[2]
With my spies near and far,
And Maun Singh through my own *Commasdár.*[3]

"Who caught Tantia Topee?
'Twas I, said Maun Singh,
Who planned the whole thing,
To save my own neck from the string!

"Who caught Tantia Topee?
Not I, said old "Mac,"[4]
But I hunted the pack,
And when they get back
We'll put in, one and all, for *the lac!*"[5]

[1] Brigadier-General Showers, whose successful attack on Tantia Topi's force at Dewása in Rájputána broke up his following and drove him to seek refuge with Mán Singh.

[2] The Gwalior Native Council of State.

[3] *Komisdár* (properly *Kamávisdár*) is a Marátha sub-collector of revenue, the same as a *tahsildar* in Northern India. *Naib-Komisdár Pirbhú Lal* was of great assistance to Major Meade.

[4] Major Macpherson, Political Agent at Gwalior.

[5] The Government of India offered a lakh of rupees reward for the capture of Tantia Topi. If any one deserved the reward it was Major Meade and those with him. But Major Meade neither asked for nor received any pecuniary recompense.

Though the surrender of Rája Mán Singh and the execution of Tantia Topi had, as we have seen, a marked effect upon the public peace, especially in the territories of Gwalior, there were still gatherings of rebels outside those territories, whose dispersal or destruction was necessary before the *pax Britannica* could be said to be completely re-established.

At length on the 1st July, 1859, Meade received intelligence of a large gathering of mutinous sepoys and local rebels in the Jhánsi district at a place called Garroya or Garwai.

Taking with him a squadron of his Horse, and a small force from Sípri, Meade made a night march of thirty miles, and early on the morning of the 2nd July was fortunate enough to surprise the enemy, whom he at once attacked and utterly dispersed with the loss of upwards of 100 men, and two of the principal local chiefs.

This successful affair virtually closed the rebellion in this part of India, and Meade and his force received the thanks of the Government of the North-West Provinces, the Commander-in-Chief, Lord Clyde, and the Supreme Government.

The success also closed Meade's career as a military officer, for now, as we shall see, a new sphere of duty was offered to him.

CHAPTER VIII.

WORK AS POLITICAL AGENT AT GWALIOR.

Meade appointed acting Agent—Letter from Lord Canning—Meade rapidly acquires influence over Sindhia—Secret of his success—Interview with Lord Canning at Agra in 1859—Is thanked for his services, and in 1860 confirmed in his appointment—Handsome testimony from Lord Canning, by whom he is frequently consulted—Negotiates the treaty of 1860 with Sindhia, and on the death of Sir R. Shakespear is offered and accepts the important post of Resident at Indore and Governor-General's Agent for Central India.

We enter now upon a new phase in Sir Richard Meade's career.

For upwards of twenty years he had served his country as a soldier, with credit, indeed, but with little opportunity for distinction, and little hope of advancement outside the ordinary routine; but he had made the best use of his opportunities, and when the time came, he displayed qualities which marked him as well fitted not only for the military but also for the political service of the Government, a service in which military training and experience are, indeed, of no small value, but in which sound judgment, patience, and an intimate acquaintance with oriental character are the most important requirements.

In July, 1859, Major Macpherson, the Political Agent at Gwalior, whose health had severely suffered from the heat of Gwalior, and the intense strain upon his mind during the Mutiny, and the difficult and anxious times which followed, applied for temporary leave, and recommended that Major Meade should be appointed to officiate for him.

Lord Canning at once acted on the recommendation. On the 9th August Meade was gazetted as officiating Political Agent of Gwalior, and on the 25th received an autograph letter from His Excellency, from which we quote the following paragraph :—

"I hope that your new functions at Gwalior will be agreeable to you. If you bring to the discharge of them the same energy, patience, and tact, which have marked your performance of other duties, I shall have good reason to rejoice that a delicate charge is in such good hands."

The Governor-General was not disappointed. Major Meade rapidly acquired a remarkable influence over the Mahárája Sindhia, as he did over every chief with whom he was subsequently brought in contact.

What was the secret of his success?

It was not the result of any acquired art of statesmanship. It could not have been so in Meade's case, for he had received no diplomatic or even administrative training.

He had, it is true, the advantage of more than twenty years' experience of native character in different parts of India. But this, though an important element of efficiency in a political officer, is by no means the most important.

Meade was also a fair linguist. He knew Persian and Urdú, and had colloquial knowledge of Maráthi. But linguistic attainments, though valuable, are by no means essential to success; the late Sir Robert Sandeman, for instance, one of the most successful politicals of modern times, knew little of the language of the tribes and races with whom he had principally to deal.

What was it then?

It was simply this: Meade added to the qualifications above described all the characteristics of the ideal "English gentleman,"—firmness and loyalty to the Government he served, deep interest in the chiefs and peoples of the States where he was employed, good sense, straightforwardness, unbounded patience, a most genial manner and a scrupulous regard for the feelings and position of the Prince to whom he was accredited. He worked with him as a friend, keeping the "representative of the Paramount Power" in the background; he educated without lecturing, and governed without seeming to do so.

He was thus enabled to bring to a successful issue many questions of difficulty which had hung fire for a long time, and in regard to which the chief had shown himself more or less impracticable. *Inter alia* he induced His Highness to assign large tracts of land required by the British Government for railway purposes in Nímár, to allow the railway authorities jurisdiction over all persons residing within railway limits, and to grant to the Agent to the Governor-General for Central India power to decide all disputes between railway servants and subjects of the Gwalior State.

Meade's success was soon recognised.

In October, 1859, Lord Canning held a grand durbar at Agra, for the reception of the loyal chiefs and gentry of the North-West Provinces, who had done good service in the Mutiny—one of the brilliant series of gatherings at which the dignity of his presence and speeches left an impression never to be forgotten. On this occasion His Excellency specially sent for Meade, and on his arrival shook him warmly by the hand, and intimated that he had particularly desired Meade's attendance to thank him, in the name of the Government of India, for his services when acting as Political Agent; and further inquired whether he would wish to be permanently transferred to the political department.

Major Meade was gratified but not elated, for in a letter to Mrs. Meade he says:—

"At Agra I received the greatest kindness from Lord and Lady Canning . . . but I fear my visit has not done me much good; for, to tell the truth, I was somewhat overwhelmed at having to occupy a position to which I was so little accustomed".

But Major Meade's idea of the impression he had created was erroneous.

On the 15th April, 1860, Major Macpherson, weary in mind and body and, as yet, unhonoured,[1] died in Calcutta, of the same disease which was soon to carry off the Viceroy himself. In the same month Meade was confirmed in the appointment, and in a private letter announcing the event Lord Canning wrote as follows:—

"I wish you to know that I never made an ap-

[1] The *Gazette* notice of his appointment as C.B. appeared after his death.

pointment regarding which I was so satisfied that it was for the interest and credit of the Government and for the honour and advantage of the native State concerned as in the case of your own appointment at Gwalior.

"The conduct of your duties, while officiating for your predecessor, has been so uniformly judicious and temperate, and so entirely in the spirit of an English gentleman—firm in the discharge of the duties prescribed to you, and thoroughly respectful, considerate and friendly to the Prince to whom you are accredited—that I have no doubt of the benefit which will result from your permanent appointment."

There was another reason why Meade's permanent appointment was specially desired by the Viceroy. Dinkar Rao, Sindhia's able minister, who was devoted to British interests, had for some time been losing favour with his master, and in December, 1859, vacated office, and thereupon Sindhia himself superintended the whole of his affairs. It was, therefore, of the greatest importance that the representative of the British Government should have personal influence over the Gwalior Chief. Though Meade was unable to prevent Dinkar Rao's dismissal, he prevailed upon the Chief to recognise his past services by the grant of a valuable *jágír*.

From this date Meade found himself in the position of confidential adviser to Lord Canning on matters of great delicacy and importance, *e.g.*, in regard to difficulties connected with the conferment of the Order of the Star of India upon Ruling Chiefs; and the appointment of Dinkar Rao to a seat in the Legislative Council of India. On both these subjects important communications passed between the Viceroy and Major Meade, showing clearly the value attached by Lord Canning to Major Meade's opinions; but we do not quote them *in extenso*, as their subject-matter, besides being confidential, is no longer one of public interest.

In the same year he induced the Mahárája to consent to the construction of a bridge over the river Chambal, thus removing a great obstacle to rapid communication between Gwalior and Agra; and, after protracted discussion, he succeeded in negotiating a treaty between His Highness and the British Government (the treaty of 1860), by which important interchanges of territory were effected between the two Governments. Lands yielding a revenue of three lakhs of rupees together with the city and fort of Jhánsi were transferred to the Mahárája; *per contra* certain of the territories assigned for the support of the Contingent Force were transferred in full sovereignty to the British Government, and the British Government engaged to keep in the place of the late Contingent a Subsidiary Force constantly stationed within His Highness the Mahárája's territories, while the Mahárája's force of all arms was increased to 5000 infantry, 6000 cavalry and thirty-six guns.

These arrangements appear simple enough on paper, but their successful negotiation involved infinite tact and patience, which only those who have been engaged in a similar task can adequately appreciate. But his work was warmly appreciated by his immediate superior, the Governor-General's Agent at Indore, who observed in his covering letter to the Government :—

"I am very deeply indebted to Major Meade, whose influence and judgment were most useful to me; and whose untiring exertions were invaluable in aiding me, not only during the conferences, but in conducting personally, when I was not present, the discussion with the Mahárája of many complicated and delicate questions".

The Government of India "gladly concurred," and the services of both officers were thus referred to in the Secretary of State's despatch of 8th May, 1861 :—

"It only remains for me, whilst congratulating your Excellency on the success of these negotiations with the Gwalior Durbár, and confidently anticipating their good results to both Governments, to express my approbation of the manner in which they have been carried out by the officers by whom you were so efficiently represented at Sindhia's court. To Sir Richmond Shakespear and to Major Meade your Excellency has conveyed your acknowledgments, and I have to request that they may be informed that Her Majesty's Government entirely concurs in the commendations which you have bestowed upon them."

A more substantial recognition was soon in store for him.

In November, 1861, Colonel Sir Richmond Shakespear, who had succeeded Sir Robert Hamilton as Resident at Indore and Agent to the Governor-General for Central India, died very suddenly, and a political appointment of the greatest importance became vacant—an appointment usually conferred upon officers of long departmental training.

At a ball given at Allahabad at the end of November, 1861, on the occasion of the investiture of Sindhia and other chiefs with the Order of the Star of India, Lord Canning sent for Meade, and, to his profound astonishment, offered him the vacant post. After a moment's hesitancy, the result of surprise and modesty, not of disinclination, the offer was gratefully accepted.

In December, 1861, he bade adieu to Gwalior, one of the hottest and most trying stations in India, and proceeded to the palatial Residency at Indore, with a far cooler climate and more genial surroundings.

An account of the new scene of Major Meade's labours, where he was destined to remain for upwards of eight years, and the new duties devolving upon him, will be given in the succeeding chapter.

THE RESIDENCY, INDORE.
(From a Sketch by Mrs. Daly.)

CHAPTER IX.

WORK AS GOVERNOR-GENERAL'S AGENT FOR CENTRAL INDIA.

Description of Central India—Its political importance—The great Marátha States—Bhopál—The "mediatised" chiefs—Contingents—The States in Bundelkhand and Baghelkhand—Conflicting interests—Differences settled, and the peace maintained by the Governor-General's Agent and seven subordinate Political Agents—The British Force in Central India—The local corps—The residency at Indore and its surroundings—Improvements effected by Meade and his successors—General condition of the States of the Agency at the time of Meade's appointment in respect to police, administration of justice, military forces, education, public works, roads, jail buildings, forest conservancy—Gwalior and its ruler—Questions to be dealt with—Indore and Holkar—Bhopál—The minor States of Málwa—Mánpur—The States of Bundelkhand and Rewah—Important political and administrative work devolving on the Governor-General's Agent.

THE jurisdiction of the Central India Agency extends over two groups of protected native States, occupying the hilly region between the Chambal and Jamna rivers on the north, and the Narbadda on the south [1]—the two groups being separated from each other by the valley of the Betwa, a picturesque but unnavigable stream, which, rising in the Vindhya mountains, near Bhopál, flows in a wide and winding and rocky channel into the Jamna near Hamírpur.

[1] A small portion of Holkar's territory extends to the south of Narbadda.

The territories of the western group include Gwalior (already described), the great Málwa plateau and the Sátpúra highlands; those of the eastern are known as Bundelkhand and Baghelkhand (or Rewah), that is, "the land of the Bundelas and Baghels," two tribes of Rájput origin, once dominant in the locality.

In all they cover an area of about 83,000 square miles—an area, that is to say, larger than England and Scotland combined—and have a population (chiefly Hindú) of about 10,000,000, and revenues roughly estimated at 300 lakhs of rupees per annum.

As might be supposed in a region so extensive the character of the country and its people varies greatly. On the south-west are desolate wilds and jungles, the home of the Bhíl tribes, an aboriginal race, abhorring labour, whose gradual reclamation from a life of savagery is one of the special functions of the Agency; farther east are the rich plains of Málwa, peopled by thrifty agriculturists, producers (*inter alia*) of the finest opium; then the hill-tracts of Ummatwára, Sironj and Kichiwára, with scanty cultivation and long stretches of dense jungle; farther north by east is the country about Gwalior, open and treeless and once desolate, but now well cultivated and prosperous; and still farther east the submontane region of Bundelkhand and Baghelkhand on the northern spur of the great Vindhya range; part of it (on the north-west) a fertile plain of black cotton soil, interspersed with granite ridges and detached hills, part rising abruptly by successive plateaus to the level of the Vindhya tableland; a region of forests and foaming rivers and grand waterfalls, with precipices overhung with foliage overlooking fertile valleys, and broad sheets of splendid cultivation carefully irrigated from wells and tanks and streams; a region, in Meade's time, comparatively little known, but now, thanks in no small measure to our "politicals," surveyed and mapped, and traversed by four lines of railway.

But the charm of Central India lies, not only in its varied scenery, but in the interest and extent and splendour of its archæological and architectural remains.

Around Bhilsa, in Gwalior territory, not far from Bhopál, is a collection of Buddhist monuments—some, possibly, of an age anterior to Asoka, but most of them ranging between B.C. 250 and A.D. 79—a collection grander than can be found elsewhere in the whole of India, from the Satlaj to Cape Comorin.[1]

At Sánchi (hard by), on a mound overlooking the valley of the Betwa, stands the most perfect *top* in India—a domed building, 106 feet in diameter, and 42 feet in height—with an inscription in the old Lát characters, which fixes its date at the first half-century of the Christian era.

Again, in the fortress of Gwalior, and in those of Ajaigarh and Kalinjar, in Bundelkhand, and at Kajrao, in Chatterpur, near Nowgong, are the remains of elaborately carved Jain temples and inscriptions, dating from the first to the tenth century A.D.

While in the petty principality of Dhár, on the western edge of the Central Indian plateau, stand the ruins of Mándú; once a Hindú stronghold, then, in the fifteenth and sixteenth centuries A.D., the capital of

[1] Fergusson.

the Ghorian (Afghán) Rulers of Málwa. The ramparts have, it is said, a circuit of thirty-seven miles, and the principal mosque and palaces are among the finest specimens of Patán architecture in India—and standing, as these ruins do, in solitude, overlooking the valley of the Narbadda, they convey "a very vivid impression of the ephemeral splendour of the Muhammadan dynasties of Central and Southern India".[1]

As to population, the dominant though not the most numerous race in Gwalior and Málwa is the Marátha—immigrants from the region south of the Narbadda, the highland home of their forefathers—a bold and vigorous peasantry, Hindús to the backbone, but not caste-ridden, whom the administrative weakness of the decaying Mughal Empire transformed into freebooters and guerilla horsemen.

It was the old story. First utilised as mercenaries, they learned their strength. Then, amid the ruins of old Hindú principalities, they challenged the existence of Muhammadan supremacy,—a supremacy no longer represented by hardy northern warriors, but by luxurious camps, by showy but ill-disciplined horsemen, and armies of slaves and menials commanded by "silken generals".

Led by Sívaji and his successors their marauding bands overran the territory of the oppressor. Their standards waved over the plains of Hindústán and the gleam of their lances was seen along the banks of the Indus. From the Indus to the Ganges, from the

[1] Among modern buildings of interest may be mentioned the tomb of Abulfazl, the chronicler, Akbar's secretary, who died in Gwalior at the close of the sixteenth century.

THE RUINS OF MÁNDÚ.
(From a Sketch by Mrs. Daly.)

Himalayas to the Káveri their desolating sway extended. For fifty years they dominated Orissa, and the "Mahratta Ditch" of Calcutta, now a municipal boundary, but once a formidable intrenchment, attests their unwelcome presence in Bengal.

For upwards of a century, they were the scourge of India, and nearly succeeded in establishing a vast Hindú empire—which promised to be much worse than that which it supplanted. But the world was saved from this calamity. Weakened by dissensions, the growth of luxury, and the uprising of subject races, and defeated and crushed in battle by Afgháns on the north and by Englishmen on the east and south, the empire fell; and a race, once the scourge of India, is now one of the most industrious in Her Majesty's dominions. But the Marátha still lives; his body as vigorous and supple and his intellect as keen as ever; his expressive language, the purest of the Sanscrit vernaculars, is now the mother-tongue of 19,000,000 souls, and he still holds his own as a ruling power among the Feudatory States of Central India.

But in Central India the Marátha is still regarded as a foreigner; and the local heads of society, in both divisions of the Agency, are the Rájput or Bundela or Baghel landholders,—representatives of the ancient conquerors and lords of the soil,—a melancholy race, too proud to work or even take service in the army, burdened with debt, fuddled with opium, and dying of ennui. The *workers* are tribes of inferior caste such as Játs, Gújars, Ahírs, Kunbis, Gonds, etc., with a sprinkling of Mussulman converts from Hinduism. In towns the bankers and traders hail chiefly from Bombay, Marátha pandits are innumerable, and a few families of Patán or Mughal origin, descendants from old Government officials and military settlers, have a good position. Brahmans are numerous in all the better callings, both in town and country, but (strange to say) are not held in much account.

Politically the region is important. The western portion includes the great Marátha States of Gwalior and Indore, with territories greatly intermixed; the compact Muhammadan kingdom of Bhopál, next to Hyderabad the greatest of the Mussulman States of India; and three other States (two Marátha and one Muhammadan), under direct treaty engagement with the British Government; and ninety-four minor chiefships chiefly Rájput;—some held direct from the British Government though not by treaty, some under engagements "mediated" between them and their feudal superiors, the great Marátha chiefs, by the British Government and known technically as "mediatised chiefships".

The principal States pay no tribute, in the ordinary sense, but are required to contribute to the military defence of the empire. This was done up to the year 1857 by providing or contributing to the provision of Contingents of native troops officered by Englishmen. But every one of these Contingents—the Gwalior Contingent, the Mehidpur Contingent, the United Málwa Contingent and the Bhopál Contingent—being composed of the same materials as our own army—mutinied in 1857, and either joined the enemy or had to be disbanded; and were, in Meade's time, represented by three newly formed local corps, organised on the "class system" and recruited from local tribesmen and races known to be loyally disposed. These corps still exist and are further described below. In addition, some of the chiefs,—notably Gwalior, Indore, Bhopál, Kashmír, the Sikh chiefs and others—have of late years formed from their own armies Imperial Service corps, some of which have already earned distinction, but these had no existence in Meade's time.

The eastern portion of the Agency includes the States of Bundelkhand—with populations similar to those of Málwa, but all holding directly, by treaty or *sanad*, as the case may be, from the British Government—and Rewah (a Baghel chiefship) and three smaller States, with domains stretching to the confines of Bengal, more backward in many respects than Bundelkhand, but in parts well cultivated, and possessing extensive treasures of timber, coal and minerals.[1]

In all the number of separate chiefs under the protection of the Agency exceeds 200, with feelings and interests frequently divergent and each jealous of his neighbour. The Rájput, proud of his ancestry, hates the Marátha "foreigner"; Sindhia, if he dared, would destroy Holkar;[2] while the Muhammadan—as a product of Mughal domination—claims (in his heart) to be the lord of all. But for the controlling hand of the Paramount Power and the tranquillising effect upon the Rájput clans of Malcolm's system of "mediatised"

[1] Little was known in Meade's time of the resources of Baghelkhand, but it is now traversed by two lines of railway, and its coal sources are being exploited by a company.

[2] This remark, it is needless to say, has no personal significance.

subchiefships, the territories would be (as they were before our advent) in a condition of perpetual unrest; harried by border raiders, plundered by Pindáris, haunted by Thugs, and desolated from time to time by intertribal conflicts and the struggles of rival chieftains.

Amid these elements of strife and war, the *pax Britannica* is quietly but firmly maintained by the Governor-General's Agent for Central India (who is *ex-officio* Resident at Indore)—the local representative of the protecting Power, the guardian of treaty engagements, the arbiter-general of differences, and the friend and adviser of all. He was aided (in Meade's time) by a couple of English assistants at head-quarters, and seven subordinate Political Agents stationed in Gwalior, Gúnah, Bhopál, Bundelkhand, Nagode, Western Málwa, and the Bhíl country; each with a staff of native subordinates and attended by *vakeels* representing the States controlled by him.

In support of the Agent's authority there were about 12,000 British troops of all arms, located in twelve cantonments or stations in suitable positions; eight garrisoned by the regular army under the General commanding at Mhau, and four by local corps under the orders of the Agent. Of the total force about one third were Europeans; the remainder were native troops officered by Englishmen, on the system successfully employed on the Punjab frontier.

At the time Meade joined, and indeed during the whole term of his office, the regular army had a quiet time; for, since the last embers of mutiny had been stamped out by Meade at Garroya, peace reigned through Central India, unbroken save by occasional disquiet on the Rájputána border, a few raids by Bhíls from the Sátpúra hills, and quarrels between petty tribal chiefs and their superiors, or other disturbances of no political importance, easily dealt with by the local corps.

These (as we have already mentioned) were three in number:—

(1) The Central India Horse[1]—into which "Meade's Horse" had recently been merged—under the immediate command of Colonel Daly, Meade's successor at Gwalior; a corps then usefully employed in protecting lines of communication and suppressing crime in Western Málwa; (2) the Bhopál Battalion, organised in lieu of the late Bhopál Contingent which had mutinied; and (3) the Málwa Bhíl Corps for controlling the wild tribes of the south-western border districts from which it was principally recruited.

Such is a brief description of the new sphere of Colonel Meade's labours and the instruments of his administration; let us now glance at his own position and surroundings.

The head-quarters of the Agent for Central India are at Holkar's capital, Indore—an ill-built, uninteresting town,—where they were finally located by Sir John Malcolm, the first Agent, after the decisive victory of Mehidpur in 1817 had placed all Málwa and its chiefs at the mercy of the British Government.

[1] The Central India Horse was formed in substitution for the cavalry portion of the Mehidpur and Málwa Contingents which mutinied in 1857.

Situated near the edge of the Málwa plateau, Indore has (for India) a fairly genial climate. April and May are hot, but, with the bursting of the rains in June, the south-west monsoon blows cool and fresh from the Indian Ocean, and all goes pleasantly till the end of March.

As for the Residency building, from a modern standpoint it could hardly be regarded as either picturesque or comfortable; but it was specially attractive in the eyes of Lady Meade from its association with her great relative. And it had the charm of being situated in grounds of singular beauty, which Meade was able greatly to improve. At the time he assumed office, they were disfigured by an unsightly water-course, dry and stony during a great part of the year, and brimming over in the rains; but by damming up and regulating the stream, generally deepening its bed and utilising the soil obtained from the excavations, Meade formed an extensive lake bordered with luxuriant foliage and dotted with islets planted with bamboo and flowering grass,—a lake, not only a thing of beauty, but a great public benefit, for it served also as a much-needed reservoir for the supply of water to the city. Following Meade's idea, successive Agents—and in particular Sir L. Griffin—have done much still further to improve the grounds, which are now said to be unequalled for beauty in the whole of India.

As Indore was unconnected by railway with the outside world, and Mhau—the military station—was fourteen miles off, the Residency, from a social point of view, was very quiet; but this absence of distraction was far from unwelcome to Meade, who found the task

View on the River in the Residency Grounds, Indore.

of mastering the details of his charge and reorganising the work of the Agency, which had suffered severely from the effects of the great Mutiny, as engrossing as it was important and laborious.

After the early morning ride, he would receive any representatives of States, or other native gentlemen desirous of seeing him, and so patient and lengthy were his discussions, that the breakfast hour, nominally 10, was sometimes protracted until 12·30. After breakfast he disappeared into his office until dark, sometimes returning to it after the evening drive. After a late dinner, a quiet half-hour with a book and a game of billiards, at which he was a great adept, usually terminated the evening. Of course, a certain number of "*bara khánahs*" or official dinners were given; but the social requirements of Indore were very small compared with those of Mysore and Hyderábád, where a "public breakfast" was given once a week, and "big dinners" were frequent; where, in fact, the family rarely sat down to any meal alone, and official visits and entertainments took up a large amount of time. In Central India Meade spent usually some five months of every year under canvas,—traversing every part of his extensive Agency, visiting Chiefs at their capitals, settling disputes, suggesting improvements, inspecting schools, hearing representations, and gaining information of every kind. But there was one thing he could not do—though an excellent shot and rider, and a sportsman to the backbone—he could find no time for either shooting or hunting. The only out-door pastime he indulged in was boating or sailing on the lake he had himself created. In Mysore, too, he had a good deal of camp life. But the work at Hyderábád kept him a good deal at head-quarters.

But we are anticipating, and must return to Central India. To enable the reader to understand the situation and gauge the progress of the Agency during Meade's incumbency, it is necessary to add a sketch of the condition of the States and their principal chiefs at the time he assumed office.

In most of the States—thanks to the influence of the Political Officers—there was some attempt at police administration, and the peace was, upon the whole, well preserved; in Bhopál and Gwalior and a few of the States which, owing to minorities or other cause, had been temporarily under British management, courts of justice with specially trained judges had been established; but, as a rule, the administration of justice, civil and criminal, was in the hands of executive officers, already overworked, who dealt with the cases, during spare moments, in arbitrary fashion, and were open to every kind of influence; for an independent judiciary, so much clamoured for by young India at the present time, is a thing unknown in native States. Except in the case of "mediatised" chiefships or States under British management, no appeal lies to the Agent from the decision of a chief or of the courts of justice in the States of Central India; but habitual and flagrant injustice would be a ground for depriving a chief of the management of his territories.

The military forces of the chiefs, especially at Gwalior, were nominally considerable, amounting in all to nearly 40,000 infantry, 13,000 cavalry and no less than 535 guns; but, except in Gwalior, the troops were ill armed and miserably drilled, and the guns more or less unserviceable.

The state of education was, as might be supposed, extremely backward. In Gwalior and Indore and some other States, schools and colleges had been established; and in a few States—notably Bhopál and Dhár—a commencement of female education had been made. But, as a rule, "education," except as a means of procuring livelihood as clerks, or shopkeepers, or priests, was not appreciated in Central India; on the contrary, many of the rulers regarded it as undesirable and objectionable; so that whatever advance was made was the result of pressure from without, or, in the case of Gwalior, through the influence of the great Dinkar Rao, Sindhia's late minister.

The revenue, as is usual in native States, was raised chiefly from the land, sometimes by division of the crop, sometimes by cash assessment. Except in Gwalior, where (thanks to Dinkar Rao) liberal assessments of land revenue had been granted for terms of years; in Bhopál, where the Rulers had been amenable to advice, and in those of the States which were, or had been, under British management, the demand was uncertain and generally excessive; sometimes collected by unscrupulous farmers of the tax, sometimes by officials ill-paid and consequently oppressive. The general principle of taxation was that the State, as lord of the soil, should "take all that it could get". The income from land revenue was supplemented by receipts from innumerable cesses, a tax on spirits, and by customs and transit duties of a particularly vexatious character. ·

Trade, as might be supposed, was much hampered by bad roads and even more by the intricate net-work of customs-lines, which caught the unhappy merchant at every turn; nevertheless in Málwa there was a brisk traffic connected with the manufacture and export of opium and cotton, and the import of English piece-goods; there was a valuable general trade in Gwalior; and Bhind was a busy cotton mart; in Bundelkhand and Baghelkhand the traffic was chiefly local; but in Rewah there was much demand for timber for railway purposes, and the diamond mines of Pannah attracted to it jewellers and merchants who trade in precious stones.

With regard to public improvements there had been considerable activity in respect of those in which imperial interests were concerned—that is to say, in the case of military works in the twelve cantonments or stations in which the British forces were located, and the construction of main lines of communication designed to open up the country. The Grand Trunk Road from Bombay to Agra, 446 miles of which passed through Central India, had made good progress. The great Deccan Road, connecting Mirzapur with Jabalpur, was being bridged and metalled. And new roads had been projected or commenced through Bundelkhand, connecting Gwalior with Etáwah on the north and with Jabalpur on the south, Saugor with Bánda, Bánda with Sípri.

These works, being more or less imperial in character, were planned (for the most part) at head-quarters and all the Indore Resident could do was to suggest and criticise, and exercise a general supervision over some portions of the lines running through Central Indian territory ;—but even this privilege was denied to him with regard to other portions; for the northern portion of his charge was, for imperial public works purposes, under the Government of the North-West Provinces, and the south-west portion under that of Bombay. This anomalous arrangement was obviously objectionable and before Meade's term of office was concluded it was remedied—all public works executed in Central India being placed under the control of the Governor-General's Agent.

But there was much to be done in promoting and carrying out—at the joint expense of the Imperial Government and local funds and the Native States interested—the construction of "feeders"—that is roads connecting main lines or railways with adjacent towns and marts, and providing both trunk-lines and feeders with staging bungalows and rest-houses.

Little had been done, either by political officers or the chiefs of States, in the matter of providing jail buildings; still less for providing medical aid for the people, but there were about a dozen dispensaries in different parts of the jurisdiction, some of them maintained by native States, to the great benefit of the population.

Nor had much been done to conserve what remained of the valuable timber—teak, ebony, and *sál*, which once abounded in the forests of Central India, but were rapidly disappearing.

For all these departments of his work Meade's early training and engineering studies admirably fitted him, and he entered upon them *con amore.*

As for the States and their Rulers, the principal State, though not the largest in area, was Gwalior, with an army of about 5000 infantry, 6000 cavalry, 600 gunners, and 163 serviceable guns; besides armed and drilled police battalions of nearly 4000 men. Gwalior and its chief have already been described. The enlightened system of administration established by Dinkar Rao was still nominally in force, but the estrangement between Sindhia and his late minister still continued with disastrous results. There was a decided falling off in the administration and the police in the Málwa portion of the territory was far from efficient. But Meade's successor at Gwalior, Colonel (afterwards Sir Henry) Daly, was the right man for the post—able, resolute and cheery, and could be trusted to do all that was possible to stimulate improvement. Sindhia himself was on the best of terms with Meade and anxious to please the Government of India; but he was deeply disappointed at the delay which had occurred in handing over to him the Gwalior fortress which had been captured from the rebels by Sir Hugh Rose's force; and the size of the new army and its concentration at Gwalior were subjects of anxiety.

Next to Gwalior the most important State in the agency was Indore. Its territories are far less extensive than those of Sindhia, but like his very scattered and intermixed with those of other chiefs. In size it

H.H. Tukoji Rao Holkar,
Mahárája of Indore.

is about as large as Wales and has a population of 1,000,000. There was an army of 5600 infantry, 3000 cavalry, and 24 guns—but far less efficient (for good or evil) than that of Sindhia.

At the time of Meade's advent the Government was centred in Maháràja Tukoji Rao Holkar, a chief with a good English education, not wanting in ability, and given to spasmodic bursts of energy; but, as a rule, inert, jealous of his power and opposed to all reform. In short, a far from promising subject for the "friendly influence" of a "political". His loyalty in 1857 had (to say the least) been less conspicuous than that of other chiefs, and he had consequently received no increase of territory like his neighbours, Sindhia and Bhopál. This was a standing grievance which did not improve a disposition not naturally contented. But, though a doubtful friend in need, distrusted by his neighbours, disliked by his subjects and difficult to move, he had, at least, one redeeming virtue; he kept a tight hand over his officials and promptly punished any oppression or peculations proved against them. Upon the whole, therefore, the administration of his territory, though open to criticism, was better supervised and more efficient than in most of the States.

At the time of Meade's appointment Holkar's relations with the Government of India were friendly, but there were serious differences with the Bombay Government in respect to the final settlement of territorial exchanges agreed upon in 1861, and constant bickerings and disputes with the Gwalior Government in regard to land in Jhabúa on the western border.

Bhopál is, next to Hyderábád, the most important

Mussulman State in India, with an area not far short of Holkar's, a population of nearly 1,000,000, and a military force of about 2000 infantry, 8000 cavalry, and 69 guns. Its ruling family is Afghán, descendants of Dost Muhammad Khan, a distinguished officer of the Mughal Emperor Aurangzeb, and it was represented at the time of Meade's appointment by Shah Jahán Begam, the daughter of Sikandar Begam, G.C.S.I., who, after the death of her worthless husband in 1844 and the usual family dissensions, was appointed Regent by the British Government in 1847.

Under the advice of a former Agent, Sir Robert Hamilton, she had introduced an excellent system of administration, and both mother and daughter proved themselves staunch friends of the British Government in 1857. In recognition of her services the mother was appointed a Knight Grand Commander of the Star of India, and Bhopál received an assignment of territory confiscated from the neighbouring State of Dhár which had rebelled.

Owing to the loss of experienced officials there had been latterly some falling off in the administration, and there were difficulties in the management of the newly assigned territory in regard to which the advice of the Agent was required; but there was no serious cause for anxiety and the relations of both the Regent and her daughter with the British Government and its representative were of the most cordial character.

The condition of Rewah, the fourth of the principal native States of the Agency, situate to the east of Bundelkhand, was far from satisfactory. The Chief was intelligent and well-disposed but inert and under evil

BHOPÁL.
(From a Sketch by Mrs. Daly.)

influence; his establishments were ill-paid and consequently oppressive, his police corrupt and inefficient, and sooner or later interference seemed likely to be forced upon the British Government.

It would be tedious to describe the condition of all the minor chiefships. Suffice it to say that—omitting for the present States under British management—those of Jhabúa, Jaurah, Ratlám, Sítamau, Bijáwar, Maihar and Pannah were well administered; for the rest little could be said, and some were so encumbered with debt and hopelessly maladministered that intervention by the Suzerain Power would ere long be necessary.

But maladministration in native States (as truly remarked by Meade) does not appear to affect the happiness of their populations so much as would be supposed; and this for two principal reasons; in the first place Asiatics will bear with equanimity from hereditary chiefs an amount of oppression and misgovernment which would drive others into rebellion; and in the second place the products of a chief's exactions, including sums spent on his extravagances, were spent, for the most part, in his own territory, where the manufacture of gold trappings, broidered garments and fire-works and dainties, offered employment to large numbers of his subjects.

Four chiefships, Dhár[1] and Barwáni in the western division of the Agency, and Saháwal and Jigni in the eastern, were temporarily under British management in

[1] Dhár (a Rájput State) rebelled in 1857 and was confiscated. It was afterwards restored (with the exception of a portion of its territory given to Bhopál), but was placed temporarily under British management.

consequence of the minority or incapacity of their chiefs. In their case the change was great. The revenues were increased, not by increase of taxation, but by just treatment of cultivators and repression of peculation; all extravagances stopped, debts paid off, roads constructed, and order and system introduced in the place of chaos, so that when the chiefship was restored, the new ruler might at any rate start well.

One small territory—that of Mánpur—belonged to the British Government and was administered under the direct orders of the Political Agent of Western Málwa. It was admirably managed in Oriental fashion, not anglicised, and thus served as a model for other States in the vicinity; and was a subject of the greatest interest to Colonel Meade.

Such is a brief description of the condition of affairs when Meade took over the duties of Governor-General's Agent for Central India. Though there were, for the time being, no burning questions to be dealt with, there were multitudes of minor ones requiring attention; in addition to the more important matters noted above, there were plenty of misunderstandings between neighbouring chiefs; an unusually large crop of boundary disputes[1]—the result of three years' absence of

[1] On Meade's accession to office upwards of 200 cases were awaiting settlement. In 1862 a code of rules was issued for the amicable settlement of these disputes by mutual agreement, or, failing that, for their judicial settlement by a boundary commission; for the demarcation of the boundary; the erection of pillars and their preservation; the punishment of the States whose subjects infringed the settlement, and appeals from the decisions given. These rules form the basis of others passed in 1877 and at present followed in settling disputed boundary cases in Central India and Rájputána.

control—and not a few domestic quarrels in which the female members of the chief's family not infrequently bore an important part. Then arrangements had to be made for the education of chiefs who were minors and the administration of their territories, while portions of the western frontier between Indore and Rájputána were more or less disturbed, requiring joint action by the Governor-General's Agents for Rájputána and Central India to preserve the peace.

This part—the most important though perhaps the least showy part of the Agent's work—involving daily references from subordinate officers from all parts of the Agency, frequent interviews and correspondence with the Ruling Chiefs or their representatives, much marching during the cold season, and careful local inquiries, was indeed no sinecure. But it was far from all. There was in addition frequent confidential correspondence with the Viceroy and Foreign Secretary on political matters of importance; official correspondence with Government departments; the control of public works; the supervision of the opium department at Indore, where upwards of Rx. 2,000,000 per annum were collected for the British Government in the shape of export or transit duties on the drug; and lastly his work as final court of appeal in judicial cases, civil and criminal, arising in cantonments or on the line of railway, or in territories under British management, or in cases of heinous crime in mediatised States.

From the above sketch it will be seen how vast and important was the field of work before him. How it was discharged during Meade's eight years of office and with what result will be the subject of the next chapter.

CHAPTER X.

WORK AS GOVERNOR-GENERAL'S AGENT FOR CENTRAL INDIA (*continued*).

Question of the restoration of the Gwalior fortress—How settled—Reduction and distribution of Sindhia's troops—Correspondence with Sir John Lawrence—Meade's successful action highly approved of—Attempts to effect a reconciliation between Sindhia and Dinkar Rao—Their partial success—Sindhia's friendly feeling to Meade—Difficulties with Holkar—The "shoe question"—His aggressive conduct in reference to the Bhíls—Impracticability in the case of boundary questions—Nevertheless continues to be on the best terms with Meade—Speech at a banquet in 1880—Administrative progress of the States of the Agency during the period of Meade's term of office—Meade's general policy—Roads and public works—Police—Administration of justice—Revenue system—Transit duties—States under British management—Ratlám—Barwáni—Their condition contrasted with Sailána, which had been restored to the chief's rule—Meade's testimony to the comparative benefits of British and native rule—Remarks of the Government of India on Meade's Administration Report—Results of Meade's work in Central India summed up.

ONE of the first of the political problems to be dealt with by Meade was the delicate question of the Gwalior fortress, to which reference has already been made.

The fort had fallen into the hands of Sindhia's rebellious troops, but had been stormed and captured by Sir Hugh Rose's forces, and was retained by the British Government. When, however, the negotia-

THE GWALIOR FORTRESS.

tions were going on which ended in the Treaty of 1860, Lord Canning gave Sindhia the conditional promise that the fort should be restored to the Mahá-rája "when this could safely be done"; and this promise was repeated by Lord Elgin. But the military authorities were strongly of opinion that it would be unsafe to allow the fort to be occupied by Sindhia's troops—who might go out of hand as they did in 1859—so long as Morár, in its immediate vicinity, was occupied by our troops. Endeavours were made to find some other suitable locality for the British troops, not commanded by the Gwalior fort, but without success. Meanwhile, as time went on, Sindhia became impatient and vexed, and Sir John Lawrence, who had succeeded Lord Elgin as Viceroy, placed himself in confidential communication with Meade, suggesting that Sindhia should waive his claim for the immediate restoration of the fort, receiving some other boon in compensation.

The matter was a delicate one and required much care and patience to arrange. At length, however, Meade was able to induce the Mahárája to agree to the continued occupation of the fort by British troops on condition that his flag should fly on the ramparts and that he should be saluted from its guns; and that if ever the British troops should be withdrawn his own should be permitted to re-enter. The Chief was further allowed, in recognition of his loyalty, to increase his artillery by twelve guns.

This solution of the difficulty much gratified the Viceroy, who wrote to Meade on the 1st March, 1864: "I am much obliged to you for the successful manner in which you have brought this affair to a right conclusion".[1]

Another matter of difficulty was this :—

Sindhia had for some time evaded the terms of the treaty, under which the strength of his army was restricted, by the enrolment of corps of *najībs* or "gendarmerie," nominally as police, but, to all intents and purposes, a military force; and had a mania for massing all his troops at the capital—a most unwise proceeding considering their liability to mutiny—which had already, on two occasions, almost lost him his throne and life, besides being a standing danger to the peace of the empire.

The Supreme Government, though cordially recognising Sindhia's loyal services and most unwilling to wound his feelings, felt it absolutely necessary to intervene and require (1) the disbandment of the police battalions as an organised force and the substitution of a local police, and (2) the distribution of the troops throughout the territories in lieu of their concentration at Gwalior.

The unpleasant duty of communicating and securing compliance with these requirements devolved on

[1] Sindhia still buoyed himself up with the hope that Morár would be abandoned and the fortress restored to him; and this was ultimately the case, but not till 1886. It was then arranged that both Morár and the Gwalior fortress should be restored to Sindhia, who was further allowed to increase his army by 3000 men. *Per contra* Sindhia restored to the British Government the town and fort of Jhánsi. But when the arrangement was carried into effect, in March, 1886, Sindhia was seriously ill and died in the following June, without being able to enter the fortress he had set his heart upon recovering.

Meade, who was thus called upon to press firmly upon a high-spirited Marátha chief two measures utterly distasteful to him, which affected (in his view) not only the dignity and honour of his State, but his own special hobby of commanding large bodies of troops and great military displays. To do this without mortally offending Sindhia and straining the friendly relations between Gwalior and the British Government was a work of great difficulty.

For the work, however, the Government of India could not have had a better instrument than Meade, and no one knew this better than Sir John Lawrence. Writing in October, 1865, he said :—

"I am quite sure from what I have seen of your acts that, when it is necessary to interfere, you will only do so in a conciliatory manner, without trenching upon the just rights of the Mahárája. But when His Highness, as in the case of the *najíbs* or in other matters, acts in contravention of the Treaty and sound policy, prompt interference becomes unavoidable."

Correspondence and discussions went on until 1867. Meade, while faithfully carrying out his instructions, took care to place fully before the Government all points in Sindhia's favour, and was able to suggest modifications in the proposals calculated to make the measures less unpalatable.[1] But the Government was

[1] One of the suggestions made by Meade is deserving of special record. He remarks in a letter to the Viceroy that the "bitterness of the pill" would be greatly softened in Sindhia's case if the British Government would do the Chief the honour of occasionally brigading his troops, or a selected portion of them, with the British forces at Morár. The suggestion was not approved of at the time, but it contained the germ of a great policy afterwards adopted,

firm, and rightly so, in insisting upon the main points, *i.e.*, a full compliance by Sindhia, in spirit as well as letter, with treaty requirements regarding his troops and arsenal.

Meade, meanwhile, took the precaution of making the path of Sindhia's duty easy. The matter was dealt with at personal interviews and by confidential communications, so that Sindhia's own officials were ignorant of what was in contemplation, and it was open to the chief to issue the necessary orders, as if *proprio motu*, and not under pressure from the Paramount Power.

At length, in March, 1867, Sindhia yielded. The *najībs* were broken up and the troops distributed according to the wishes of the Government of India, and a standing danger to public tranquillity removed.

To the breaking up of the police battalions little objection was offered, but the removal of two-thirds of the troops from the capital was a sore trial. But, under Meade's influence, Sindhia met the British Government in a kindly spirit, and accepted the situation with dignity; and he was, in a measure, comforted by receiving from the Viceroy a letter expressing appreciation of the Mahárája's loyalty, and adding that "nothing but a sense of the paramount necessity for the measure would have led the Viceroy to press for it so strongly," and that "by his compliance the Mahárája had established a strong claim upon the good will and

which has led to the establishment of "Imperial Service Corps" in the armies of feudatory chiefs. At the present time five Imperial Service Detachments from the armies of the chiefs are brigaded with our troops and co-operating heartily in the defence of the British frontier. (October, 1897.)

friendship of the British Government," all which was duly endorsed by the Secretary of State for India.

Meade, as may be supposed, received the thanks of the Government and established his position as a Political Officer of the first rank.

Another matter of importance dealt with about this time was an endeavour to effect a reconciliation between Sindhia and his able and patriotic minister Rája Sir Dinkar Rao, K.C.S.I. Since his dismissal from office the latter had further incurred Sindhia's displeasure by absenting himself from a *darbár*, at which the chief had announced his adoption of a son, and in consequence the *jágír*, which had been conferred upon him in recognition of his services, was resumed and a sentence of exile from Gwalior passed upon him. The reconciliation was effected to some extent. The *jágír* was restored and the ex-minister was permitted to return to Gwalior. But he was never re-employed, and on his deathbed Sindhia specially desired that Dinkar Rao should have nothing to do with the administration of his territory. A regrettable episode, but not without precedent in European history.

We have been somewhat anticipating events, but it seemed desirable to complete the history of Meade's personal relations with the great Marátha Chief. Let it be added that Sindhia retained to the last the warmest friendship and respect for Meade as well as gratitude for the service he had rendered in days gone by; and after Sindhia's death his successor, then a bright and promising youth, in reply to a letter of condolence, speaks of Meade as one of his father's "old and sincere friends".

With Holkar there were difficulties, but none of a very serious character.

His first difficulty involved the celebrated "shoe question".

Holkar (unlike Sindhia) insisted, or, at any rate, tried to insist, upon the strict observance of Oriental customs at his court. His hall of audience was, ordinarily, unprovided with chairs, and the Resident and his suite, on paying an official visit, were expected to divest themselves of their boots in the vestibule, and on entering the presence-chamber to make profound obeisance (*kormish*) to the Ruling Prince as he reclined upon a cushion (*gadi*), and then to seat themselves cross-legged upon the ground beside him.

In the days when the East India Company was a mercantile body, seeking to obtain from native princes concessions of trade privileges or territory, such conformation to Eastern usage, however humiliating and even painful, may have been expedient; but when the Company ceased trading and the British Government assumed the position of Paramount Power of India it was entirely out of place.

It was also unreasonable.

An Indian Prince is allowed to pay respect to the Queen's Viceroy in Oriental fashion—by removing his shoes without removal of his head-dress. If so, the representative of the Viceroy can reasonably claim the right of paying his respects to an Indian potentate in English fashion, by taking off his hat without removal of his shoes.

But customs die hard, and the old form of ceremonial still lingered at Indore and in the court of the Nizám.

During his brief tenure of office as Indore Resident Colonel Durand declined to submit to the humiliating ordeal, but his successor, Sir Richmond Shakespear, was more complaisant.

Accordingly, when Meade and his suite presented themselves for the first time, on his appointment, no chairs were provided, and he and those accompanying him had a very *mauvais quart d'heure*.

But this was the first and last occasion. Meade courteously but firmly declined a repetition of the unpleasant operation, and insisted that, in future, chairs should be invariably provided for the Resident and those accompanying him.

There was much correspondence, but ultimately Holkar yielded—and the old ceremonial of obeisance and squatting has been long a thing of the past (in the case of British officers), not only at Indore, but even in the still more strait-laced court of the ruler of Hyderábád.[1]

[1] Another phase of the "shoe question" was for many years a cause of much difficulty and disquietude in India, *viz.:* how far was the half-anglicised Indian to be excused from compliance with the ordinary forms of Oriental respect? Members of the Young India party were prone to wear tight-laced boots incapable of easy removal, and at the same time objected to remove their head-dress—a proceeding which often led to unpleasant altercations. At length the question came before the Viceroy in connection with the regulation of ceremonial at *darbárs*. The knotty point was solved by the Viceroy (Lawrence) thus: It was decided that, if a native of India so far conformed to English notions of respect as to wear *patent leather shoes*, he should not be required to remove them, and, at the same time, should not be required to remove his head-dress. The decision caused much grumbling, and was, perhaps, not very logical, but it had the merit of settling a much vexed question. It has prevented unpleasant altercations, has done no harm to any one, and has greatly benefited the manufacturers of patent leather.

But there were more serious difficulties than "shoe questions". Holkar had to be curbed in his desire to assume sovereignty over two independent Bhíl chiefs or Bhúmias,[1] of Jamnia and Rájgarh; a proceeding in which His Highness was aided by the clever advocacy of his new minister, Sir Mádhava Rao.

Pressure had to be put upon him to do justice to another Bhíl chief, whom he nearly drove to desperation by withholding for years dues payable for the protection of passes in the Sátpúra range. After some years of correspondence Holkar ultimately paid the amount due.

In 1861 it was deemed desirable, with the view of making the British boundary compact, to enter into negotiations with Holkar for the mutual exchange of territory—Holkar ceding some scattered villages in the North-West Provinces and Deccan, and receiving land of equal value on the Bombay border. Boundary commissioners were appointed and transfers of territory effected from time to time; but owing to difficulties raised by Holkar the negotiations were protracted throughout the whole time of Meade's tenure of office, and were not finally concluded until 1880, when a boundary was at length fixed to the great advantage of Holkar. But he was dissatisfied.

In 1864 it was deemed expedient to demarcate the boundary between Holkar's territories south of the Narbadda and the Bombay district of Khandeish—in accordance with the treaty of 1818. This was done after searching inquiries by two British officers, whose decision Holkar promised to accept. Holkar

[1] Alluvial proprietors.

was dissatisfied and appealed to the Supreme Government. The Supreme Government upheld the award. Holkar was aggrieved. At length, on the occasion of the Imperial Assemblage of 1877, Lord Lytton's Government agreed, as an act of grace and with a view of removing all possibility of complaint, to enlarge Holkar's boundary by the grant of 360 square miles of British territory in Khandeish. Holkar received this generous gift and—was dissatisfied; because he hoped to have got more.[1]

There were other boundary cases between Indore and the neighbouring States, notably one with Dhár, in which Holkar's claim had to be rejected.

In 1869 Holkar offered the British Government a loan of £1,000,000 for the construction of a railway at Indore. This was accepted and a railway has been made. But Holkar was dissatisfied because he was not allowed to levy a tax on the materials used for the railway.

All these cases caused a good deal of trouble and required much patience to adjust; but in spite of his having to decide them unfavourably for Holkar, Meade's relations with that Chief were, up to the last, of a most cordial character. In 1880, ten years after Meade had left Indore, Holkar entertained him at a banquet, and in a speech delivered on the occasion referred to Meade as "his oldest friend in India," and described him as one who "was popular with the Government he served and popular with the States to which he had been accredited". He continued to

[1] It is fair, however, to state that Holkar's successor, the present Mahárája, expressed to the writer the warmest gratitude for the grant of territory referred to.

correspond with Meade long after the latter had retired, and in his last letter, dated 15th May, 1885 (about a year before Holkar's death), he speaks of Meade as his "intimate friend".

In reference to other States there were no political difficulties of any moment; there might have been many if the Agency had been in less experienced and cautious hands.

With regard to the administrative progress of the States, in 1866 Colonel Meade prepared the first general report of the territories under his political control. Commencing with a general description of their physical features, population and resources, he proceeds to sketch the condition of the several States in respect to police and military forces, the administration of justice, jails, education, roads and public works, revenue, trade, forest conservancy and the character and efficiency of the ruling chiefs.

It is a report of great value and interest, and for its preparation Meade received the thanks of the Government of India. From that date reports have been annually submitted and contain a mass of material from which the administrative history of the territories can be gathered; and we are thus in a good position to judge of the progress made during Meade's *regime*.

There was progress, undoubtedly, but, except in the case of public works of imperial concern, which were very vigorously pressed, the progress was slow. For in regard to internal reforms of every kind—taxation, police, justice, sanitation, road-making and the like—Meade's policy was *festina lente*. It was his policy—or rather, we should say, it was the policy of the Government of India which he faithfully pursued—to endeavour to carry the Chiefs with him in all he did, and even when he was constrained to press unwelcome reforms to do his best to make them as palatable as possible. No man was more anxious for improvement than Meade, but no man was more convinced of the necessity for caution.

To begin with public works:—

In regard to military buildings and imperial lines of communication, an immense amount of work was done. The Grand Trunk Road from Agra to Bombay, 446 miles of which lay in Central India, was completed; and so was the great Deccan Road connecting Mirzapore with the capital of the Central Provinces; and all the other main lines of communication mentioned in the preceding chapter were finished.

In 1867 the two great Indian railway systems—the G.I.P. Railway and the E.I. Railway—at length met at Jabalpur and there was now through traffic from Bombay to Calcutta. This was an enormous benefit to the general public; but its immediate effect upon the States of Central India was to deprive them of transit duties on goods to the value of about £200,000 per annum. But the uniform good will with which this loss of revenue was accepted by the chiefs and the liberality with which they provided the land required for railway purposes were highly creditable, not only to the chiefs themselves, but to the political officers by whom they were advised and influenced.

Of the roads of the second class—that is cross-roads connecting important towns—those connecting Mhau with Nasirábád, Gwalior with Jabalpur, Indore and Bánda with Saugor, were for the most part completed; and, in addition, roads connecting Jhánsi with Naugong and Sutna on the G.I.P. line, and with Gwalior and Sípri, and another connecting Pannah with Jabalpur, and a multitude of other "feeders" connecting the principal towns with the main lines or with the railway, were taken in hand.

Some of the "feeder" roads were works of considerable importance, notably the road from Indore to Bulwára on the G.I.P. line, which descends, at a gradient of 1 in 20 feet, from the high plateau of Málwa to the Narbadda Valley (1200 feet below) by three *ghâts*, the Simrol, the Bhai and the Bhor; "now crossing a ravine by a handsome stone bridge, now passing through a ridge of hard rock by a cutting of many feet, the road winds down the hill and excites admiration by the magnitude of the work, its evident commercial utility and picturesque scenery".

So much for imperial or quasi-imperial works; with regard to works carried out by the Chiefs themselves there was little to record. The very idea of executing works of public benefit with no immediate pecuniary advantage to the rulers was in Central India a novel one. Some viewed it with dislike, some with surprise, others with indifference. But there were signs of better things. Some of the States, notably Dhár, Ratlám and Jaura, were induced to contribute liberally to the construction of new roads; and even Sindhia, who had hated improvements of every kind, agreed, on the advice of Colonel Daly, to grant a subvention of Rs. 75,000 per annum for this purpose. The Rája of Pannah went a step further. On his own initiative he made a road forty miles long, from his capital to Simmíah, with the view of opening up his territory; while the chief of Dattia constructed the portion of the main road between Gwalior and Jhánsi passing through his territory entirely at his own expense. The section of road so constructed is twenty miles in length, with twenty-four bridges, and raised, metalled, and planted throughout with trees.

At Indore and Bhopál works for the supply of pure water were completed; and at Indore and in Ratlám and one or two other States something was done towards providing proper jail accommodation. In the former place a central jail was constructed for the reception of prisoners (from cantonments or States under British management) sentenced for long terms by the Agent or his subordinates.

In matters of police and the administration of justice little advance was made; but in Bhopál and Dhár the Indian Civil and Criminal Procedure Codes were introduced with suitable modifications.

Endeavours were made to introduce better systems of revenue management, but the subject was a delicate one. In Gwalior, indeed, and Bhopál, and some of the States which had been placed temporarily under British rule, such as Maihar, Pannah, Nagod, etc., good systems were in force, but in most of the States matters were as bad as ever. In Indore, however, and one or two other States, besides those above referred to, settlements of land tax for short terms of years (on the British system) were tentatively introduced, and of late years there has been much improvement.

Trade.—One of Meade's first efforts was directed towards effecting the removal of the vexatious tolls and transit duties which so seriously interfered with it. But he found the feeling of the native rulers strongly opposed to anything like a general remission of such duties, so he wisely confined his endeavours, in the first instance, to obtaining their remission on *main lines* of communication. This he succeeded in doing and the boon was an immense one. But this was not all. Two chiefs in Bundelkhand—Dattia and Maihar—convinced by the arguments of the Political Officers, set a good example by abolishing *all* transit duties on traffic passing through their territories, and their example has been since followed by other States. At the present time transit duties have been abolished in all the States of Bundelkhand and Baghelkhand, and also in Gwalior, and seventeen States in Málwa.

But in one important department, education, there was a very perceptible improvement. Many new schools were opened in Indore, Bhopál, Dhár, Jaura and other States; at Gwalior the Central School is described in the report for 1866-7 as "excellent," and eighty-five schools originally established by Dinkar Rao are said to be maintained in working order. That at Sehore (Bhopál) was affiliated to the University of Calcutta. While even in backward Bundelkhand, where education was once almost non-existent, the number of chiefs who opened or assisted in the opening of schools increased in Meade's time to the respectable figure of twenty-eight, and the number of schools to sixty-five, with an attendance of 2000 scholars.

The number of hospitals and dispensaries was increased during Meade's term of office from twelve to forty, that is to say, was more than trebled. A commencement of forest conservancy was made by the issue of a code of rules drafted by the Inspector-General of Forests for adoption, *mutatis mutandis*, by States with forest tracts. But Bhopál (as usual) set a good example by appointing a trained officer to conserve the forests in that State, and something was done towards protecting the teak forests in the Bhíl hills. On Meade's recommendation the young Rája of Rewah sanctioned a topographical survey of his territory ; and he has since placed his forests under scientific supervision and granted a concession for working the coal sources of the State.

Hitherto we have been dealing chiefly with self-governed States ; but the greatest progress effected during Meade's time was in those States which were or had been (owing to the chief's minority or other causes) under British management. Thus Ratlám—a Rájput principality, the principal mediatised State in Western Málwa—was singularly prosperous under the enlightened management of Mir Shahámat Ali. There was a substantial surplus revenue, part of which was spent in paying off debts, part in the extension of education, part in the establishment of a school of industry and a State garden for agricultural experiments. The land revenue was assessed and settled on liberal terms and every branch of the administration put in thorough order.

Again the condition of Barwáni, another Rájput State under British management, is thus described :—

"Our management was introduced in 1860, since which year the revenue has risen from Rs. 23,512 to Rs. 76,209; a debt of Rs. 29,430 has been discharged; and a cash balance was exhibited of Rs. 50,812. Instead of a distempered atmosphere of disorder and confusion surrounding a population given up to lawlessness and plunder, there are now the freedom and security which result from the establishment of courts of justice, with a strong and well-organised police, and the community has become quiet and peaceable. Schools have been established; a road twenty-eight miles in length has been constructed; and miles of territory over which a man could with difficulty find his way are now intersected by fair-weather cart roads and good bridle roads. . . . Over a tract of fifteen miles in the Goi valley smiling corn-fields have taken the place of unreclaimed and useless jungle; a similar change being visible in other parts." [1]

Per contra we have the case of Sailána, a small Rájput State in Western Málwa which, after being placed under British management, was restored to its chief's rule. "No improvement," writes Meade, "is reported in the management of this State, or the debauched habits of its ruler, who, while profuse in promises, pays no real attention to the advice and ex-

[1] The State was restored to the chief's management in 1873, but the administration has not been satisfactory.

postulations repeatedly addressed to him. The treasury is empty and debts increase; while the town presents a melancholy appearance, one quarter being in ruins, and the school-house, built while it was under British management, having been pulled down."[1]

But such a relapse was not invariable; and it is expressly mentioned in the report that the States of Dattia, Maihar and Nagod (in Bundelkhand) were "continuing the systems of administration introduced during their temporary management by British officers".

As, however, it is a modern fashion to assert the superior happiness of the peasantry in native States to those in British territory, let us hear the testimony of one of the best friends of native Governments, who had ample experience of the administrative systems both of British and Feudatory India.

Writing in 1866-7 Meade observes: "The superiority of the condition of the mass of the population in British territory to that of the same class in native States, with which it is impossible to be otherwise than struck when passing from the latter into the former and *vice versâ*, is, beyond doubt, in a great measure due to the benefits conferred by the equitable and liberal character of all the British systems of managing the land revenue; while the generally depressed condition of the same classes in native territory may be fairly attributed to the absence of these advantages and the

[1] Matters have apparently improved since this was written, for we find that in 1887 the Rája, on the occasion of Her Majesty's jubilee, abolished all transit duties in his State excepting those on opium.

blighting effect of the oppressive systems to which they are subjected".

The Report from which these words are taken is the last submitted by Meade for the States of Central India. The final paragraphs of the Supreme Government's review of it are as follows :—

"His Excellency in Council is well aware of the difficulties which you had to encounter while carrying on the administration of Central India, in the shape of apathy on the part of some chiefs or of the debased and dissolute habits in others. He is conscious that the direct management or the general superintendence of so many petty States, involving disputes as to boundaries, the decision of points of jurisdiction, inquiries into robberies and the escape of criminals, and the settlement of divers other questions intimately connected with the welfare of all classes, is a task calculated to draw forth qualities of tact, discretion and firmness, such as are to be looked for in high political officers; and he considers that the responsible duties of your Agency have been by you discharged in a manner calculated to win the regard and confidence of the chiefs and people, as well as to satisfy the legitimate expectations of the Government of India."

To sum up the results of Meade's work in Central India :—

There is nothing of a sensational character to record; but plenty of useful work done with a minimum of fuss or friction. It was, indeed, a time for laying foundations rather than achieving results. But much was effected nevertheless.

For eight years he maintained the *pax Britannica* in

a territory far larger than England, the scene, a few years previously, of war and plunder and rapine—*without once calling out the regular troops*; and restored to working order the complicated system of political control under which a multitude of States and tribes, full of intestine enmities and jealousies, are made to live in harmony with each other and in subordination to the protecting Power,—a system which had been rudely shaken by the events of 1857.

This alone was a work deserving the thanks of the community. But Meade did a good deal more than this.

With the help of his efficient staff of subordinates—civil and military—he settled quietly and wisely many political difficulties, which *might* have led to strained relations between some of our most powerful feudatories and the Suzerain Power. Through his influence with the Chiefs he opened out the country from north to south and from east to west with miles and miles of road; abolished transit duties on the main lines of traffic; multiplied rest-houses, and postal lines and dispensaries; and prepared the way for surveys and scientific forest conservancy.

If no startling reforms of administration were effected in the States themselves, he laid the foundations of improvement; for by wise and just administration of States coming temporarily under British rule he furnished examples of good government, which afterwards bore fruit.

And all this was done not by *force majeure*, but by the willing co-operation of the Chiefs themselves, with all of whom—whether Hindú or Muhammadan; whether Marátha or Rájput or Patán or Bundela or Brahman—he was on the best of terms.

And if, in later years, the States of Central India have been conspicuous for loyalty and progress; if roads and railways have been carried through their territories, not only without exciting ill-feeling, but with the liberal assistance of the Chiefs; if their lands are being surveyed and mapped and their forests scientifically conserved; if Sindhia and Holkar and Bhopál and other States are vying with each other in co-operation with the British Government for purposes of Imperial defence, the result is doubtless, in some measure, due to the friendly feelings and confidence engendered and established during the eight years of "Meade Sáhib's" *régime*. For these services in April, 1866, during the Viceroyship of Sir John Lawrence, Meade received the honour of a Companionship of the Star of India,—and never was the decoration better earned.

CHAPTER XI.

WORK AS CHIEF COMMISSIONER OF MYSORE AND COORG.

Meade takes furlough—On return is offered and accepts the Chief Commissionership of Mysore and Coorg—Account of Mysore—Its physical features, population, climate, products, revenue, history—Administration assumed by the British Government in 1831—Entrusted to General Cubbon, who conducts it for twenty-five years—Financially successful, but becomes in time inadequate—Mr. Bowring succeeds and reorganises the province—Great improvements effected—The Chief petitions for reinstatement—His prayer four times rejected—But policy changed in 1867 and a promise given that the Government would be made over to his adopted son on coming of age—Administrative arrangements have therefore to be reconsidered—Discussions—Qualifications required in the *ad interim* administrator—Letters from Lord Mayo and Sir H. Durand—Coorg—The new appointment a great change for Meade—He adapts himself to the situation and throws himself heartily into the work—His report for 1872-3 quoted—The young Mahárája—His education—Succession in 1881 and early death—His correspondence with Meade—Meade's life as Chief Commissioner of Mysore—Appointed on special duty.

In February, 1869, Meade took his first and only furlough to England and it was a very brief one; for it was the particular wish of Lord Mayo, who had succeeded Sir John Lawrence as Viceroy, that Meade should return in time to be present at his post during the visit of H.R.H. the Duke of Edinburgh in the ensuing cold season.

Accordingly he left India at the end of February and returned in the following November.

Soon after his return Mr. Lewin Bowring, C.S.I., Chief Commissioner of Mysore and Coorg, applied for leave preparatory to his retirement from the service, and it became necessary to select a suitable successor.

Owing to circumstances the selection required especial care.

The modern State of Mysore is a tract of hilly table-land, about twice the size of Switzerland, on the south-western side of the Indian Peninsula, between the Western and Eastern Gháts—forming the water-parting between two river systems, the Tunga Bhádra and Krishna on the north and the Káveri on the south.

The most elevated portion of the plateau is Bangalore (on the south-east corner of the province), 3000 feet above sea-level; but scattered here and there, are lofty piles of rock known locally as *durgs*,[1] many of them fortified and doubtless the strongholds of robber chieftains in days gone by. One of them, the fortress of Nandidrug, attains the height of 4700 feet, and contains the precipitous cliff called "Tippu's Drop," whence (during the struggles of 1783, 1793 and 1799) European prisoners of war are said to have been hurled. It was long believed to be impregnable, but was taken by escalade by British troops in 1791. Towards the Western Gháts are ranges of similar altitude, some covered with dense forest, others green with coffee plants.

Mysore has a population of nearly 5,000,000, of which 94 per cent. are Hindús; the prevailing language is

[1] *Durg* is a Hindí word meaning a place difficult of access. Durgai, the Tírah fastness, with which recent events have made us familiar, has, doubtless, the same origin and meaning. When used as a name-terminant *durg* is transmuted into *drúg*.

Canarese, but Támil, Telúgú, Hindustáni and Maráthí are spoken.

The climate is (for India) temperate. There are two monsoons, and in the greater part of the territory[1] the rainfall, in ordinary years, is about thirty inches; but from ancient times water for irrigation has been stored with infinite pains and ingenuity in artificial lakes and tanks, in number nearly 40,000,[2] and their proper repair and up-keep is a matter of extreme importance. The storage, however, though wonderfully extended, does not suffice for times of protracted drought. In the great famine of 1877 the tank-supply completely failed and upwards of 1,000,000 of people perished.

The produce of the fields consists of the ordinary Indian grains, but the rich red loam of the primeval forests of the Western Gháts is found suitable for coffee, which was introduced from Mecca many years ago and now forms a staple industry. The cardamum grows spontaneously in the western jungles and its cultivation is now carried on with profit. Forests of teak clothe the western ranges; bamboos flourish in the eastern, and sandal-wood (a State monopoly) is found in the western portion of the province. Iron abounds everywhere, but gold (now an important industry) was, in Meade's time, found only in small quantities by washing the alluvial soil of the Kolár district.

The revenue, which, at the time of our assuming control of the territory, amounted to fifty-five lakhs of rupees per annum, amounted in Meade's time—in spite of vast reductions—to nearly twice as much.

[1] In the vicinity of the Western Gháts the rainfall is much heavier.

[2] Indian Famine Commission Report.

As for the history of the tract, 300 years ago Mysore formed a portion of the ancient Hindú principality of Vijáyanagar, the most powerful native monarchy which has ever existed in Southern India.

For upwards of two centuries it withstood the encroachments of the Muhammadans of the Deccan; and the extensive ruins near Hampi in the Bellary district attest the size and splendour of the capital; but it fell in A.D. 1564 and out of its ruins the modern Mysore Ráj arose.

In 1763 its government was usurped by a Mussulman adventurer from the Punjab—the well-known Haidar Ali, our inveterate foe, whose son and successor, Tippú Sultán, was conquered and slain at Seringapatam in 1799.

At the close of the war the Earl of Mornington, afterwards Lord Wellesley (then Governor-General of India), conferred a portion of the conquered State upon a descendant of the old royal family, upon condition of his providing the cost of a Subsidiary British Force to be located in his territory and assisting the British Government pecuniarily in time of war.

At the same time power was reserved to the British Government, if failure of payment was apprehended, to resume the whole or a portion of the grant or regulate its administration.

In 1831 the contemplated contingency arose. Gross and continued misgovernment by the chief plunged the State in debt and drove the population to rebellion, and even Lord William Bentinck, the most pacific of Governor-Generals, found it necessary to depose our *protégé*. The administration was, accordingly, assumed by the British Government, and entrusted ultimately to General (afterwards Sir Mark) Cubbon, an illustrious member of the patriarchal school of Indian administrators; who conducted it, for twenty-five years, in "a manner honourable to the British name"—on the lines of a benevolent despotism worked by selected British officers.

"The history of the province under his rule," said Meade, "affords a brilliant illustration to those who maintain the superiority of British over native rule; for it is the history of a people made happy by release from serfdom and of a ruined State restored to financial prosperity." During this period peace and order were restored; peculation checked, and affairs conducted with such prudence and economy that, though the land tax was greatly reduced and upwards of 700 vexatious imposts ultimately swept away, the revenues largely exceeded the expenditure. State debts to the amount of Rs. 85,00,000 were paid off, credit restored, and a nest-egg of forty lakhs of rupees invested in British Government securities. At the same time the country was opened up for traffic by inexpensive but practicable roads, and all transit duties were abolished.

But the millennium had not arrived. As wealth and population and intelligence and business increased a system of administration, which answered well in early times and justly evoked the gratitude of all, became more and more inadequate. For though the territory had been opened out with roads and the finances put in order, yet, in other matters, such as law and justice, police, jail management, survey and settlement of land, education, public works, irrigation, medical aid, sanitation, forest conservancy and the like,

Mysore, though blessed with a large surplus, was far below the standard of a British province.

Such was the situation when Sir Mark Cubbon was succeeded by Mr. Bowring, a distinguished member of the Bengal Civil Service, formerly Lord Canning's private secretary, by whom the administration was successfully conducted for upwards of seven years, whose courtesy, culture and deep interest in oriental studies, combined with great energy and practical ability, won him the respect of all.

He found an overflowing treasury, and it was considered that the time had come for conferring upon the province a more "up-to-date" administration. It was determined, accordingly, that it should be reorganised, *mutatis mutandis*, on the lines of the Punjab—a province regarded in those days as a "model" administration—a happy mean between "patriarchalism" and "red-tape," or, to put it even more colloquially, between "government by the rule of thumb" and "government by the rule of three". The reorganisation was carried out by Mr. Bowring, an old Punjab officer, with care and judgment, and the administration more or less assimilated to that obtaining in British territory, and, in the absence of competent native agency, free use was made of the agency of British officers.

But the Punjab model was not blindly followed; in matters of survey and settlement of land the Bombay system was found more suitable, and in dealing with *inám* or tax-free tenures the principles applied were those obtaining in Madras. In a word the new administration of Mysore, as introduced by Mr. Bowring, may be described as the scientific result of the administrative experience of the three provinces.

The result was eminently beneficial.

The records and accounts of the province, then in a chaotic condition, were systematised and simplified, and a proper audit of expenditure maintained.

Regular courts of justice took the place of corrupt and dilatory *punchayats*, or committees of arbitration, to the great delight of all but influential suitors.

Surplus revenue was no longer hoarded, but spent liberally on public works.

Miles and miles of admirable roads were constructed, rivers bridged, irrigation tanks repaired, public offices (a great want) erected, municipalities established, sanitation, conservancy, etc., looked after to an extent previously unknown.

Large sums were spent on higher education, and measures taken for the establishment of village schools.

Jail management was thoroughly reformed and the Bangalore Central Prison became a model institution.

And lastly the survey and settlement of the land, and inquiries into claims to hold lands tax free—the weak points of every native administration—were diligently taken in hand.[1]

Prosperity increased. Capital was attracted to the province. English planters were encouraged, and British interests in the shape of coffee estates and mines began to be developed.

Meanwhile the ex-Chief kept petitioning for reinstatement, but his prayer was rejected by four

[1] See farewell memorial to Mr. Bowring from the native community of Bangalore.

successive Governor-Generals, Lord Dalhousie, Lord Canning, Lord Elgin and Sir John Lawrence, and the rejection was confirmed by the Secretary of State for India; and when the Mahárája adopted a son, the adoption was not recognised. Everything pointed to the early absorption of Mysore into British territory.

But in 1867 all was changed. Her Majesty's Government, reversing its previous decision, agreed to recognise the Chief's adopted son, and undertook, on his coming of age and being found qualified for the discharge of the duties of the position, to entrust the government of the country to him—"subject to such conditions as may be determined at the time".

The change of policy necessitated a reconsideration of administrative arrangements; for, whereas Mysore had been latterly administered in view of its ultimate absorption into British territory, it was now to be administered in view of its continuance as a native State.

And it led, as might have been expected, to much discussion. The decision to maintain the dynasty was, indeed, very gratifying to the Mysoreans, as well as to the chiefs and people of India generally; but many who had the welfare of Mysore at heart dreaded the possibility of a return to barbarism. So the "conditions" under which the native rule should be restored, in other words, the lines on which the principality should be administered, were very anxiously considered. Local feeling was strong, and, as usually happens on such occasions, doctrinaires and faddists made their voices heard. But their views were various and conflicting.

"Nothing," said one writer, "can be worse than the present administration of the country."

"The expectations of the success of your administration," so runs the farewell memorial to Mr. Bowring from the native community of Bangalore, "have been more than realised."

As for the future :—

Many heartily approved of Bowring's work and deprecated material change;

Some were for a return to "patriarchal government" with no law and a strong executive;

Some were for an absolutely separate judiciary—with lawyers rampant and the executive paralysed;

Some were for reduction of the land tax, already light; some for increased expenditure on "developing the resources";

Some grudged expenditure on education, especially on village schools, but asked, in the same breath, for costly institutions for scientific and industrial training;

Some advocated gradual, some immediate change; while the holders of comfortable appointments (a powerful class) were greatly averse to any change at all!

But one criticism was just, *viz.*, that the administration was costly and too much anglicised for a native State.

So there was much to be considered and the new Chief Commissioner, whoever he was to be, was promised a somewhat lively time.

In these circumstances, it was, doubtless, considered important that the officer selected for the post of *ad interim* administrator should be a man of power and mark; that he should (1) be one of proved ability in guiding and influencing native rulers and their councillors; (2) should have wide experience of both English and native administrations; (3) have an open mind; (4) should be tolerably pachydermatous, and (5) strong enough to withstand undue pressure from vested interests, to deal justly between the sometimes conflicting claims of European and native, and—hold his own with the doctrinaires and faddists of the period.

Lord Mayo—passing over a number of distinguished civil servants—selected Meade; who certainly combined the qualifications above described; and his selection, though it caused some surprise, was ratified by the public opinion of the time. Meade, though greatly regretting to leave Central India, could not do otherwise than gratefully accept the post; and his acceptance was acknowledged by the Viceroy (on the 3rd February, 1870) in the following flattering terms:—

"My dear Colonel Meade,—I am glad that you have accepted the offer of the Chief Commissionership of Mysore.

"I can assure you—without flattery—that my object in offering it to you was principally to testify my sense of the services you have performed to the Government in the discharge of your difficult duties as Governor-General's Agent for Central India.

"In taking Mysore you have assumed a most responsible and interesting task, which will require the exercise both of political and administrative duty of the highest importance.

"It is needless for me to recapitulate the relations under which the British Government now stands to that State; they are unique in India, and though the fate of the State in future may be still uncertain, it is our duty to endeavour by every means in our power, during the period in which it remains wholly in our hands, to place every part of its administration upon a firm and efficient basis.

"I shall be happy to hear from you from time to time and wish you every success in your new sphere.

"I remain, yours faithfully,

"MAYO."

Two days afterwards Sir Henry Durand, then a member of the Governor-General's Council, wrote as follows :—

"MY DEAR—MEADE, I think you have done right to accept Mysore. I feel, at the same time, and said so in council when the fact of the offer being made to you was mentioned by Lord Mayo, that your influence in Central India and your management of its chiefs, more especially the leading ones—Sindhia and Holkar—had been so valuable to the Government that I should regret your leaving.

"At the same time I should deem it unfair that your advancement should be stopped or detriment caused to your career in consequence of your great utility in Central India. . . .

"I am certain the administration of Mysore will be conducted with the same sound judgment and ability as Central India has been under you; and it is almost a duty to acquiesce in the decision of Government in its selection of you for a post of such importance in which it feels it requires your services.

"Yours very sincerely,

"H. M. DURAND."

The Chief Commissioner of Mysore was also (*ex-officio*) Commissioner of Coorg.

COORG is a small highland district on the Malabar coast adjoining Mysore, inhabited by a Hindú race of sturdy hill-men.

Its inhabitants bravely defended their mountain homes from the domination of Haidar Ali and in 1790 came under the protection of the British Government.

Coorg remained a protected State till 1831, when, after years of misrule and cruelty, the Chief was deposed (after an armed conflict with British forces) and the territory, at the universal wish of the inhabitants, was annexed to the British Crown.

In 1837, when a rising took place against British rule, the people rose *en masse* in our support, defeated a rebel force in Canara and recaptured the treasure which was being carried off. In 1857, during the great Mutiny, a band of armed Coorgs, moving into Mysore territory, held in check the disaffected Muhammadans of Seringapatam, and, in recognition of the service then rendered, the Coorg head-men are permitted to this day to wear arms without a licence.

Since annexation Coorg has been administered as a British "non-regulation" province under the Mysore Commissioner. It has given no trouble; is the happy home of English coffee-planters, and in matters of education, one of the most advanced districts in British India; and it is particularly proud of having a separate administration under the direct control of the Supreme Government.

But the move to Mysore and Coorg—though highly gratifying to Meade—was undoubtedly a great change. All his service hitherto had been either as a soldier, or as a political officer in Northern and Central India; and his administrative experience was confined to the case of petty States, in a most backward condition, placed temporarily under British rule. He was now called upon to conduct the administration of an important province in the South of India, with a population widely differing in language, customs and feeling from those he had dealt with before, and under new and unique conditions. But Colonel Meade quickly adapted himself to the new situation and was soon immersed in work.

We find him prospecting new lines of railway; pressing forward the repair of irrigation tanks; arranging for surveys and settlements of land; improving the administration of justice by effecting a partial separation of judicial and executive functions; reorganising the police, on a system which recognised and utilised the indigenous village watchman; transforming the cavalry of the local force, known as *Silladárs*, from a disorganised rabble into a tolerably efficient body of irregular horse; reorganising the commission for inquiring into claims to hold lands tax-free; extending primary education among the masses; opening new dispensaries; supervising the experimental cultivation of new products—such as cinchona, Australian maize, Java grass, etc.; and extending scientific conservancy to district forests; and in 1872-3, by request of the Supreme Government, he prepared an admirable report, giving a history of the administration of Mysore from the date of its assumption by the British Government, and an account of its resources.

This report contains in a brief form Meade's answer to the vexed question of the day: How should Mysore be prepared for its early reversion to the status of a native principality?[1] And we give it nearly *in ex-*

[1] Meade also submitted to the Government a much fuller statement of his views upon the subject, but his report being confidential is not available.

tenso because it comes with all the weight due to the opinion of one who had a wider experience of native governments than any living Englishman. Meade's weighty opinion carried the day—and Mysore has still a civilised administration.

"There are some"—we quote from the general summary of the report for 1872-3—"There are some who oppose every reform tending towards the introduction of a 'regulation system' on the ground that 'the administration may become too elaborate' and that 'the system of government,' usually termed *patriarchal*, 'is best adapted to a native State'. These, however, are not the views which during the last ten years, under the directions of the Government of India, have actuated the administration. . . . The present Chief Commissioner believes that, while over-elaboration in the system of government cannot but be an evil, as well in a native State as in British territory, the patriarchal system is even less adapted to a native State than to a province under British rule; for the reason that those personal qualities in the ruler which can alone secure for such a system even a moderate and transient success are rarely possessed by the natives of India. . . . On the other hand in these days of high education, no difficulty will ever be experienced in procuring the services of native officers who are qualified to work any system, however elaborate. Nor, if we examine the condition of those States which are now governed by native rulers, do we find any tendency to allow subordinate officers to improvise decisions for themselves unchecked by law, precedent or central authority. . . . The patriarchal system in a native State is a synonym for anarchy and corruption, and the most successful

H.H. CHÁMA RAJENDRA WADIAR,
Mahárája of Mysore
(*æt.* fifteen years).

native States are those which strive to imitate a European model.

"The Chief Commissioner, therefore, believes that the closing years of British rule in Mysore should witness—not disorganisation in the vain pursuit of a phantom system of native administration—but a thorough consolidation of what has already been done, to the end that the province may be handed over to His Highness the Mahárája in perfect order."

On one point, however, and that an important one, Meade very properly modified, or rather, we should say, adapted to present circumstances the policy of his predecessor. He took decided steps to gradually substitute (so far as possible) native for European agency; and he sought to raise the tone of the native service by the appointment of probationary *attachés* of good family and traditions—a plan which has been followed in other branches of the Indian public service.

The Mahárája referred to in the last paragraph but one was the excellent young Chief who has so recently passed away, to the great sorrow of his subjects and of all who knew him.

During Colonel Meade's term of office the Chief, then a boy under twelve years of age, resided at Mysore under the charge of his tutor Colonel Malleson, C.S.I.[1] Every endeavour was made to preserve him during his childhood from the demoralising influences which contributed to his adoptive father's failure as administrator, and to impart a liberal and manly tone to his tastes by proper education, by travel, and by

[1] Who has just passed away.

encouraging him to vie in sports with companions of his own age. And the result was all that could be wished. On the 25th March, 1881, he was formally invested with the administration of the Mysore State.[1] His Highness succeeded, not indeed to an overflowing exchequer, for the accumulated surplus had been more than swallowed up by the outlay on the great famine, but to an administration organised in all its details, with its system of land revenue thoroughly settled and its

[1] The following are the principal conditions under which the Mysore chief now holds his territories :—

(1) He is to pay a tribute of thirty-five lakhs of rupees per annum. (2) He is not to build or repair fortresses or strongholds, or import arms, ammunition or military stores without the sanction of the British Government. (3) He is to allow British cantonments to be established whenever and wherever the Governor-General in Council may consider such cantonments necessary. (4) He is to limit his forces to the strength fixed by the British Government. (5) To abstain from interfering in the affairs of any other State and have no communication or correspondence with any other State except with the sanction and through the medium of the Governor-General in Council. (6) He is not to employ persons not natives of India without previous sanction. (7) Have no separate coinage. (8) Grant land for telegraphs and railways. (9) Extradit offenders. (10) Comply with the wishes of the Governor-General in Council in the matter of prohibiting or limiting the manufacture of salt and opium. (11) Maintain the laws in force. (12) Make no material change in the system of administration without the consent of the British Government. (13) Maintain title deeds and settlements. (14) Conform to advice. (15) No succession to be valid until approved by the British Government.

The practical result is that Mysore resumed its position as a native principality with a good administration ready-made; is secured against undesirable changes; compounds for the cost of its protection and feudal obligations by a moderate annual payment, and—subject to such payment—enjoys the full benefit of its own surplus.

finances in a sound condition; and, if regard be had to future prosperity,—a prosperity based not only on material but moral considerations, not only on the resources of the province, but the character and training of its Chief—seldom did a monarch assume the reins of government under fairer auspices. He proved himself an enlightened ruler, and his death in 1894, at the early age of thirty-one years, was a calamity.

Colonel Meade had a deep regard for the Mahárája. They corresponded long after Meade had left Mysore, and copies of two characteristic letters from the young prince, one written when a child of twelve, and one as a Ruling Chief, are appended to this chapter.

Meade's life as Chief Commissioner of Mysore, while full of engrossing work, was very pleasant. Government House is situate at Bangalore, the head-quarters of the Subsidiary Force. There was therefore plenty of society and valuable friendships were formed. During the summer months he and Lady Meade usually stayed at Nandidrug—once the "Bastile" of Tippú Sultán, then a British sanitarium, and now giving a name to a successful gold-mining company—which, besides being cool and agreeable and only thirty miles from Bangalore, has beautiful surroundings; the rest of the year he spent chiefly at head-quarters, where he was busily engaged in overhauling every department of the administration, that it might be handed over to its chief "in as perfect a state as possible". But he paid frequent visits to the capital, where the young Mahárája resided with his guardian; or moved with his camp through the charming scenery of the Mysore territory, inspecting improvements, planning roads and irrigation works, visiting schools and hospitals, testing settlements and listening to representations; or proceeded to his second province, the little British district of Coorg, in the welfare of which he took the deepest interest and where he always received the heartiest welcome.

So time went on delightfully. But in the summer of 1872, an event occurred which filled him with profound sorrow, the death of his revered friend and chief, Lord Mayo, who was assassinated by a convict at the Andamans.

Irrespective of personal feelings, the departure of one Viceroy and the advent of another is naturally a matter of interest and importance to those who—as Chief Commissioners and officers in high political appointments—work under the Viceroy's immediate direction. In Meade's case, however, there was no cause for apprehension; the late Viceroy's successor, Lord Northbrook, at once recognised his abilities and worth, and assured him of cordial support; so Meade hoped to be allowed to carry on his deeply interesting and useful work as Chief Commissioner of Mysore for some years to come.

But in September, 1873—when planning his operations for the ensuing cold season—he received intimation that his services were required on special duties of very great importance.

APPENDIX TO CHAPTER XI.

LETTERS FROM THE LATE CHIEF OF MYSORE.

(1) From the Mahárája of Mysore (*æt.* 12 years) to Sir R. Meade on the latter's transference to Hyderábád :—

" MY DEAR SIR RICHARD MEADE,—Colonel Malleson delivered to me this morning your letter of the 18th inst., at the same time that he explained to me the reasons of duty which had caused you to accede to the wishes of H. E. the Viceroy, and to leave Mysore for Haidarábád.

" I can easily understand your preference for a place which you know, when the other is comparatively unknown. I used to experience a similar feeling when it was proposed to take me from Mysore to Bangalore. But I trust the results in both cases may be the same.

" At all events you have given me the example of sacrificing inclination to duty; though, I must admit, since my journey to Bombay, my previous prejudices against change have been removed.

" My best wishes will go with you; and it will always be a pleasure to me to hear that you and Lady Meade are happy.

" I remain,
" dear Sir Richard Meade,
" Your sincere friend,
" CHAMA RAJENDRA WADIAR.

" MYSORE, 23*rd December*, 1875."

(2) From the Mahárája of Mysore (*æt.* 21 years) to Sir R. Meade, in reply to a letter of congratulation :—

"BANGALORE, 26*th July*, 1884.

"DEAR SIR RICHARD MEADE,—I have to thank you very sincerely for your kind congratulations on the birth of my son and the honour of the G.C.S.I. recently conferred on me. Both these events were the occasion of very sincere rejoicing in the province.

"I regret to say that, up to this time, the monsoon has been rather a failure; but we are not without hope that the season may yet prove a fair one. The arrangements with regard to the High Court are completed, and I think we have now a court which will command the respect of the people.

"You will be glad to hear that we are gradually getting on with our railways. Besides the line between this and Mysore, over fifty miles from Bangalore towards Tiptur are on the point of completion and will be open to traffic next month. This line runs through the country that suffered most in the last famine.

"Please give my very kind regards to Lady Meade,

"and believe me,

"Yours very sincerely,

"CHAMA RAJENDRA WADIAR."

CHAPTER XII.

BARODA.

(FIRST COMMISSION.)

Meade appointed president of a commission to inquire into the affairs of Baroda—Account of Baroda—Its territories, population, capital, reigning family and history—Loyalty of Khandi Rao in 1857, but falling off in his administration during the last six years of his reign—His death in 1870—Succeeded by Malhar Rao—His maladministration—Colonel Phayre becomes Resident in 1873 and brings to notice the grievously oppressive character of the Gaekwar's administration and neglect to fulfil his treaty obligations—Members of the committee—Their instructions—The inquiry—Report submitted in March, 1874—Its findings and proposals—Meade's conduct of the inquiry greatly approved of—Letter from Colonel Etheridge—Meade created K.C.S.I.—Orders of the Government of India on the report—The Gaekwar allowed eighteen months in which to carry out necessary reforms.

THE intimation referred to in the last chapter was contained in the following letter from the Viceroy :—

"GOVERNMENT HOUSE,
"CALCUTTA, *16th September*, 1873.

"DEAR COLONEL MEADE,—I am sorry to say that the condition of affairs is so serious, or represented by Colonel Phayre to be so serious, at Baroda that we have found it necessary to appoint a commission to inquire, and report both the facts and the remedies which should be applied. I believe no one is better able to fill the difficult office of chairman of the commission than you; I therefore hope that there is no reason to prevent you from undertaking the duty.

"Yours very truly,
"NORTHBROOK."

Meade deeply regretted that his labours at Mysore should be interrupted, but as his services were required, he of course at once placed them at the disposal of the Government.

BARODA (properly *Virodra*), though less extensive than Gwalior, is the senior of all the Marátha States of India, and its chief, the Gaekwar,[1] receives a salute of one and twenty guns.

It exercises direct control over an area larger than Wales, or five times that of Hampshire, and receives tribute from a multitude of minor chiefships, all forming part of the old Mughal province of Guzerat.

The area under direct control consists of five divisions or tracts separated from each other by intervening British or native territory; three situate in the lowland plain between the Western Gháts and the Gulf of Cambay, two in the west and north-west of the Káthiáwár Peninsula.

Of the tributary States some seventy-eight are in Káthiáwár, others in the Political Agencies of Pahlanpur, Mahe Kantha and Rewa Kantha—tracts adjacent to or intermixed with the mainland divisions, above referred to. But, under an arrangement in force for nearly eighty years, the political control over the tributary States is exercised, not by Baroda, but by the British Government, through whose officers the tributary payments are collected.

The population of Baroda (exclusive of the tributary States) amounted in 1891 to nearly 2,500,000 persons, and the revenue (including tribute) to about 133 lakhs of rupees per annum. It has an army of 3500 cavalry,

[1] A family title signifying "herdsman".

5000 infantry and thirty-four serviceable guns, besides irregular cavalry and police.

The language ordinarily spoken is Gujeráthi, the mother-tongue of 10,000,000 people, a language closely resembling the Hindi of the northern provinces, and largely used for commercial purposes throughout the West of India. Maráthi is also spoken at Baroda in court circles and by the household troops and retinues, and in the Trans-Tapti portion of the territory, but is regarded elsewhere as a foreign language; Urdú (or Hindústáni) is a medium of communication between educated persons of all parts of India.

Of the outlying divisions in Káthiáwár that of Okhamandal, in the north-west corner, is a dreary expanse of treeless plain, with a seaward fringe of sand-dunes; having an annual rainfall of only ten inches and no rivers, but the advantage of a healthy and bracing climate.

It is interesting as the home of the Vághers, a turbulent clan of hereditary pirates, who for years gave serious trouble, until taken in hand, at the request of the Baroda State, by British officers. They are now disarmed, watched by a military force, kindly treated, and gradually settling down to peaceable pursuits.

The second of the Káthiáwár divisions consists of a group of districts of which Amreli is the centre. It has a larger rainfall, about twenty-four inches annually, is fertilised by streams, and has a small port (Porbandar) on the west. Till lately it was a neglected part of the Gaekwar's dominions, but, thanks to improved administration, is now prosperous and traversed by two lines of railway.

The three mainland divisions, especially the centre

one in which the capital is situated, are blessed with a most copious rainfall and a large and industrious population. The latter—that is the central division—is described by a recent traveller[1] as "one of the gardens of India"—"a fine fertile plain, perfectly flat, beautifully wooded, with rich alluvial soil of great fertility, well watered by streams that never dry up, and good wells and reservoirs. . . . Luxuriant crops are grown of grain, cotton, tobacco, opium, sugar cane, and oil seeds, and Baroda is famous for a kind of white cattle, of great size and strength."

The plains are traversed by three large rivers—the Mahe, the Narbadda, and the Tapti—none of them, unfortunately, of much use for navigation but full of fish, with affluents utilised (but only to a small extent) in irrigating crops during the dry season. Torrents from the mountains bring fertilising silt, and on the hill ranges south of the last-named river, are forests of teak, bamboo and blackwood, covering an area of 600 square miles.

Baroda, the capital city, has a population (according to the census of 1891) of upwards of 116,000. It is situate near the banks of a small deep-set river, crossed by four fine bridges, one (the most ancient) with a double tier of arches. It is surrounded by luxuriant groves of trees, overshadowing mosques and tombs and mausolea of Mussulman grandees and interspersed with *baolis*, or covered wells, spacious and deep and cool, with successive galleries of carved stone connected by broad flights of steps leading to the water's edge, through rows of stone pillars and pilasters.

[1] Caine, *Picturesque India.*

As for the city itself, "the three or four main streets," says Caine, "are singularly picturesque, lined with fine houses belonging to merchants, bankers and nobles, many of the façades being of finely carved teak wood. The rest of the town is a labyrinth of narrow and crowded alleys. . . . Near the western gate are interesting aviaries and menageries and extensive *filkhana*, or elephant stables, where in the old days a hundred of the finest animals, with golden trappings, were collected, housed and tended at an enormous cost." There are numerous Hindú temples and some fine specimens of Mussulman architecture, and in the matter of art and handicraft Baroda was, and still is, in the judgment of an expert,[1] "one of the most fascinating of the great polytechnical cities of India".

Meade's first impressions were less favourable. "Baroda," he says in a letter to his eldest daughter, "is a most uninteresting place and has nothing to recommend it. It has a very sinister reputation with us, as your grandfather [Colonel Duncan Malcolm] and your grandmother both died here within a month of each other in September, 1855." But many of the present attractions of Baroda—the public gardens, the new palace, the Maharáni Jamna Bai's hospital, the public library, etc., had no existence in Meade's time.

The dynasty, though senior to Gwalior and Indore, is not an ancient one.

The reigning family traces its descent from Damaji Gaekwar, second in command of the Marátha armies in the commencement of the eighteenth century. By force or fraud he and his nephew, Pilaji, and his grand-

[1] Sir G. Birdwood.

nephew, Damaji II., gradually occupied the greater part of Guzerat, but had afterwards to share their acquisitions with the Peshwa; and in 1753 the capture of Ahmedábád by the joint forces of the Peshwa and the Gaekwar destroyed the last vestige of Mughal domination.

We will not attempt to describe the complicated and unedifying history of the subsequent relations of the Gaekwar with the Peshwa, on the one hand, and the Government of Bombay on the other; suffice it to say :—

(1) That, under a series of treaties and engagements, commencing with the treaty of 1802, Baroda became a British Protected State;

(2) That, in accordance with the usual conditions, the Gaekwar agreed to receive a British Subsidiary Force, the cost of which was provided by a territorial cession; and to provide a Contingent of 3000 cavalry, to be utilised in time of peace in maintaining order in the tributary States; and

(3) That, in 1820, the Gaekwar assigned to the British Government the duty of collecting the tribute from the States in Guzerat—an arrangement which has formed the basis of the political control which has since been exercised over the States in question.

In 1857, the reigning Gaekwar, Khandi Rao, identified his cause with that of the British Government and was liberally rewarded—receiving the honour of G.C.S.I., while a payment of Rs. 300,000 per annum, made heretofore for the cost of horsemen employed in Guzerat, was remitted for ever.

But in the last six years of his rule the system of Government, always bad, became particularly arbitrary and oppressive. New cesses and levies were recklessly imposed to pay for court extravagancies and collected by the harshest measures. No complaints were listened to, and no redress granted for proved grievances. And discontent became general among all classes except a limited number of court favourites.

Khandi Rao died in 1870 leaving no son, but his younger wife, Jamnabai, was at the time of his death *enceinte.* The next heir was his younger brother Malhar Rao. This prince had been accused in 1863 of being concerned in a conspiracy to compass the death of his brother, the reigning chief, by poison or other means, and was, in consequence, confined as a state prisoner during the remainder of Khandi Rao's life; his associates in the plot, who were in his service, being sentenced to long terms of imprisonment.

But the then Resident, having regard to the fact that Malhar Rao's guilt had not been proved, and that it was not improbable that he was the innocent victim of a tyrant's jealousy, summoned him from his place of confinement and at once installed him on the throne, subject to the approval of the British Government; and the British Government, accepting this view of the case, agreed to recognise him as chief presumptive; it being understood that if the widow's offspring was a son the child should be recognised as Gaekwar. The posthumous child being a girl Malhar Rao retained the throne.

The administration of Malhar Rao proved even worse than that of his predecessor. He passed his time in wreaking vengeance upon the adherents of the late chief, and there were tales of cruelty and recklessness current regarding him not less revolting than those alleged against his brother.

In March, 1873, a new Resident came into office in the person of Colonel (afterwards General Sir Robert) Phayre, an officer with a distinguished military career, who had filled for a time the post of Political Superintendent of the Sind Frontier District and more recently of the States of Pahlanpur.

The new Resident was greatly shocked at the misgovernment which prevailed, and the widespread discontent among all classes of the people, and finding remonstrance ineffectual, submitted to the Bombay Government a series of despatches reporting on the state of affairs—the alleged oppression of British subjects and others in the administration of justice; general discontent culminating, in one district, in armed rebellion; serious and general maladministration; the bribery of the minister and other officials in connection with the sale of offices; the abduction of respectable women from their families for purposes of domestic slavery and other unlawful ends.

They further brought to notice the inefficient state of the Contingent of 3000 horse, which the Gaekwar was bound by treaty to maintain, and his refusal to comply with treaty obligations, or to co-operate in improving the administration of Kathiáwár.

The Government of Bombay, in forwarding the despatches to the Government of India, expressed the opinion that the British Government would be guilty of dereliction of duty if it failed to inquire into and, if necessary, apply a remedy to so discreditable a state of

H.H. MALHAR RAO,
Gaekwar of Baroda
(deposed for maladministration).

things; and suggested that it should be empowered to call upon the Gaekwar to remove certain officials and appoint a Commission of inquiry.

The Government of India, recognising the gravity of the representations, decided to take the matter into its own hands and itself to appoint the Commission referred to in Lord Northbrook's letter.

It was composed of the following members:—

Colonel R. J. Meade, C.S.I., Chief Commissioner of Mysore, President (an officer "whose character for calmness of judgment is well known, who has an extensive knowledge of native States and who throughout his career has shown that he is ready to make every allowance in their favour and that he has no wish to enforce a standard which it would be unreasonable to expect in a native administration"[1]).

Nawab Faiz Ali Khan Bahadur (for many years Prime Minister of the Jaipur State).

Mr. E. W. Ravenscroft, of the Bombay Civil Service (of great experience in land revenue administration).

Lieutenant Colonel A. T. Etheridge, an officer of the irregular cavalry (well acquainted with Baroda and its people).

With Mr. McKenzie, of the Bombay Civil Service, as Secretary.

They were instructed to inquire carefully into the specific charges made by Colonel Phayre; and also into the charge of general maladministration. But in regard to the latter, the Viceroy in Council was especi-

[1] Lord Northbrook's minute of the 29th April, 1875.

ally anxious that they should not apply to the Government of Baroda the same high standard which would be expected in a British province, or to descend into minute details.

"His Excellency in Council"—so run the instructions—"has no wish unnecessarily to interfere with the details of the Gaekwar's administration; for the good government of his country the Gaekwar is responsible, and in isolated cases of complaint His Excellency in Council would look to His Highness to take the necessary measures to redress individual grievances, or remove evils that may be brought to his notice.

"But when evils of the kind indicated pervade all departments of the administration, as is officially reported to be the case in Baroda, it becomes the duty of the British Government to institute an inquiry, and, if necessary, to use the power it possesses under treaty of offering advice to the Gaekwar and requiring His Highness to conduct the affairs of Baroda in accordance with that advice.

"In entering on this branch of their duties the Commission will be careful to give no encouragement to frivolous or vexatious complaints, and their inquiries should be conducted, not so much with the view of the redress of individual grievances, as for the purpose of ascertaining whether such general maladministration exists as to call for the further interference of the British Government.

"Should the Commission be satisfied that such misgovernment exists, they will report fully the grounds of their conviction, and suggest such measures as they may consider should be adopted to bring about and maintain for the future a more satisfactory state of affairs, without entailing a minute and vexatious interference on the part of the British Government."

The Commission assembled at Baroda to make inquiry in November, 1873. They commenced their sittings on the 10th *idem* and continued them daily, Sundays excepted, till the 24th of December. They inquired into thirteen cases of complaint by British subjects; sixty-five complaints by Baroda subjects of general misgovernment, and fourteen miscellaneous complaints, examining in all upwards of 200 witnesses. The evidence was taken in the presence of the Resident and of a representative of the Baroda Government, who was allowed to cross-examine and record replies or remarks upon the statements made.

In March, 1874, the Commission, after frequent meetings to consider the evidence, submitted their report. It was admirably drawn up by Meade and unanimously adopted.

The Commission considered the charges of oppressing British subjects to be exaggerated, but found the complaints of misgovernment and oppression made by Baroda subjects to be substantially true. They found that: (1) The agricultural classes were grievously oppressed by the levy of arbitrary demands over and above their previously heavy burdens.

(2) That the nobility and military classes had their appointments abolished and allowances arbitrarily reduced, rather in a spirit of vengeance, than from a feeling of State necessity.

(3) That cases of personal ill-treatment by the Gaekwar's officials were not of infrequent occurrence.

(4) That sentences were passed altogether excessive and out of all proportion to the offence.

(5) That highly arbitrary proceedings had been taken against bankers and other wealthy persons not in favour with the Mahárája.

(6) That respectable married and unmarried women at Baroda had been seized for compulsory service as household slaves in the palace.

(7) That measures of unusual harshness had been adopted by the Chief towards his predecessor's relatives and towards his favourite followers and dependants.

(8) That payments were unjustly withheld from the State creditors, and grants of the last Gaekwar unjustly repudiated.

(9) That the state of the prisons was bad; that female prisoners had been subjected to corporal punishment, and that torture of accused persons with the object of extorting confession undoubtedly obtained to some extent.

(10) That the minister and his officials were, for the most part, quite unfitted to hold responsible and important posts, and the chief minister a man of evil repute.

In regard to the remedies to be applied the Commission suggested a series of administrative reforms—such as revision of the land assessments, abolition of fees on appointments, suppression of torture, reform of the judicial department and jail management, etc.—the adoption of which would do much to prevent a recurrence of the evils; but they added :—

"It appears to us it is hopeless to look for any effectual measures of reform and improved government at the hands of the present ruler and his advisers, and we are convinced that these can only be introduced through the intervention and under the auspices of the British Government".

They therefore recommended that a new minister should be appointed having special administrative experience, who, while enjoined to secure the Chief's good will and confidence and to work in respectful subordination to him, should be supported by the Resident, and not be liable to removal without the special orders of the British Government, and that he should have power to eliminate and dismiss incompetent or unfit officials and appoint others in their place.

The Government of Bombay, through whom the report was submitted, generally agreeing in the report, strongly supported the last recommendation; one member of the Council considered that the report, though true as far as it went, gave an inadequate idea of the intolerable tyranny and oppression of the Gaekwar's rule, and two others expressed the opinion that more drastic measures would soon be necessary.

The reform of the Contingent was separately dealt with.

No orders were passed on the report until the 25th July following.

Meanwhile Meade's conduct of the inquiry had gained universal approval, as being at once able, dignified and impartial; while he was scrupulously careful to avoid any proceedings calculated to make the inquiry more distressing and painful to the Mahárája than was absolutely unavoidable.

In reference to the scope of the inquiry and regarding some points of procedure there were differences of opinion with the Resident and his immediate superior, the Government of Bombay, but Meade's views were supported (on reference) by the Supreme Government. "The spirit and tone of your letter"—wrote the Foreign Secretary—"are precisely what His Excellency expected from you, and your proposals are entirely approved."

And on the termination of the inquiry one of his colleagues (Colonel Etheridge, a Bombay officer) thus wrote to him:—

"I have been thirty-three years in public life and have served with all classes and sorts of official men, but, with the exception perhaps of Sir Bartle Frere, I could not point to one who, to my idea, was capable of handling the matter with the tact, judgment and correct appreciation of the rights of all concerned, as you have done. . . . I now understand the secret of your great success as a political officer. It is so long since the Mutiny, that I did not realise, till close upon your departure, that you were the self-same Meade of whom we had heard so much at that dismal time, and, also, that *you* were 'Meade's Horse'. I hope you will soon reap the reward which has been so long delayed."

The hope was soon fulfilled. On the 2nd June, 1874, Meade, who had returned to Bangalore, received the following telegram:—

"From Viceroy, Calcutta.

"Her Majesty has created you a Knight Commander of the Star of India."

The announcement was well received by the public and followed by a shower of congratulations, and among them delightful letters from his former military superior,

Lord Napier of Magdala, and his friend and late subordinate, Colonel Daly.

At length on the 25th July the Government of India replied.

The Government acknowledged the "care and impartiality" with which the Commission "had discharged their difficult and delicate duties"; accepted all their findings and approved of the scheme of reforms suggested.

But in respect to the action to be taken, the Government shrank from the responsibility of selecting a new minister for the Baroda State and placing the Mahárája under tutelage. It determined, instead of adopting the course proposed by the Commission, to give the Gaekwar an opportunity to carry out himself the necessary reforms, with the help of British officers, should he require their services; but warning His Highness that, if by the 31st December, 1875, the necessary reforms had not been carried out, the only course left would be to deprive him of the throne. He was further advised to dismiss his present minister and certain other officials.

The decision was excellently intended, but in its immediate result unfortunate.

Events showed that Meade and his colleagues (one the minister of a native State) and the Government of Bombay were probably right. "Reform by the chief himself" turned out, as was expected, a fiasco, and the object had to be ultimately effected by the means originally proposed, that is to say by a native minister appointed and upheld by the British Government and supervised by a British officer; and this had to be done after a series of calamitous incidents which probably would not have occurred if there had been more decisive action at an earlier stage.

This is true. But it by no means follows that the Government of India was wrong.

In exercising the functions of the Suzerain Power a Viceroy has to consider not only the justice and propriety of measures in themselves, but their effect. And the effect of interference with the autonomy of States is apt to be far-reaching. However just and called for, it is liable to be misunderstood, and to alarm the very class whose good-will and confidence we are anxious to maintain. Again, tinkering a bad Government with foreign tools without changing the ruler seems, at best, a hazardous experiment, and change of ruler was not proposed by the Commission. In these circumstances the course adopted by the Government—admittedly a choice of difficulties—had much to recommend it, even though it involved rejection of the advice of Meade.

But whether right or wrong, its ultimate result was good, better perhaps than would otherwise have been the case. The Augean stable has been cleansed, the dynasty maintained, and an evil brood of sensuous oppressors for ever swept away.

CHAPTER XIII.

TRIAL OF THE GAEKWAR.

The Gaekwar commences his term of probation badly—Mr. Dadabhai Naoroji—Proceedings of Colonel Phayre—His recall asked for—He is superseded by Sir L. Pelly—Serious state of affairs—Mr. Dadabhai Naoroji resigns—Sir L. Pelly recommends deposition of the Gaekwar—Inquiries into the poisoning case—Confessions of Raoji and Nársú—Government determines to temporarily depose Malhar Rao and proceed with the criminal inquiry—Proclamation—Gaekwar dethroned and placed under honourable surveillance in a house in British cantonments—Excitement amongst the Maráthas of Western India—Further development of the case—Damodur, private secretary to the Gaekwar, confesses—Government of India forms a special tribunal—Its composition—Lord Northbrook's minute—Meade appointed one of the judges, and Sindhia, Jeypore, and Sir Dinkar Rao agree to serve—Notification of trial—Comments of the *Times*—Baroda trial an important event in the political history of India—Form of inquiry, why adopted—Association of chiefs in the inquiry a measure of doubtful expediency; but the idea a noble one.

THE Gaekwar commenced his term of probation badly. He carried out the Viceroy's wish for the dismissal of his principal officers in letter but not in spirit.

He dismissed his minister, but conferred upon him the honourable rank of *Priti Nidhi*; and, instead of appointing in his place a "new minister," with special administrative experience, "and with full power to dismiss unfit officials," appointed the late minister's associate, Mr. Dadabhai Naoroji, a Parsee gentleman of unexceptionable character, high academical distinction and some mercantile knowledge, but with no administrative training, and without the prestige and influence necessary for overcoming opposition ; and, meanwhile, left the "old gang" practically in power.

The arrangement was not acceptable to the British Resident, and was one, no doubt, unlikely to succeed, but it was one to which the Government did not and could not object, and he was bound to allow it a fair trial, helping, if called on, to make it a success.

But Colonel Phayre pursued a different course. Actuated by the best intentions, he endeavoured to keep the new minister "up to the mark" by constant and irritating pressure, at the same time weakening his position by readily listening to complaints. The result was that the relations of the Resident with the Gaekwar and his officials—though perfectly courteous—became less and less cordial ; and, in respect to the Gaekwar personally, matters reached an acute stage when, in October, 1874, the Resident, in accordance with his interpretation of previous instructions, refused to recognise directly or indirectly as heir to the throne a child born to the Gaekwar by a woman named Laxmi Bai,—a person of low character and position whom His Highness had married in the previous May, to the disgust of his own relatives and subjects—she being at that time his kept mistress and the reputed wife of another man.

The antagonism culminated on 2nd November, 1874, in two despatches, one being an elaborate report from Colonel Phayre to the Government of Bombay on the state of Baroda affairs, and the other a letter from the Mahárája to the Viceroy, written by the minister, praying for the recall of Colonel Phayre.

On the 5th, the Resident further irritated the Gaekwar by expostulating with him privately on the attempts made by his agents to secure the recognition of Laxmi Bai's child by bribing officials at Bombay.

Four days afterwards, on the 9th November, an attempt was made to poison Colonel Phayre by putting arsenic and diamond-dust into his sherbet. The Colonel at once reported the circumstance to the Government, and tried to find out the authors of the crime.

Meanwhile, the Viceroy in Council, having become apprised of the strained relations between the Resident and the authorities at Baroda, and disapproving of the manner in which the former had carried out his instructions, deemed it desirable—while recognising the integrity of Colonel Phayre's intentions and the difficulty of his position—that the office of Resident should be placed in other hands.

Accordingly, on 25th November, Colonel Phayre, who declined to resign, was superseded[1] by Colonel Sir Lewis Pelly, K.C.S.I., C.B., an officer of high position in the political service, having acted for years as Resident for the States of the Persian Gulf and more recently as Governor-General's Agent in Rájputána. He was appointed "Agent to the Governor-

[1] Colonel Phayre's removal from political service, though it caused indignation at the time, proved to be a blessing in disguise. His services were "replaced at the disposal of the Military Department," and, on the outbreak of the Afghan War, he was given the command of a Division. For his services in the campaign he received the honour of K.C.B., and ultimately that of G.C.B. As a political officer he could not have expected anything higher than K.C.S.I.

General and Special Commissioner for the affairs of Baroda" and relieved Colonel Phayre on the 30th *idem*.

Sir Lewis Pelly found the state of affairs very serious indeed—the cultivating classes discontented to an unusual degree, the nobles in combination against the authority of their ruler, the administration of justice venal and corrupt, and the general voice of the community loud in condemning the ruler's reckless expenditure on personal favourites, palaces and other selfish objects.

Sir Lewis succeeded in quieting apprehensions and did his utmost to co-operate heartily with the Gaekwar's minister in carrying out reforms, but, elated perhaps by their triumph over Colonel Phayre, the court party, against whose influence the minister was powerless, steadily opposed improvement, and, within a month from Colonel Phayre's departure, the minister, Mr. Dadabhai Naoroji, finding himself quite helpless, very properly resigned.

And early in January—before it had been decided to have a public trial—Sir Lewis Pelly felt himself constrained to "submit his solemn recommendation that the Gaekwar State be saved by the deposal from power of its ruler, and the inauguration of a minority or other mode of government under suitable conditions".

Meantime, Sir Lewis Pelly prosecuted inquiry into the poisoning case, and obtained the assistance of Mr. Souter, C.S.I., and the police officers of Bombay. For some time they could obtain no evidence of importance, but in the middle of December they discovered that Malhar Rao had been in the habit of holding secret communications by night with the Residency servants. They also discovered that one of those servants, Raoji, had been spending large sums of money; they arrested him on suspicion, and he confessed that he had committed the offence, and alleged that he had done so at the personal instigation of Malhar Rao; and his confession was subsequently corroborated by the discovery of a packet of arsenic secreted in his belt. At the same time another Residency servant, Nársú, who had been arrested in consequence of the statements of Raoji, made a similar confession. Raoji made this confession on receiving the promise of a pardon; but Nársú was distinctly told by Sir L. Pelly that he must expect none. "From his condition of overwhelming grief, from his tone, his manner and language, and from the general concurrence of his statement with that of the havildár[1] (Raoji), whom he had not communicated with, he induced in my mind," said Sir L. Pelly, "the conviction that he was a man of somewhat stupid nature who had been led into an atrocious conspiracy, and was unable, under mingled feelings of shame, dejection and horror, any longer to refrain from disburdening himself of his crime." He soon afterwards attempted to drown himself in a well and was with difficulty rescued.

After consulting the Advocate-General of Bombay and the Advocate-General and Standing Counsel to the Government at Calcutta, the Government of India was constrained to consider that there was strong *primâ facie* reason to believe that the attempt to poison Colonel Phayre had been instigated by Malhar Rao.

The next step taken was a serious one, and its

[1] Native corporal.

nature and the reasons for it are thus described by Lord Northbrook :—[1]

"It was impossible to pass over an attempt on the life of a British Resident at the court of a native Prince. The sanctity attached to the lives of Ambassadors extended, in the opinion of the Government of India, if possible in a greater degree to British Residents at the courts of native States; no crime, therefore, could be more serious than an attempt upon the life of a British Resident, instigated by the Ruler of a native State. The evidence as it then stood would not have justified the Government of India in at once condemning Malhar Rao, because he had had no opportunity of making his defence, and the witnesses had not been subjected to cross-examination. Some inquiry, therefore, was essential.

"In deciding upon the course to be adopted, the Government of India could not overlook the character and antecedents of Malhar Rao. He had been accused of having been engaged in a conspiracy to murder his brother Khanderao Gaekwar in 1863, and had in consequence been kept in seclusion during the lifetime of his brother. After Malhar Rao's succession to the Government of Baroda, Bhau Sindia, the minister of the late Gaekwar, had died in prison under suspicious circumstances, and was generally supposed to have been poisoned. The Government of India had expressed to Malhar Rao their regret that, in consequence of his having omitted to follow the advice given by the Assistant Resident, the only satisfactory means of clearing up the doubts that rested on the

[1] Minute of 29th April, 1875.

death of Bhau Sindia had been neglected. Moreover the whole tenor of the report of Sir Richard Meade's Commission was highly unfavourable to Malhar Rao's personal character.

"Having regard to these circumstances and to the strong *primâ facie* case against Malhar Rao, it appeared that there was no probability of a fair inquiry being made into the attempt to poison Colonel Phayre, so long as Malhar Rao remained in the position of Ruler of Baroda. And that it would have been improper for the Government of India to continue friendly communications with him pending investigation. It was therefore determined to suspend Malhar Rao from power, and to assume, on behalf of the Queen, the administration of the State of Baroda, pending the result of the inquiry. This action was not based on considerations of law, it was an act of state, carried out by the Paramount Power."

Accordingly, on 14th January, 1875, the following proclamation was issued :—

"PROCLAMATION.

"To all whom it may concern : Be it known that, Whereas an attempt has been made to poison Colonel R. Phayre, C.B., the late Resident at the Court of His Highness Malhar Rao Gaekwar, and evidence has been adduced to the effect that His Highness Malhar Rao Gaekwar instigated the said attempt to administer poison to Colonel Phayre, and whereas to instigate such attempt would be a high crime against Her Majesty the Queen, and a breach of loyalty to the Crown, under which Malhar Rao Gaekwar is recognised as Ruler of the Baroda State ; and whereas, moreover, such an attempt would be an act of hostility against the British Government, and it is necessary fully and publicly to inquire into the truth of the charge, and to afford His Highness Malhar Rao Gaekwar every opportunity of freeing himself from the grave suspicion which attaches to him; and whereas, in consequence, it is necessary to suspend Malhar Rao Gaekwar from the exercise of power, and to make other arrangements for the administration of the Baroda State: it is hereby notified that, from this date, the Viceroy and Governor-General in Council temporarily assumes the administration of the Baroda State, and delegates all the powers necessary for the conduct of the administration to the Agent of the Governor-General and Special Commissioner at Baroda. The administration will be conducted, as far as possible, in accordance with the usages and customs of the country. All Sirdárs, Inamdárs, Zemindárs and other inhabitants of Baroda territories, and all officers and persons whatsoever, in the military and civil service of the Baroda State liable to be called upon for such service, are hereby required to submit to the authority of, and render obedience to, the said Agent of the Governor-General and Special Commissioner during such time as the State may be under the administration of the British Government.

"In accordance with the gracious intimation made to the Princes and Chiefs of India that it is the desire of Her Majesty the Queen, that their Governments should be perpetuated, and the representation and dignity of their houses should be continued, a native administration will be re-established in such manner as may be determined upon after the conclusion of the inquiry, and after consideration of the results such inquiry may elucidate.

"By order of the Viceroy and Governor-General of India in Council.

"C. U. AITCHISON."

The same day the British garrison in Baroda was strengthened by one European and one native regiment and a battery of artillery, and Sir Lewis Pelly, having informed the Gaekwar of the charge against him, suspended him from power and placed him under honourable surveillance. His Highness offered no resistance and the operation was effected without the slightest indignity. He was driven in the Resident's carriage to a comfortable house in the British cantonments, where he remained, under charge of a European guard, until he was finally removed from Baroda territory after sentence had been passed against him.

His Highness was treated with the greatest respect and consideration, and it was specially directed that his confinement should not be stricter than was necessary to ensure the proper investigation of the case; that he should be afforded every facility for appearing before the Commission, either in person or by counsel, for submitting statements or explanations, for producing evidence and consulting legal advisers. He was allowed carriage exercise in company with his medical attendant (Dr. Seward) and the services of a pipe bearer, three cooks, three valets, two heralds, a Brahman, a doctor, a barber, an interpreter, and two story-tellers.

After disposing of the Gaekwar, Sir L. Pelly proceeded to occupy the city of Baroda, and took the administration of the Government into his own hands, and charge of all the State palaces and property. The Gaekwar's troops showed no disposition to fight for their master, and were not even disarmed. Some of the nobles were annoyed at the interference of the British Government; but the population of Baroda generally acquiesced in the transfer of power from the Gaekwar to the Viceroy's Agent; and all signs of local discontent quickly disappeared.

But outside Baroda the news that the Gaekwar had been summarily suspended from power, pending trial, was received with great concern, and though the measure was obviously necessary (if the inquiry was to be anything but a farce), and was carried out with the greatest consideration for His Highness's feelings, it created a widespread sympathy for the accused Prince. Among the Maráthas of Western India especially the excitement became intense; and Púnah in particular, the old capital of the Peshwas, showed the keenest sympathy with Malhar Rao. Matters were not improved when the Anglo-Indian press, in its comments on the Viceroy's proclamation, expressed doubts on the expediency of appointing a Commission of Inquiry, and strongly advocated summary annexation. Thereupon the priestly class (with whom Malhar Rao was careful to be on good terms) was deeply moved at the prospect of the absorption into the British Empire of a native State noted for its charities to Brahmans, while the nobles trembled for the loss of the pensions and other advantages secured to them by their relations at Baroda. Púnah, therefore, became the headquarters of a vehement agitation on behalf of Malhar Rao—an agitation not limited to processions to the temples and prayers to the gods, but modernised by the educated natives into the form of public meetings and memorials to the Viceroy, praying that at all events the Commission of Inquiry might be equally composed of natives and Europeans. The excitement rapidly spread among all sections of the native community, many of the Parsees even catching the infection; the gross misgovernment, the cruelties, the follies, the horrible charge now made against the Chief, were all forgotten, and the cause of

Malhar Rao was identified with that of the subject races of the country.[1]

While political excitement in favour of the Gaekwar was growing outside Baroda, the suspension of His Highness from power led to further development of the case against him.

On the evening of the 14th January Damodur Trinbhak (or Pant), Brahman, private secretary to the Gaekwar, was stopped at the city gate when endeavouring to leave Baroda in company with the late minister. He was detained on suspicion of being privy to the poisoning, and was taken to the palace, where the box containing the Gaekwar's private accounts (which had been under his control) was unsealed in his presence and its contents taken charge of. After some days' detention Damodur offered to confess on a promise of pardon; this was granted, and on the 29th inst. and following days, he made a full confession, which was taken down by Mr. Richey, J.P., in the presence of Sir Lewis Pelly.

His statement was to the effect that shortly before the attempt to poison, he had, by direction of the Gaekwar, on two occasions procured arsenic and diamonds (for diamond dust, believed by natives of India to be poisonous), and made them over to Salim and Yeshwant Rao, the Gaekwar's servants, from the former of whom according to Raoji and Nársú the poison was received. His statement was supported by the private accounts referred to in the last paragraph, which were based, in accordance with Marátha

[1] Statement published by the *Bombay Gazette* and apparently derived from official sources.

usage, on a series of detailed memoranda explanatory of each item. The accuracy of some of these memoranda was proved by external evidence, and in explanation of the absence of any recorded payment for *arsenic*, Damodur stated that the seller was, for obvious reasons, to be rewarded in another way. He further showed how, after the attempt to poison had taken place, some of the memoranda had been defaced and blotted in order to conceal their meaning. He pointed out the sources from which the funds were obtained and the manner in which accounts had been falsified in order to disguise the character of the transactions. While the jeweller (Hemchand) from whom the diamonds had been purchased proved that he had been required to destroy all record of the sale.[1]

While the case was being completed the Government of India was engaged in determining what form the inquiry should take, and its conclusions are thus described in Lord Northbrook's minute:—

"Notwithstanding the objections to which a public inquiry was open, it was decided that a public inquiry was more advisable than one conducted in private, which might have given occasion for suspicion.

"The composition of the Commission was next considered. In order that it should be so constituted as to command complete confidence, the services of Sir Richard Couch, the Chief Justice of Bengal, and the highest judicial authority in India, were secured as President. Sir Richard Meade, whose character has

[1] A statement he afterwards repudiated.

been already described,[1] and Mr. Philip Melvill, an officer who had been Judicial Commissioner of the Central Provinces and acted as a Judge of the Chief Court at Lahore, who had no connection whatever with Baroda affairs, and whose character for independence and ability is well known, were appointed Commissioners.

"The Government of India further considered that it was desirable to obtain the assistance of natives of India of high rank and position as members of the Commission. Rája Sir Dinkar Rao was summoned to Calcutta and consented to serve. I requested Mahárája Sindhia, Mahárája Holkar, and the Mahárája of Jeypore to join the Commission. Mahárája Holkar, while expressing his complete concurrence in the course which had been taken, excused himself from serving, but the other two Princes consented to serve.

"In making public the suspension of the Gaekwar and the institution of the inquiry, it was announced that whatever the result might be, a native administration would be established at Baroda."

At length, on 15th February, 1875, the following notification was issued:—

"Whereas an attempt has been made at Baroda to poison Colonel Phayre, C.B., the late British Resident at the Court of His Highness Malhar Rao Gaekwar; and whereas the following offences are imputed against the said Malhar Rao Gaekwar, that is to say:—

"I. That the said Malhar Rao Gaekwar did by his agents and in person hold secret communication for improper pur-

[1] See p. 163.

poses with some of the servants employed by Colonel Phayre, the Resident at Baroda, or attached to the Residency;

"II. That the said Malhar Rao Gaekwar gave bribes to such servants or caused such bribes to be given;

"III. That his purposes in holding such communications and giving such bribes were to use the said servants as spies upon Colonel Phayre, and thereby to improperly obtain information of secrets, and to cause injury to Colonel Phayre, or to remove him by way of poison;

"IV. That in fact an attempt to poison Colonel Phayre was made by persons instigated thereto by the said Malhar Rao Gaekwar;

"And whereas the Viceroy and Governor-General in Council has temporarily assumed the administration of the Baroda State for the purpose of instituting a public inquiry into the truth of the said imputations, and of affording His Highness Malhar Rao Gaekwar an opportunity of freeing himself from the grave suspicion which attaches to him:

"Therefore the Viceroy and Governor-General of India in Council appoints you the said Sir Richard Couch, you the said Mahárája of Gwalior, you the said Mahárája of Jeypore, you the said Sir Richard John Meade, you the said Sir Dinkar Rao, and you the said Philip Sandys Melvill, Esq., to be Commissioners for the purpose of inquiring into the truth of the said imputations and of reporting to the Viceroy and Governor-General in Council how far the same are true to the best of your judgment and belief.

"And the said Viceroy and Governor-General in Council appoints you the said Sir Richard Couch to be President of this Commission, with full power to appoint times and places of meeting, to adjourn meetings, to adjust and arrange the method of procedure, to settle the course which the inquiry shall take, to call for and to receive or reject evidence documentary or otherwise, to hear such persons as you shall think fit on behalf either of the Viceroy and Governor-General of India in Council, or of His Highness Malhar Rao Gaekwar, and generally to guide the whole course of the proceedings of this Commission as from time to time shall appear to you to be proper for the purposes thereof. . . .

"And the said Viceroy and Governor-General of India in Council hereby appoints John Jardine, Esq., of the Bombay Civil Service, to be your secretary.

"By order of the Viceroy and Governor-General of India in Council.

"C. U. AITCHISON,
"Secretary to the Government of India."

The place appointed for the inquiry was a bungalow in the British cantonments with a large room suitable for a court, in the immediate vicinity of the mansion occupied by the accused.

The prosecution was placed in the hands of the Advocate-General of Bombay, Mr. (now Sir Andrew) Scoble. For the defence, the Gaekwar's advisers secured the services of Mr. Serjeant Ballantine, who came from England for the purpose.

The importance of the occasion and the novelty of the tribunal and proceedings attracted the greatest attention both in India and in England. And the *Times* of 24th February honoured the subject with a leading article, from which we extract the following passages :—

"The arraignment of His Highness the Gaekwar Malhar Rao before a tribunal appointed to sit at Baroda by the Viceroy of India will probably be recorded in history as one of the most remarkable of state trials—unique in the judicial annals of British India and perhaps of the world.

"The Viceroy of India, acting in the name and by the supreme authority of the Empress-Queen Victoria, has delegated to the Commission the right to inquire into the guilt of the accused Prince—not to pronounce a sentence or even to give a conclusive verdict. The supreme exercise of power is reserved for England as the victor and successor of the Mogul Empire."

As for the accused : "The follies, the cruelties, the incredible abominations that are attributed to the late Gaekwar, the brother and predecessor of Malhar Rao, can only be paralleled from the worst pages of Suetonius, and, according to his enemies, the present Prince of Baroda was not behind his brother in cruelty and recklessness".

As to the Viceroy's actions: "Every step in the proceedings against the Gaekwar, the reception of complaints against him, the warning given to him last summer, his arrest, his temporary deposition and the investigation of the charge against him, have been one and all acts of prerogative, having root neither in statutes nor in custom, nor in the consent of those over whom it is exercised. The Viceroy has acted as any of the Mogul Emperors might have acted if a similar charge had been brought against any of the tributary Princes of the Empire; and Judges to whom no exception can be taken are to investigate the matter."

"Among the Judges is a Prince of similar origin, the Mahárája Sindia, Ruler of Gwalior; among them also the Mahárája of Jeypore, a Rájput Prince, a Hindú Ruler of the purest blood and educated in the strictest code of Oriental chivalry. But alongside these peers of the accused appears a man who specially represents the results of English rule in India, a high caste Hindú gentleman, with all the energy of the Mahratta and all the culture acquired by contact with Europeans. Sir Dinkar Rao is a native politician who has risen by means which in the old days of violence and intrigue would have led him to nothing but ruin. He has governed great States and well, and won the admiration of Anglo-Indian statesmen.

"But these three native notables are not to try Malhar Rao alone. They are aided by an English lawyer trained in the practice of the English bar, and in the procedure of the Indian codes, and by an Anglo-Indian political officer, who knows, it may be presumed, why the power of Government has been brought to bear, under the uncertain conditions of a legal process, on the Ruler of Baroda."

These remarks are just. They recognise the gravity of the occasion and admit that the action taken is within the prerogative of the Paramount Power of India, and, though doubting the desirability of proceeding by legal process, admit the fairness of the tribunal, and note that it is no jury but simply a committee of inquiry to inform the mind of the Viceroy in Council.

But there is one memorable fact connected with the inquiry which deserves more prominent mention, namely, that this is the first occasion on which England's jurisdiction as Paramount and Protecting Power in India, to inquire into and punish (if need be) the misfeasances of native Rulers, was formally recognised by the Chiefs themselves.

Such jurisdiction, as rightly stated in the article, is not founded upon statutes nor is it expressly declared (though often implied) in treaties, but results directly from the position we have assumed. For the Power which protects from internal as well as external foes, which prevents uprising against oppression, is in justice bound to deal with the oppressor.

It is a jurisdiction which has been exercised, submitted to, and acquiesced in since the commencement of the present century, but never received such formal and complete acknowledgment as in the Baroda trial, —when the Rulers of two of the principal States of India, one representative of the most ancient dynasties, one of the dynasties of modern date, consented to take part in the grand inquest held by the Suzerain Power into the alleged misdeeds of one of the greatest of its Feudatories.

As to the question why the power of Government was brought to bear upon the Baroda Chief "under the uncertain conditions of a legal process," Lord Northbrook explains in his minute that it was so brought to bear to prevent our motives from being suspected. This is doubtless true, but there was probably another reason present to the minds of His Excellency's advisers. In deciding to give the inquiry a quasi-judicial character, the Government of India was probably influenced by the attitude of Parliament and the statements of the Secretary of State for India when the Nawab of Tonk (in Rájputána) was deposed, in 1867, for having instigated a murderous outrage.

On that occasion public opinion was much exercised, owing to the secrecy of the inquiry and to its being conducted by Political Officers without judicial training; and it was proposed that an appeal in such cases should be allowed to Her Majesty's Privy Council.

To this proposal Her Majesty's Government very properly objected, holding that the proper remedy for the evil was to improve and strengthen the political court of first instance, not the establishment of a remote tribunal of appeal upon the facts. It was therefore promised that in future the tribunal or court or committee appointed to inquire into the misconduct of native Princes should have a strong judicial element.

Whether in a public inquiry, conducted by Englishmen after English methods, it was advisable to associate Oriental Rulers quite unaccustomed to such methods and bound to sympathise profoundly with their brother Prince, may be well open to dispute, but it will be seen that the object was a laudable one; and many will be of opinion that the idea of associating our Feudatories with high officers of the British Government in the administration of Imperial justice was, in itself, statesmanlike and noble, and that its failure (for it was a failure) is a matter for profound regret.

CHAPTER XIV.

TRIAL OF THE GAEKWAR (*continued*).

The so-called trial—Opening scene described by Serjeant Ballantine—Account of the proceedings—Brief abstract of the evidence—Serjeant Ballantine's defence—Mr. Scoble's reply—Serjeant Ballantine's testimony to the fairness of the inquiry—His conduct of the defence—Comments on the evidence made by the press before decision—Native opinion—The Commissioners, not being able to agree, submit separate reports—English members of the Commission find all the charges proved—Two, Sindhia and Dinkar Rao, find the principal charge not proven; one, Jeypore, finds the accused not guilty—Meanwhile Meade succeeds Sir L. Pelly, who leaves on account of ill-health—The Government of India supports the view of the English Commissioners and recommends Gaekwar's deposition on the ground of his guilt and also on the ground of misgovernment—The Home Government sanctions his deposition on the ground of misgovernment, but leaves out of view the report of the Commission—Before the decision is generally known Meade quietly deports the Gaekwar to Madras—Proclamation of Gaekwar's deposition quietly received in Baroda, but announcement unfavourably received in England and India until publication of Baroda Blue Book, when all opposition ceases—General result of proceedings.

THE proceedings in the so-called "trial" of Malhar Rao Gaekwar commenced at 11 A.M. on Tuesday, 23rd February, 1875.

We say "so-called trial" because it was not a judicial proceeding, but an inquiry made for the purpose of informing the mind of His Excellency the Viceroy in Council, representing the Paramount Power of England in India, in respect to alleged misconduct by a

Feudatory. The Commissioners were to give no verdict but simply to report their opinions for the consideration of higher authority.

But the inquiry, though political, was conducted on judicial principles, and in the regulation of procedure and the admissibility of evidence the practice of the British Indian law-courts was generally observed.

All the English members of the Commission were holding or had held high positions as judicial officers, and had more or less experience in dealing with Maráthа-speaking as well as other native witnesses.

The President (the Hon. Sir Richard Couch), who regulated the procedure, was Chief Justice of Bengal and had served previously as Puisne Judge and Chief Justice of the High Court of Bombay.

Mr. Melvill was a Judge of the Chief Court of the Punjab, and had served previously as Judicial Commissioner of the Central Provinces, with a large Marátha population.

Sir Richard Meade, when Governor-General's Agent for Central India, exercised the function of High Court Judge in respect to appeals in civil and criminal cases arising in the twelve cantonments of the Agency and in native States under British management and along the line of railway.

Of the three Indian members of the Commission, two were ruling Princes of the highest rank, and the other was a successful administrator of native States; but none had received any special judicial training, and all were quite unused to the practice and procedure of British courts.

As might have been expected, the occasion was

one of great public interest, and we cannot do better than quote the following graphic description of the opening scene from the pen of Mr. Serjeant Ballantine :—

"It is superfluous to mention that shortly after daybreak on the morning of 23rd February, 1875, Baroda was in a blaze of sunshine; for such was the case every day during my sojourn. No rain, no dew. The grass, a few blades of which did meet my eye ten days before, was burnt out of sight, and the heat threatened a sunstroke to those who were exposed to it for a moment.

"Yet on this particular morning everything was as much alive as it could be. The ruler of a country covering 4400 square miles was about to be put upon his trial for the attempted murder of an English officer, holding the post of British Resident, and great potentates had consented to take part in the solemn duty, whilst the Chief Justice of India had been deputed to conduct the inquiry, after European fashion, with the assistance of a military and civil officer, each one distinguished in his respective position.

"A guard of Infantry and a troop of Lancers did no more honour than is due to Mahárája Sindhia, the great Marátha potentate, the tried and trusted friend of England. His appearance was such as to command respect in any country, and I cannot deny myself the pleasure of copying a few lines of description from an admirably conducted paper, *The Times of India*, of what it presented on that memorable day, 'burly and princely, an Asiatic Harry the Eighth'. The writer might have added 'before the English monarch had imprinted upon his features the marks of gross indulgence, selfishness and cruelty'. For Sindhia's is a courteous mien and pleasant to look upon. Sir Dinkar Rao, a Hindu possessing great weight with his fellow-citizens and esteemed as a very able administrator, was another of the Judges, and the third native member of the Commission was the Mahárája of Jeypore, highly esteemed by the British Government.

"Sir Richard Couch, Colonel Sir R. J. Meade, and Mr. Philip Sandys Melvill composed the English element.

"Naturally Sir Richard Couch conducted the proceedings.

"The Hon. A. Scoble, Advocate-General of Bombay, and Mr. Inverarity appeared for the prosecution. With me were Mr. Branson, Mr. Purcell, Shant Aram Narain, and Wassudeo Juggonath. For myself I cannot forbear saying that my reception was most cordial and kind, both by the bench and my brethren at the bar.

"The accused Mahárája sat upon the bench, Colonel Sir Lewis Pelly sitting beside him. . . . I do not think his face was unprepossessing.[1] His dress was in singularly good taste, his demeanour quiet and dignified."

The proceedings lasted for twenty days, until the 18th March. In all forty-five witnesses were examined, including, besides the principal witnesses (Raoji, Nársú, and Damodur Pant), the native Inspector of Police

[1] Opinions differ on this point. Writing to his eldest daughter (shortly after his first arrival in Baroda) Meade remarks of the Gaekwar: "He is one of the most awful-looking men I have ever seen, and I have seen some strange ones in my time. He is, however, very civil and anxious to please."

(Akbar Ali), Hemchand (the jeweller), Colonel Phayre and his informant Bhau Púnakar, Dr. Seward (the Residency Surgeon), Dr. Gray (the chemical examiner), Mr. Souter (Commissioner of Police), Mr. Richey, J.P., and Sir Lewis Pelly. Nearly six days were occupied by the speeches of counsel.

All the witnesses but one adhered to the statements they had made during the preliminary investigation, and the single case of repudiation of previous testimony given in the presence of Sir L. Pelly was explained and exposed by the counsel for the prosecution.

As the result of the inquiry was ultimately abortive, we do not propose to go into the evidence at any length.

Suffice it to say that it was clearly proved that Colonel Phayre's sherbet was poisoned; that Malhar Rao was desirous of being rid of him; that for some time past there had been secret communications for improper purposes between His Highness the Mahárája and some of the servants employed by Colonel Phayre or attached to the Residency, and that large bribes were received by those servants as reward. Whether the poisoning of the sherbet was done at the instigation of the Mahárája depended upon the credibility to be attached to the self-criminating statements of Raoji and Nársú, two of the Residency servants referred to, and those of Damodur Pant, the Gaekwar's private secretary, supported by accounts and memoranda discovered in the palace. If these statements (which were made independently) or any of them were substantially true the Mahárája's guilt was clear.

All these witnesses, and, indeed, all the important

witnesses in the case, were subjected to a severe cross-examination, and, as might have been expected, certain discrepancies and contradictions were elicited, though on all material points the testimony was unshaken.

But the counsel for the defence naturally made the most of these discrepancies; urged the insufficiency of the corroboration of the confessions; dwelt on the absence of any written orders from the Mahárája, and the fact that most of the witnesses had been kept under police surveillance (a proceeding necessary to protect them from violence, and prevent their being bribed or made away with); abused the police and hinted, though he did not prove, that the whole thing was a conspiracy on their part, or that Damodur Pant or Bhau Púnakar were the real culprits; and finally urged that the Mahárája could have no possible motive for instigating the murder of Colonel Phayre, seeing that he had applied for his recall. But he called no witnesses for the defence, not even the Gaekwar's own servants Salem and Yeshwant Rao, to rebut the statement that it was through them that the arsenic had been conveyed to the Residency orderlies.

Mr. Scoble in an able reply on the whole case contended that the evidence for the prosecution had not been shaken on any material point, and had not been in any way rebutted; as for the suggestion that the case was "got up" by the police, there was not a tittle of evidence in support of it, beyond a worthless statement by the jeweller in repudiation of his previous testimony; the police were not Baroda men but from Bombay; they were all picked men of the highest character, and worked under the immediate direction of

Mr. Souter, Commissioner of Police; and the statements of all the more important witnesses were taken before an English Justice of the Peace, and generally in the presence of Sir L. Pelly, in whose official residence the investigations were carried on. He claimed, therefore, to have fully substantiated the case against the accused.

At the conclusion of Mr. Scoble's reply, "the English Commissioners," says Mr. Serjeant Ballantine, "closed their note-books" (Meade's consisted of two volumes of closely written MS.), and departed, and the Chiefs retired under a roar of artillery salutes, "but not a word was spoken—not a hint given of what the decision was to be". Later in the day the Commissioners proceeded to Bombay to consider their report.

So ended the public proceedings of the inquiry. There was no charge by the President and no verdict was given, for the Commissioners were not a jury. But though the *finale* was not dramatic, though there was no "breathless silence" preceding the delivery of a momentous verdict, there can be no doubt that the proceedings must have left a most favourable impression of the earnest desire of the President of the Commission and his colleagues, as well as of the Government, to arrive at the truth and do justice.

"It is impossible," generously observes Mr. Serjeant Ballantine, "that any inquiry could be conducted with greater fairness and impartiality. No impediment of any kind was presented to the defence, and certainly the earnest attention paid by every member of the court showed their full appreciation of the importance of their position, while Sir Lewis Pelly's demeanour towards the accused Prince was characterised by all the courtesy and consideration that his duty could permit."

We must add that Serjeant Ballantine himself discharged a difficult duty very creditably, under novel conditions, which must have severely taxed his powers of cross-examination. He did not demur to the jurisdiction or raise unnecessary difficulties; abstained from touching upon questions of *la haute politique*, and, though indulging in some pardonable rhetoric about "a cruel and groundless prosecution" and a "persecuted prince," dealt with the case generally with fairness and moderation.

Long before the Commissioners had prepared their reports, indeed throughout the progress of the case, the press both of England and India was busily engaged in expressing its opinion in no measured terms; for, unfortunately, the rule of law requiring the press to abstain from commenting upon proceedings pending the decision of a case is not applicable to a political inquiry, and, even if applicable, could not be enforced over so vast an area.

The opinions expressed were very various. The *Times* Calcutta correspondent of the period observed: "There is much diversity of opinion as to the future results of the inquiry. On the one hand, a large class of persons hold that the evidence has brought guilt home to the Gaekwar in a most conclusive manner, and that the cross-examination of the witnesses wholly failed in shaking the case made against the accused. On the other hand, there are not wanting many who look upon the case as a conspiracy cleverly planned by the police." *Per contra*, the reporter of one newspaper, hostile to the Government and anxious to applaud the efforts of the great English counsel, admits that the native inspector of police, by whom the investigations were made, more than held his own with Serjeant Ballantine.

In England some of the leading newspapers had, from an early period in the progress of the case, ranged themselves, unaccountably, on the side of the defence.

As for native opinion there was, no doubt, a strong revulsion in favour of the Gaekwar; not so much on the ground of his probable innocence of the crime charged, as in view of the indignity he had suffered from his summary dethronement on the *ex parte* statement of men of inferior position, and from the publicity of the proceedings. "The Chiefs' feelings on the subject," says Meade, in a letter to the Viceroy, "have appeared to me to have come at last to regard the poisoning question as a secondary matter; and this seems to me very much the light in which it is generally viewed by the public who sympathise with His Highness."

Amid this hubbub of popular criticism, the Commissioners proceeded to consider their report. But it soon became apparent that the English and Indian Commissioners could not agree as to the trustworthiness of the testimony against the Gaekwar. In these circumstances Sir Richard Couch (the President), Sir R. Meade and Mr. Melvill drew up a joint report of seventy-eight paragraphs, in which, after carefully reviewing the evidence, and considering the arguments of counsel, and also the opinions of their Indian colleagues, they express their unanimous opinion that there was no ground whatever for suspecting the police, and that all the charges were proved.

The two Mahárájas and Sir Dinkar Rao prepared brief separate reports, Sindhia and Dinkar Rao finding that the charge of instigating the attempt to poison was not proved; the Mahárája of Jeypore that the accused was not guilty.

The reports were delivered to the Government of India on 4th April, but it was not until the 22nd that the decision was announced.

Meanwhile Meade was looking forward with anticipation to an early release from his somewhat unpleasant duty, but he was doomed to disappointment, as Sir Lewis Pelly's health broke down and he had to leave for England. For the important post thus vacated at a critical time, Lord Northbrook felt that Meade was the best, if not the only man, and he asked him accordingly to undertake, for a time, the duties of Governor-General's Agent and Special Commissioner for Baroda. Meade promptly, but with a heavy heart, consented, and relieved Sir Lewis Pelly on 10th April.

During this time the Government of India, including, besides the Viceroy (himself an English magistrate), the Commander-in-Chief, experienced in reviewing the findings of courts martial, the Law member of Council, Mr. (now Lord) Hobhouse, Q.C., and three civilians, more or less experienced in dealing with native testimony, were engaged in considering the reports of the Commissioners. On the 19th inst. they arrived at a conclusion which is embodied in a resolution of fifty-six paragraphs. The conclusion is to the effect that it was their decided opinion that all the offences charged against the Gaekwar had been substantiated.

The reasons were summed up as follows :—

"Notwithstanding the doubts entertained by the Mahárája Scindia and Sir Dinkar Rao, and the more positive opinion of the Mahárája of Jeypore, the examination of the evidence by the Government of India leads them to concur with the three Commissioners who signed the joint report, that it bears on its face a trustworthy character, and contains no such contradictions and obscurities as would justify them in disbelieving the witnesses on their own showing. Counter-evidence, it has been already stated, there is none ; the Gaekwar's advisers have refrained from calling upon his agents to attest his innocence. His counsel, at the close of his argument, boldly maintained that it was not for him to make out a case on behalf of the Gaekwar. The Government of India think differently. One of the main objects of the inquiry was to afford the Gaekwar an opportunity of freeing himself from the grave suspicion which attached to him. The Government of India think it was for the Gaekwar's advisers to make out a case, if they could honestly do it, to rebut the strong evidence brought against him, and cannot see any ground for their refusal to do it, except their inability. Neither is there any counter-theory to explain the evidence before the Commission. It is true that the Gaekwar's counsel rather suggested than argued that Damodhur Punt or Bhow Poonekur might be the authors of the attempt to poison. But there is not a particle of evidence to support either suggestion, and both are justly dismissed in very brief terms by the three Commissioners who have signed the joint report."

There was therefore the concurrence of very weighty opinion in favour of the Gaekwar's guilt.[1] But it was further brought to the notice of the Government of India that in the interval between the report of Sir Richard Meade's Commission and Malhar Rao's suspension from power several instances occurred in which he gravely misconducted himself,—such as his marriage with Laxmi Bai (which disgraced him in the eyes of his people and was of questionable legitimacy), his cruel treatment of Rakmabai, his late brother's younger widow, and his arbitrary conduct towards his Sirdars; and after the assumption of administrative power by Sir Lewis Pelly, further information was obtained which added materially to the previous evidence of the misgovernment of the Baroda State; such as the suspicious circumstances connected with the death of Bhau Sindhia, the late Gaekwar's minister, and the death of Govind Naik, believed by Sir L. Pelly, after full inquiry, to have been tortured to death under Malhar

[1] As the findings of the Commissioners were left out of account in deciding the fate of Malhar Rao their correctness or otherwise has little more than an academical interest; but it may be worth while to mention that the view of the Government of India and the English Commissioners was strongly supported by Mr. (afterwards Sir James) Fitz James Stephen, in a series of articles. On the other hand, Mr. Serjeant Ballantine in his *Experiences* (published in 1882) repeats the views he advocated upon the trial. General Sir R. Phayre, to the day of his death, firmly believed in Malhar Rao's guilt. Malhar Rao died in 1882 leaving no male issue, his son by Laxmi Bai having predeceased him in 1880. His two widows returned to Baroda, where they lived (and may be still living) under the protection of the Baroda Government.

Rao's orders, and the disastrous state of the finances resulting from extravagance and waste. "Daily, almost hourly," said Sir Lewis Pelly, writing in February, 1875, "fresh cases of iniquity are discovered."

Taking all these matters into consideration the Government of India recommended that Malhar Rao should be deposed, and his issue declared incapable of occupying the throne.

Her Majesty's Government, to whom these conclusions were telegraphed, sanctioned the proposals, on the ground of the Chief's misgovernment and incapacity, but wisely, perhaps, under the circumstances, left out of view the report of the Commission.

Accordingly on 23rd April the following proclamation was issued :—

"PROCLAMATION BY THE GOVERNMENT OF INDIA.

"To all whom it may concern: His Highness Mulhar Rao Gaekwar was suspended from the exercise of power, and the administration of the Baroda State was temporarily assumed by the British Government, in order that a public inquiry might be made into the truth of the imputation that His Highness had instigated an attempt to poison Colonel R. Phayre, C.B., the late representative of the British Government at the Court of Baroda, and that every opportunity should be given to His Highness of freeing himself from the said imputation.

"The proceedings of the Commission having been brought to a close, Her Majesty's Government have taken into consideration the question whether His Highness Mulhar Rao Gaekwar shall be restored to the exercise of Sovereign power in the State of Baroda.

"The Commissioners being divided in opinion, Her Majesty's Government have not based their decision on the inquiry or report of the Commission, nor have they assumed that the result of the inquiry has been to prove the truth of the imputations against His Highness.

"Having regard, however, to all the circumstances relating to the affairs of Baroda from the accession of His Highness Mulhar Rao Gaekwar, to the present time, his notorious misconduct, his gross misgovernment of the State, and his evident incapacity to carry into effect the necessary reforms; having also considered the opinion of the Government of India that it would be detrimental to the interests of the people of Baroda and inconsistent with the maintenance of the relations which ought to subsist between the British Government and the Baroda State that His Highness should be restored to power, Her Majesty's Government have decided that His Highness Mulhar Rao Gaekwar shall be deposed from the Sovereignty of Baroda, and that he and his issue shall be hereafter precluded from all rights, honours and privileges thereto appertaining.

"Accordingly, His Excellency the Viceroy and Governor-General in Council hereby declares that His Highness Mulhar Rao Gaekwar is deposed from the Sovereignty of the Baroda State, and that he and his issue are precluded from all rights, honours and privileges thereto appertaining.

"Mulhar Rao will be permitted to select some place in British India, which may be approved by the Government of India, where he and his family shall reside with a suitable establishment and allowances to be provided from the revenues of the State.

"Her Most Gracious Majesty the Queen, in re-establishing a native administration in the Baroda State, being desirous to mark her sense of the loyal services of His Highness Khundi Rao Gaekwar in 1857, has been pleased to accede to the request of his widow, Her Highness Jumnabaee, that she may be allowed to adopt some member of the Gaekwar House whom the Government of India may select as the most suitable person upon whom to confer the Sovereignty of the Baroda State.

"The necessary steps will accordingly be immediately taken to carry into effect Her Majesty's commands. In the meantime, with the consent of His Highness the Máháraja of Indore, Sir Madava Rao, K.C.S.I., will at once proceed to Baroda, and conduct the administration of the State as Prime Minister, under instructions which he will receive from the Governor-General's Agent and Special Commissioner at Baroda.

"In conferring the Sovereignty of the Baroda State, no alteration will be made in the treaty engagements which exist between the British Government and the Gaekwars of Baroda, and the new Gaekwar will enjoy all the privileges and advantages which were conveyed to the Gaekwar of Baroda in the sunnud of Earl Canning, dated the 11th of March, 1862.

"By order of His Excellency the Viceroy and Governor-General of India in Council.

"C. U. AITCHISON,
"Secretary to the Government of India.

"SIMLA, *19th April*, 1875."

The case was concluded by a masterly despatch from Lord Salisbury, a copy of which is given as an appendix to this chapter, reviewing the proceedings *ab initio*, explaining the action of Her Majesty's Government, and expressing their high appreciation of the services rendered by Lord Northbrook.

Meanwhile—the evening before the issue of the proclamation—the dethroned Prince, with his suite, was (thanks to Meade's foresight) quietly moved into a special train, and next morning, when his deposition was announced was well away on his journey to Madras. The circumstances will be described in the next chapter.

The proclamation caused no excitement in Baroda, but the telegraphic announcement of the decision of

Government was most unfavourably received, both in India and in England.

And certainly, when stated without explanation, it was one calculated to call forth very adverse comment. "The Government have not found the Gaekwar guilty of the attempt to poison, yet depose him on the ground of misgovernment, before the expiration of the period allowed him for reform"—such was the common and very obvious criticism.

So strong was the feeling that even the usually calm-minded *Spectator* demanded "the immediate restoration of Malhar Rao"; and notices of hostile motions were threatened in both Houses of Parliament.

But when the Baroda Blue Book appeared early in June, and the public read Sir Lewis Pelly's despatches of the 5th and 7th January, 1875, Lord Northbrook's minute of 29th April, and Lord Salisbury's despatch of the 3rd June—a revulsion of feeling took place, the opposition collapsed, hostile notices were withdrawn and there was a general feeling that justice had been done.

And the general result of the great Baroda "trial" was this:—

1. The jurisdiction of the Paramount Power to inquire into and punish the misconduct of its Feudatories was formally recognised and admitted by the Chiefs themselves.

2. Baroda was relieved of a tyrant and given a new lease of life.

3. The character of the Government of India, which, for a time, was ruthlessly assailed, was completely vindicated. "There will be reams of criticism," wrote Mr.

Secretary Aitchison, as he sent Meade a copy of the proclamation of dethronement; "there will be reams of criticism, but our intentions have been upright from the beginning and time will vindicate our integrity." And so it proved.

The Government was accused of grasping at annexation, of folly, inconsistency and breach of faith.

It was shown :—

That there was not the slightest desire on the part of the Government of India to annex Baroda, or even to interfere with its autonomy if such a course could possibly be avoided, consistently with our duty to the Baroda people and the inhabitants of adjoining British territory.

That, on the contrary, the Government made all possible allowance for shortcomings of administration, and was supremely careful not to exact too high a standard of government, and carried forbearance to its utmost limits.

That no breach of faith or anything approaching it was committed, as fresh grounds for deposition (of a most serious character) had been ascertained or accrued since the orders passed on Meade's report; while any prospect of reform was clearly hopeless if the Chief remained in power after the failure of the minister he had himself selected.

That in all the arrangements, in the choice of the mode of inquiry, the selection of the members of the Commission, the treatment of Malhar Rao during his suspension from power and in the final course adopted the Government was inspired by the sole object of doing what was just and right and acting for the best interests of the Baroda State.

But, on the other hand, two important lessons had been learnt :—

1. That it is a mistake to associate Oriental Rulers with English Officers on a Commission for judicial or quasi-judicial inquiries, conducted after English methods.

That it should be so is no discredit to the Oriental Rulers. "Princes and Nobles," says Lord Salisbury, "are not qualified by forensic training for the conduct of a delicate judicial investigation ; and those of India, to whom the customs of an English court of law and the skill of an English advocate are strange, enter upon such novel duties under special disadvantage."

If it is deemed desirable to have a native member of such Commission he should be chosen, we would suggest, from the ranks of native High Court Judges who have been trained to appreciate evidence tested by cross-examination and the arguments of counsel.

If Feudatory Chiefs are associated it should be as Assessors and not as Judges.

2. That inquiries into the conduct of native Princes should not be held in public. They should be held *in camera* (as is done in England in certain classes of cases) in the presence of representatives of the parties immediately interested, of the Chiefs and of the public. And the evidence (if published at all) should not be published until after the decision is arrived at.

Confidence in the tribunal would be sufficiently secured by appointing as President a high judicial officer ; but the publication during the progress of a case of evidence affecting the conduct and character of Princes —an evil which cannot be prevented if the public are admitted—is regarded with profound dissatisfaction by the Chiefs of India; while the newspaper commenting (favourable or unfavourable) which went on merrily during the Baroda trial and will go on again, should such an inquiry unfortunately recur, is at once unfair to the Commission, an interference with the course of justice and in other ways open to grave objection.

These remarks and suggestions have no claim to be original; they are mere expressions of "wisdom after the event," and are not intended to cast the slightest reflection upon the proceedings of a Viceroy whose acts were inspired, not only by love of justice, but by "that earnest and watchful consideration of the feelings of Her Majesty's Indian subjects" which consistently marked Lord Northbrook's administration.

APPENDIX TO CHAPTER XIV.

Lord Salisbury's Despatch on the Gaekwar Case.

"To His Excellency the Right Honourable the Governor-General of India in Council.

"India Office, London, *3rd June*, 1875.

"1. I have received and considered in Council Your Excellency's Despatches quoted in the margin; also the evidence taken upon the recent inquiry before Sir R. Couch's Commission; the Report of the Commissioners; the Resolution of the Government of India in respect of it; the Proclamation in which you declared the Gaekwar of Baroda deposed; and a Minute by Your Excellency, reviewing the recent history of the Baroda State.

"2. I have to inform you that Her Majesty's Government approves of the course you have pursued in directing the deposition of Mulhar Rao, the late Gaekwar of Baroda.

"3. The maladministration of that State, which for many years has caused anxiety to the Government of India, was reported by the Commission which sat under Sir R. Meade to have reached to a point 'urgently calling for reformation'. The Commission further recorded their opinion that it was 'hopeless to look for any effectual measures of reform and improved government at the hands of the present Ruler and his advisers; but that these could only be introduced through the intervention and under the auspices of the British Government'. They accordingly recommended the appointment of a Minister, who should be invested with the requisite powers, and who should not be removable except with the consent of the Government of India.

"4. Your Excellency decided not to accept this recommendation. The plan of setting aside the authority of a tyrannical Sovereign by the appointment of an independent Minister, while the Sovereign still remained nominally on the throne, had not in your judgment been sufficiently successful in other cases to justify its renewal. You justly preferred to seek a remedy by charging Mulhar Rao himself with the duty of immediate reformation.

"5. In a khureeta, dated 25th July, 1874, you pointed out to the Gaekwar the responsibility which his misuse of power had imposed upon the British Government. The fact that you are bound to protect his throne against insurrection laid on you a sacred obligation to protect his subjects against misgovernment. The sentences in which Your Excellency pointed out this consequence to the Gaekwar forcibly express the principles on which your relations with the Sovereigns of protected States must always be conducted,—

"'Your Highness has justly observed "that the British Government is undoubtedly the Paramount Power in India, and the existence and prosperity of the native States depend upon its fostering favour and benign protection". This is especially true of the Baroda State, both because of its geographical position, intermixed with British territory, and also because a subsidiary force of British troops is maintained for the defence of the State, the protection of the person of its Ruler, and the enforcement of his legitimate authority.

"'My friend, I cannot consent to employ British troops to protect any one in a course of wrong-doing. Misrule on the part of a Government which is upheld by the British power is misrule in the responsibility for which the British Government becomes in a measure involved. It becomes, therefore, not only the right, but the positive duty, of the British Government to see that the administration of a State in such a condition is reformed, and that gross abuses are removed.'

"6. You then proceeded to draw His Highness's attention to the practical course which these principles would impose upon you. You expressed your wish to give him a fair chance of reforming his administration, and you warned him of the inevitable consequences if he failed to take advantage of it:—

"'I must hold Your Highness responsible for the amendment of the serious evils disclosed, and I leave to you the selection of your agents, with a distinct intimation that, if Your Highness fails to attend to the advice I now offer you, and the counsel which the Resident, who possesses my full confidence, will be instructed to offer you, and if, in consequence, the condition of the Baroda administration remains unreformed, the only course left will be to remove Your Highness from the exercise of power, and to make such other arrangements, consistent with the maintenance of the integrity of the Baroda State, as I may deem necessary to secure a satisfactory administration.'

"Without pledging yourself to leave him in authority to the end of the present year, you fixed that date as the one beyond which your indulgence would certainly not be prolonged.

"7. The experiment was not destined to last so long. It proceeded for some months under the guidance of Colonel Phayre, and though the imperious tone of that officer's communications, and his disregard of your instructions, justified you in removing him, there was nothing in his conduct which need have hindered the Gaekwar, had he been anxious to do so, from prosecuting the necessary reforms. No desire of this kind, however, was discoverable in his acts. Up to the time when his apparent complicity in the poisoning of Colonel Phayre compelled you to suspend him from power, no substantial progress towards improvement had taken place. On the contrary, as Your Excellency shows in your Despatch of the 29th of April, this period was marked by a treatment of his predecessor's widow which threatened her life, a marriage which aggravated his difference with his Sirdars, and a continuance of that reckless prodigality which, on the one hand, had reduced the cultivating classes to despair, and, on the other, by leaving unprovided the necessary payments of the native soldiery, threatened to plunge the State into disorder.

These symptoms indicated no change in Mulhar Rao's characteristic weaknesses. Almost the last incident in the history of his reign, before it was closed by his arrest on the charge of poisoning, was the mysterious resignation, without reason given, of the reforming Minister who had been appointed under the pressure of Sir R. Meade's report.

"8. Whether, supposing no charge of poisoning to have arisen, it would have been more expedient to act upon these indications or to defer the final decisions until the close of the year, it is not now necessary to inquire. It is only proper to observe that, whatever course might have been taken, it must and could only have been dictated by a regard for the interests of the people of Baroda. It might have been more politic to avoid the popular excitement and apprehension consequent on any sudden change of policy, than to anticipate by a few months the redress that was due to many suffering classes in the State. But there was nothing in the conduct of the Ruler to call for such indulgence, or to impose on your Government a further delay in the vague hope of an improved administration.

"9. Any such question was necessarily insignificant compared with the grave suspicion of poisoning that was the subject of the inquiries conducted by Mr. Souter. Her Majesty's Government entirely concur with Your Excellency in the opinion that you could not have left this charge unnoticed. It would have been a scandal to continue relations of friendliness and apparent cordiality with a Prince lying under a charge so horrible, made by those who professed to be his instruments; and it would not have been just to the able servants of the Crown who perform delicate political duties, often under circumstances of difficulty and peril, to announce to the world that you held their lives so cheaply.

"10. In deciding upon the mode of inquiry to be adopted Your Excellency was guided by weighty considerations. You desired that the sufficiency of the evidence on which you proceeded should be known to the world, and therefore you determined that the proceedings should be public. You further desired, as you informed the Mahárájah Scindia, 'that the

Commission should be constituted in such a manner as to command the confidence of the whole of India'. In this spirit you resolved that one half of it should consist of Natives, and that of these one should be, like the accused, a Marátha Prince, and one a distinguished Marátha statesman. In so doing you were inspired by that earnest and watchful consideration for the feelings of Her Majesty's Indian subjects which has consistently marked your administration, and of which Her Majesty's Government have always expressed their emphatic approbation.

"11. Whether the result of this mode of proceeding has in all respects corresponded to your anticipations may be open to question. It has been undoubtedly attended with grave inconveniences, from which a sufficient argument might be drawn against the adoption of a similar procedure, if, unhappily, a similar occasion for it were ever to arise. Princes and nobles are not qualified by forensic training for the conduct of a delicate judicial investigation; and those of India, to whom the customs of an English court of law and the skill of an English advocate are strange, enter upon such novel duties under a special disadvantage. The experience, moreover, of the present case has shown that our judicial forms are little suited to the trial of a Sovereign Prince within his own dominions; for the publicity of the proceedings and the preliminary restraint which is politically necessary, inflict on him a grave indignity, which, in the eyes of his subjects and of other princes, could only be justified by proved crime, and so create for him a sympathy which easily becomes a bias in his favour. The rules of procedure again, enforced by our law, are less appropriate in cases where witnesses are easily tampered with between their first examination and their production in open court, where the means for such operations are abundant, and where the temptation to use them is overwhelming. Under such conditions there must always be a risk that the evidence at a trial will seem imperfect compared to that which was available when it was first determined that a trial should be held.

"12. These various inconveniences were of a character whose importance it was not easy for Your Excellency to estimate beforehand, but they were brought into notice, and they grew in importance as the inquiry proceeded. They account sufficiently for the difficulties of the native Commissioners, and for their reluctance to concur in the unhesitating decision of their more practised colleagues.

"13. Whatever explanation may be given of the reasons which guided the native Commissioners to their decision, it could not, in the opinion of Her Majesty's Government, be ignored. My instructions, conveyed to Your Excellency by telegraph, gave expression to this view. The appointment of native Commissioners had little meaning unless its object was to assure the natives of the equity of the tribunal, and that assurance would have been illusory if the judgment of the native Commissioners had been allowed to count for nothing in the decision of the issue. Moreover, in a case which wholly turned on the credibility of three witnesses, their bearing under examination was of the utmost importance; and the judgment of those who had watched it could not under the circumstances be properly submitted to the revision of any authority, however high, which had not the same opportunity. It is true that, in your orders constituting the Commission, you designated its proceedings as an inquiry, not a trial. But this circumstance did not, in the opinion of Her Majesty's Government, neutralise the force of the considerations to which I have referred.

"14. If Mulhar Rao had been found guilty by the Commission of the heinous offence imputed to him, there would have been no ground for inflicting on him any milder punishment than that which would have been thought just if he had occupied a humbler position. His crime would have been aggravated by the character of the office held by the person against whom it was directed, and it would not have been extenuated by his own exalted station. He was, however, neither convicted nor acquitted. The opinion of the Commission, though it inclined against him, was not decisive; for of the six members, while three, including the learned President, were for conviction, only one was for acquittal. Under these circumstances, considering that the three Commissioners who declined to convict him were the men of his own race, who had been placed upon the tribunal in order to insure for it the confidence of the people of India, Her Majesty's Government were of opinion that Mulhar Rao could not be treated as having been proved guilty of the crime of poisoning. His guilt accordingly was not assumed in the proclamation issued by you under the instructions of Her Majesty's Government, and he has been spared the penal consequences which would probably have followed a conviction for that crime.

"15. It by no means followed as a necessary consequence that he should be replaced upon the *gadi*. Of the issue of the inquiry the utmost that could be said was that the inability of the Commission to pronounce a definite opinion upon his guilt protected him from the punishment of a criminal. He had so acted that three Europeans of great experience had declared him guilty of poisoning, and two of his own race had, in giving judgment, abstained from declaring him innocent. Whatever inference might be drawn from this finding, it could not be regarded as an assertion of his fitness for an office of the highest trust, and would, even if considered alone, have placed a serious difficulty in the way of his restoration to sovereignty over the people of Baroda.

"16. Other reasons, however, in themselves amply sufficient, existed for refusing to invest him again with power. The period which had elapsed since the holding of Sir R. Meade's inquiry had shown no abatement in the vices to which the misgovernment of Baroda had been due. Before his arrest the reforming Ministers had resigned their offices, and Sir Lewis Pelly had submitted to you his 'solemn recommendation that the Gaekwar State be saved by the deposal from power of its Ruler'. A few weeks later evidence was discovered of crimes which, had they been known sooner, would have brought this oppressive reign to an earlier close. The poisoning of Bhow Scindia, former Prime Minister of Baroda, and the still more horrible details of the death of

Govind Naik by torture, were proved before Sir Lewis Pelly, after the proceedings of Sir R. Couch's Commission had commenced. Both crimes were committed by persons in authority under Mulhar Rao, and the latter was directly traced to his orders. Had they been established while he was still upon the throne, it would have been impossible for the British Government to have abstained any longer from terminating a power used for such atrocious purposes.

"17. On these grounds, had he lain under no suspicion of poisoning Colonel Phayre, it was necessary that he should be deposed. The British Government, which had deprived his Sirdars and ryots of the power of righting themselves, would not be justified in using its supremacy to compel them to submit again to a Ruler whose incurable vices had been established by a full experience. You were accordingly instructed to rest his deposition in your formal proclamation on these general grounds. The danger of seeming to visit the crime of poisoning a Resident with the simple penalty of deposition, as well as the opinions recorded by the native members of the Commission, made it inexpedient to include matters arising out of the inquiry among your grounds of action. Such a course would have only added a superfluous justification for a necessary act. It might have obscured the principle that incorrigible misrule is of itself a sufficient disqualification for sovereign power. Her Majesty's Government have willingly accepted the opportunity of recognising in a conspicuous case the paramount obligation which lies upon them of protecting the people of India from oppression.

"18. I have, in conclusion, to express on behalf of Her Majesty's Government their high appreciation of the services which have been rendered by Your Excellency during this painful case. I have also to request you to convey to Sir Lewis Pelly, and the officers acting under him, the sense which is entertained by Her Majesty's Government of the efficient manner in which their difficult duties have been performed.

"I have, etc.,

(Signed) "SALISBURY."

CHAPTER XV.

REMOVAL OF THE GAEKWAR — SELECTION OF HIS SUCCESSOR — REORGANISATION OF THE GOVERNMENT.

Signs of disturbance—Meade arranges quietly for Gaekwar's deportation immediately on receiving orders for dethronement—Orders received and conveyed to Gaekwar—He protests but ultimately consents to start that evening—Gaekwar and suite sent off by train at 6 P.M., after which Meade holds a reception of notables and explains to them the situation—Army informed—Proclamation issued and quietly received—But delay in announcing his successor leads to a disturbance on 28th April, during which the child of Laxmi Bai is placed on the throne and proclaimed Gaekwar—Meade calls out detachments of the Subsidiary Force, which marched through the town, occupied the palace and disarmed the palace guard—Laxmi Bai and the elder Ráni sent to join the Gaekwar—State reception of Maháráni Jamna Bai—Quiet restored and rioters punished—Claimants for succession—Gopál Rao of the Khandeish branch of the family selected and adopted by Mahárání—Installed as Gaekwar on 28th May under the name of Syaji Rao and holds his first reception on the 16th—Account of the young Chief—Arrangements for his education—Correspondence with him and his adoptive mother—Reorganisation of the Government—State of affairs—Lines of policy sketched by Lord Northbrook—Sir Mádhava Rao—Meade prepares a plan of administration, etc., and hopes to be relieved—But is asked to stay till November—Correspondence with Lord Northbrook—Is at length relieved by Mr. Melvill—Letter to Lady Meade—Impression left by Meade at Baroda—His services acknowledged by Government in a special *Gazette* notification and his term of service extended for five years.

REMOVAL OF THE GAEKWAR.

LONG before the decision of the Government there were ominous signs that any attempt to remove the

Gaekwar would be the signal for disturbance. Secret appeals were made to the armed forces of the State, the Marátha party, and the populace, to prevent the deportation of the Chief. Anonymous communications, couched in violent language, calling on his subjects to take up arms were freely circulated, and threatening letters sent to Meade himself. The situation was made more difficult by a severe outbreak of cholera among the British troops, which necessitated their being moved, a fact pointed to as a step towards annexation; while the precautions taken to prevent the spread of cholera necessarily caused much friction and annoyance.

In these circumstances Meade felt that, if the Prince was to be dethroned and exiled, the sentence should be promptly carried out, before the elements of disorder had time to gather force; and, as the exact time of deportation was left for Meade's decision, he decided to effect it immediately on receiving the order for dethronement and before its publication.

Accordingly (in communication with Sir Philip Wodehouse, Governor of Bombay) he quietly made arrangements for a special train to be in waiting, which was to convey the dethroned Prince (accompanied by a European guard) to his destination without going through Bombay or stopping at Púna—then, as now, the headquarters of Marátha disaffection.

At 10 A.M. on the 22nd of April, 1875, Meade received the orders of the Government and a telegraphic copy of the proclamation.

At 2 P.M., after having a copy and translation of the proclamation made, he waited on the Gaekwar, by appointment, and had the proclamation carefully read and explained to him in Maráthi, and intimated to His

Highness that it was the wish of the Government of India that he should leave for Madras at 6 P.M. that day, adding that he would be accompanied by Dr. Seward, who would see that every provision was made for his comfort.

The Gaekwar received the announcement with profound surprise, protesting that he had not been found guilty of any offence and had had no sufficient time allowed for reforming his administration.

In reply he was referred to the grounds for removal stated in the proclamation and courteously informed that the decision was final.

He then begged that his son by Laxmi Bai should be allowed to succeed him.

But it was pointed out to him that by the terms of the proclamation his son was declared incapable of succession and that his brother's widow was to adopt a suitable successor.

He then protested against being sent to Madras and desired to live at Púna.

He was informed that his living at Púna was impossible and that it was the wish of the Government that he should go to Madras for the present at all events.

He prepared a telegram for the Viceroy on the subject, which was duly despatched; but ultimately, finding Meade immovable, he yielded and gave directions to his servants to make ready for the journey.

Then a new difficulty arose.

When it was announced that Madras was to be the Prince's destination, his "devoted" followers, one and all, positively refused to accompany him. The *chobdar* ("Silver Stick in waiting"), it is said, collapsed; the *patawallahs* (orderlies) removed their badges; the cooks (all Brahmans) would not hear of it; the heralds proclaimed their intention of remaining at home; and the "story-tellers" ceased to be amusing.

Ultimately, however, Dr. Seward, whose kindness combined with firmness gave him great influence over both the Mahárája and his household, prevailed upon them all to go.

The Mahárája was asked if he desired to be accompanied by any members of his family or to see any of them before his departure, but he replied in the negative.

At 6 P.M. all was ready, the Prince and his suite were driven to the station and placed in the train, which proceeded on its journey without the slightest demonstration on the part of the few persons present.

After seeing the Gaekwar safely on his way Meade proceeded to the Residency, where he had prudently arranged to have a reception of the principal members of the nobility and men of influence.

He explained to them the orders of the Government and informed them of the departure of the Gaekwar and the measures taken for appointing a successor.

The nobles were flattered by being taken into confidence and received the announcement without any hostile feeling, merely observing that no delay should be allowed to occur in the appointment of a successor.

The same evening the orders were explained to the Mahárája's troops, and early the next morning the officers were received by Meade at the Residency and appeared fully satisfied with all that had taken place.

The minds of the Baroda community having been

thus prepared, the appearance of the proclamation caused no excitement and it was considered that the prompt removal of the ex-Chief was a most desirable measure.

All had gone off quietly and the revolution would have probably been effected without disturbance if the successor had been ready; but this was impossible, as the selection of a suitable occupant of the throne from a number of claimants, in communication with the Mahárání Jamna Bai, required some little time.

Meanwhile the disaffected took advantage of the delay to excite in the minds of the well-disposed suspicions of the Government's good faith in promising to restore the native administration, while the trading classes felt keenly the stoppage of trade resulting from late events and the cessation of the lavish expenditure of the late Ruler.

On the morning of the 28th April the shopkeepers of Baroda, carrying out a preconcerted design organised by emissaries from Bombay in communication with the ex-Chief's family, began to close their shops, saying that there could be no trade while there was no Gaekwar; and when the police attempted to interfere they were assaulted by the mob. The *émeute* soon assumed formidable dimensions. The detachment of Gaekwar troops in the town was quickly overpowered. The palace guard, consisting chiefly of sepoys from Hindústán, sympathised with the rioters, and their commandant, one Jaikarn Sing, took Laxmi Bai's child and placed it on the throne amid the plaudits of the multitude, and then passed it to the keeping of Malhar Rao's senior wife, Mahálsa Bai, who promised to adopt it. The crowd then wrecked the premises occupied by Damodur Pant, the ex-Chief's private secretary, who had given evidence against him.

Meanwhile Captain Jackson, Sir R. Meade's Assistant, who had proceeded to the spot on hearing of the riot, and General Devine, commander of the Gaekwar's troops, were pelted with bricks and stones and otherwise maltreated, the latter's carriage was burnt, and the former only saved himself by firing his revolver among the crowd who were assailing him with sticks and stones.

The disturbance having become serious Meade found it necessary to call out detachments of the Subsidiary Force. Two detachments of native troops were sent, the second accompanied by two guns, and ultimately a company of Europeans. The detachments entered the town and occupied the palace without bloodshed, the rioters flying in all directions, and captured and disarmed the palace guard. Laxmi Bai's child and the elder Ráni were, by Meade's orders, moved into the British cantonments, and by the next morning all was quiet.

On 30th April Laxmi Bai and her child and the elder Ráni were sent to join the Gaekwar, and on 2nd May the Mahárání Jamna Bai, who had been summoned from Púna, arrived at Baroda and was conducted with great ceremony from the Moti Bágh palace to the palace in the city, where her little daughter, Tára Bai, was placed on the *gadi* to represent her, and received in her name the gifts of honour presented by members of the nobility and others who crowded the throne room.

This solemn reception of the late Khandi Rao's widow was regarded by the inhabitants of Baroda as a guarantee that the dynasty of the Gaekwar would be continued, and there was no subsequent attempt to disturb the peace.

The ringleaders of the disturbance were punished but not vindictively. The palace guard were disbanded and the foreigners among them sent away, at the State's expense, to their homes in Hindústán.

SELECTION OF A SUCCESSOR.

According to the terms of the proclamation of the 19th April the Mahárání Jamna Bai was to be allowed to adopt some member of the Gaekwar's house whom the Government of India might select as the most suitable person on whom to confer the sovereignty of the Baroda State.

There were two groups of claimants, one claiming legitimate descent from Mháloji, elder brother of Pilaji, founder of the dynasty (known as the Baroda group); the other from Pratáp Rao, a younger son of Pilaji, living at Nassik in Khandeish (known as the Nassik group).

A committee, *viz.*, Colonel Etheridge, Inám Commissioner, and Mr. Elliot, Collector of Nassik, was appointed to report on the claims of the candidates, and reported in favour of those of the Nassik claimants. The accuracy of its finding was contested by the Baroda claimants, but the legitimacy of the Khandeish branch was considered sufficiently established by the Gaekwar's family priest and the Mahárání Jamna Bai, who herself was particularly anxious to be allowed to adopt one of the Nassik boys.

The Government of India (without attempting to decide the genealogical merits of the respective claimants) considered that the selection of a lad of the Khandeish group was best in the interests of the Baroda State; and accordingly the Mahárâni, with the concurrence of Sir Richard Meade, selected Gopál Rao (the present Gaekwar), the eldest and most promising of the three boys of the Nassik group, and the selection was ratified by the Government of India. Meanwhile Meade took the precaution of quietly explaining matters to the three disappointed candidates of the Baroda group, and induced them all to acquiesce in the decision and promise to do homage to the new Ruler.[1]

By the public generally the decision was received with great satisfaction, and on 27th May (the first propitious date available) the adoption and installation ceremonies were performed with great *éclat*. The young Gaekwar assumed the ancestral name, Syaji Rao, and on 16th June, after paying a state visit to the shrines of the Gaekwar family in accordance with ancient custom, held his first reception, when a letter of congratulation from the Viceroy was read, and the new Minister, Sir Mádhava Rao, was formally presented.

"The young Mahárája," says Meade in his report, "has already acquired a singular amount of quiet self-possession. His disposition is extremely amiable and he is most anxious to learn what he ought to do, and I have no doubt that with proper care and attention he will turn out well."

[1] Two out of the three fulfilled their promise, but one of them subsequently gave much trouble and had to be exiled from Baroda.

H.H. SYAJI RAO, Gaekwar of Baroda
(*æt.* twelve years);
THE MAHÁRÁNI JAMNA BAI (his adoptive mother);
TÁRA BAI (her daughter).

With this object in view the greatest care was taken in arranging for the young Chief's education. And one of Meade's last official acts, as Special Commissioner, was to select as His Highness's tutor Mr. J. A. Elliot, of the Bombay Civil Service, an old Harrow boy, who had served in the Education Department in Berár, a selection which proved a happy one; and to draw up a scheme of training and instruction based upon the system successfully pursued in the case of the Mahárája of Mysore.

The scheme provided that His Highness should be well grounded in the three languages likely to be of practical use to him as Ruler—Guzaráti (the vernacular of his territory), Maráthi (the language of his tribe) and English, and in all the elements of a high class education.

But his education was by no means to be confined to book-learning, but include athletic and military training, riding and games; and every opportunity was to be taken to improve his mind by travel and make him personally acquainted with every portion of his scattered territory.

Moreover he was to be taught, not in seclusion, but in a class composed of lads about his own age, of good position and intelligence, who could compete with him in his studies and join in his games and sports; and on the 18th October, about a month before Meade left Baroda, he had the pleasure of laying, in the grounds of the Moti Bágh Palace, the foundations of a college for the education of His Highness and the sons of the nobility. The speeches on the occasion are of such interest that extracts are given as an appendix to this chapter.[1]

[1] Appendix A.

In all these matters, as in others, Sir Richard Meade received the most cordial assistance from the Mahárâni Jamna Bai, herself a lady of strong and cultivated intellect and, as such, able to appreciate the proper training of the future Ruler of Baroda, and, thanks to her co-operation and unceasing vigilance, the young Chief was kept perfectly free from the contaminating influences which usually surround an Oriental Prince.

Before leaving Baroda Meade had the pleasure of conveying to Her Highness the expression of Her Majesty the Queen's sense of the Mahárâni's judicious conduct during these eventful days, as well as her sincere good wishes for the well-doing and prosperity of the young Gaekwar.

Long after Meade had left Baroda he continued to correspond both with the Gaekwar and his adoptive mother, and copies of some of their letters will be found appended to this chapter.[1]

REORGANISATION OF THE GOVERNMENT.

This was a subject in which the Government of India and the Viceroy personally took the deepest interest.

Affairs were, indeed, in a state of grave confusion, full of elements of disorder with no adequate means for dealing with them. A discontented body of sirdárs, descendants, for the most part, of the military companions of the founders of the dynasty, with hereditary claims to place and power; a peasantry grievously overtaxed and oppressed by farmers of the revenue;

[1] Appendix B.

Yours very truly
T. Madava Row

numerous claimants for tax-free lands (*grassias*) impatient of delays which had occurred in the investigation of their cases; merchants and traders clamorous for settlement of demands against the State; a city populace not yet recovered from the disturbing effect of the late riots, and plenty of intrigue going on with the supporters of the ex-Gaekwar and one, at least, of the disappointed claimants. On the other hand, no properly organised police or judiciary; and the Contingent, on which the peace of the tributary States depended, in a most unsatisfactory condition. As for the finances "it was an exchequer," said Sir Mádhava Rao (quoting from Burke), "where extortion was the assessor, fraud the cashier, confusion the accountant, concealment the reporter and oblivion the remembrancer". The "public works department" was so corrupt and inefficient that it had to be abolished—and it soon became evident to Meade that there was not a man in Baroda fit to be entrusted with any high office in the State.

For dealing with this tangled web of difficulties the Government of India felt it incumbent upon them to afford Baroda the services of the best and ablest Marátha-speaking statesman they could find. Their choice fell on Sir Mádhava Rao, K.C.S.I., a Marátha Brahman, who, after a distinguished career at the Madras University, became successively *Diwán* or Minister of Travancore and Indore—a man of rare intelligence, indomitable powers of work, a perfect knowledge of English, great administrative experience, very liberal ideas combined with intense loyalty to the British Government, and the highest character for probity. He took charge at Baroda on the 16th June, 1875.

Meanwhile Lord Northbrook had sketched out to Meade the broad lines of the policy to be carried out, in a letter of the 22nd May, from which we quote the most material paragraphs :—

"One of the first matters which will have to be dealt with is the education of the young Prince.

"The exact position and duties of Sir Mádava Rao will also have to be determined. He will, I presume, be much in the same position as Sir Sálár Jang at Hyderabad, with the difference which follows from our Treaty engagements with Baroda giving the British Government greater power to interfere, if necessary, with internal affairs than we may have by our treaties with the Nizam.

"Would it be well to establish a consultative Council composed of the principal Sirdárs? anything which would associate them in the government and give them an interest in the new order of things, would appear to be of advantage.

"Some unpopularity must necessarily follow from the sweeping out of the old corrupted and debauched hangers-on of the late *régime*, but it seems desirable to make as few changes at first as possible consistently with the carrying out of the necessary reforms.

"As regards the interference of the Resident with the Minister, you will probably agree with me that it should be confined to indicating the nature of the reforms to be made, which indeed have been pretty completely described in the report of the first Commission over which you presided. But there is one of some consequence which was advisedly postponed. I allude to the arrangements connected with the Contingent and the military strength of the Baroda State. Our policy seems to me to be to relieve the State from the Treaty obligation to keep up 3000 Horse and accept the substitute of an efficient police, the military force of Baroda being limited to such a small number of troops as will be sufficient to support the dignity of the Court on ceremonial occasions.

"In making these concessions from our Treaty rights we

should have an understanding that we are not bound to keep the full representative of our Subsidiary Force in Baroda. The reason for the stipulation has ceased with the pacification of the country and the improvement of means of communication.

"Military reductions are ticklish measures in most countries, and would, of course, have to be carried out in Baroda with deliberation and with a due regard for its vested interests.

"There are other questions, such as the transit duties, the arrangements for united police action, where British and Baroda territory is intermingled, in prevention of opium smuggling, etc., which will have to be arranged as time goes on.

"The first thing will be to establish the popularity of the new Government and to show that we are caring for the real interests of the people; if Sir Mádava Rao is the man I take him for he ought to be able to put the conduct of the British Government in such a light as will ere long remove the unfavourable impression which, from whatever cause it has been derived, has been circulated through the press in Western India and partially elsewhere.

"I have not forgotten your very natural desire to be relieved, as soon as the public interests will allow you to return to Mysore, from your temporary employment at Baroda; you will soon be able to tell me what probability there is of affairs being sufficiently settled to enable the work to be handed over to a successor."

With the help of the indefatigable Minister Meade was able in a short time to lay the foundation of a well-ordered Government on the lines sketched out in Lord Northbrook's letter. He submitted a plan for the administration of the territory during the minority of the Ruler; prepared a scheme for the latter's education which has already been described, and drew up reports upon a variety of important questions requiring settlement, with the exception of the proposed military reforms, which were advisedly left in abeyance for a time. With his concurrence the Minister prepared a programme of administrative improvements to be gradually and cautiously carried into effect,[1] and before the middle of July he was able to report that the organisation of the new Government seemed to him to be sufficiently advanced to admit of his departure. But he was again doomed to disappointment.

On 19th July Lord Northbrook asked Meade to continue at Baroda until after the Prince of Wales's

[1] The programme is thus given in Sir Mádhava Rao's first Administrative Report for the Baroda State:—

"(*a*) To maintain public order and tranquillity with firmness and moderation;

"(*b*) To redress the accumulated complaints arising out of past maladministration, whether of Sirdárs, bankers, ryots or others;

"(*c*) To establish a proper and sufficient machinery for the dispensation of justice in all its branches;

"(*d*) To provide a police commensurate with the extent of the country and the density and character of the population;

"(*e*) To provide for the execution of necessary or useful public works;

"(*f*) To promote popular education;

"(*g*) To provide suitable medical agencies for the benefit of the people;

"(*h*) To reduce the burden of taxation where it is excessive, to readjust taxes where they require to be readjusted, and to abolish such as are totally objectionable;

"(*i*) To enforce economy in expenditure, restrain waste, reduce extravagance, and prevent losses resulting from corruption and malversation;

"(*j*) To quietly strengthen the executive establishments.

"For the first time," he adds, "in the annals of the State the fundamental principle has obtained recognition that the object of Government is to promote the happiness of all classes alike."

visit, which was expected to take place about the middle of November.

Meade, while placing his services as in duty bound at the disposal of the Government, ventured to make a mild remonstrance, urging that he had important work at Mysore and that as His Royal Highness intended to visit Mysore, it was fitting that he should, as Chief Commissioner of the Province, be present to receive him.

To this Lord Northbrook sent a reply conveying a rebuke so complimentary in its terms that we give it almost *in extenso* :—

"13*th August*, 1875.

"MY DEAR SIR RICHARD,—I feel considerable difficulty in answering your letter of the 4th on the subject of your leaving Baroda, for I am exceedingly sorry to interpose any obstacle in the way of your very natural desire to receive the Prince of Wales when His Royal Highness visits Mysore, and the more so because I have always regarded your employment at Baroda to be temporary, and told you so. Moreover, the great service you have rendered at Baroda would of itself make me anxious to consult your wishes.

"At the same time I have very reluctantly come to the conclusion that it would not be for the public interest that you should leave Baroda before I meet you at Bombay and the Prince of Wales has paid the visit now contemplated to Baroda. . . . I see no reasonable probability of the important questions to which you referred in your letter being brought to a head in a shorter time than there is between now and the beginning of November, and in addition to those questions there is the one upon which you either have received or will shortly receive an official letter, namely, the record of the manner in which the Government of Baroda is to be carried on during the minority of the Gaekwar.

"Moreover, if the Prince of Wales visits Baroda I should

not feel comfortable unless the arrangements are made by you and you are there to prevent any difficulties.

"I feel sure, from the manner in which you have shown upon several occasions your feeling that the interests of the public are the first consideration to which we all of us who have the honour to serve Her Majesty have to look, that you will cordially accept my decision in this matter.

"From what I have said you will require no further assurance from me that I am very sorry I have felt bound to come to a conclusion contrary to your wishes and even perhaps your legitimate expectations.

"Yours very truly,

"NORTHBROOK."

After all Meade was not destined to receive the Prince of Wales at Baroda, for His Royal Highness decided at first to omit it from his programme. In these circumstances it was arranged that Meade should accompany the Gaekwar and the Mahárání to receive the Prince of Wales on landing at Bombay and then make over charge to his successor, Mr. Philip Sandys Melvill.

To Meade the prospect was delightful, and his feelings are thus described in a letter to Lady Meade then in England :—

"BARODA, *26th September*, 1875.

". . . We are making our preparations for the trip to Bombay, and I can hardly realise that in less than two months I shall again, please God, be at Bangalore with dear old Fred,[1] and looking for the return very soon after of one still more dear, *viz.*, your dear self! I was at the palace for upwards of two hours with the Minister yesterday, settling various matters with him and the Mahárání about the Bombay journey and other things. They are in great disappointment at the news I had to give them that the Prince of

[1] His youngest son, to whom he was much attached.

Wales would not be able to come here; the trip being too hurried and fatiguing. The young Rája is getting on very well, and will turn out a nice lad. I am getting a young civilian for his tutor. The Ráni told Sir Mádava Rao to tell me, after a long conversation on all the matters in hand, that 'the name of Sir Richard Meade would never be forgotten in Baroda, and would be inseparably connected with its history'. The remark was made quite spontaneously, and it is gratifying to me to feel that my deputation here has really been a success, and that I have, under Providence, been able to fulfil the objects for which I was sent to this place. You will, I trust, be able to look back upon the time of my stay here, though a period of distress and anxiety to you, as an occasion during which I have had an opportunity of rendering some return for the great benefits I have enjoyed during so many years, and for the great mercies that have throughout attended me since coming here you and I should be ever most thankful. . . ."

After taking part with his Chief, in the public reception of the Prince of Wales at Bombay on 8th November, the official visit to His Royal Highness on the 9th[1] and the return visit by the latter on the 11th,

[1] "All eyes were dazzled when Maháràja Syajee Rao, the little boy whom the Government of India installed as the Gaekwar of Baroda, stood at the threshold of the door—a crystallised rainbow. He is a small delicately framed lad for his twelve years and more, with a bright pleasant face. He was weighted, head, neck, chest, arms, fingers, ankles, with such a sight and wonder of vast diamonds, emeralds, rubies and pearls, as would be worth the loot of many a rich town. . . . He was met at the edge of the carpet and strode with much solemnity to his seat side by side with the Prince. Sir Madhava Rao, Sir R. Meade and a noble train of Chiefs came with him. The first is one of the most noteworthy men in India; the second is distinguished as a soldier and diplomatist and is deemed by the Government as worthy of the highest trust and the most responsible posts."—Russell's *Prince of Wales's Tour*.

Meade returned to Baroda, and on the 16th made over charge to Mr. Melvill. He then hastened back to Bombay *en route* (he hoped) for Bangalore. But it was otherwise ordered. Next day he had to retrace his steps to Baroda in company with the Prince of Wales, who, after consulting Meade, decided after all to include it in his programme.

The visit of His Royal Highness to Baroda was a great success, and a graphic description of its incidents—the grand elephant procession from the railway station, the picturesque *darbár*, the displays of wrestling, the combats of wild beasts, the deer stalking with *cheetas*, the boar-hunt, at which His Royal Highness won his first spear, the weird scenes at the night of the illuminations, the state banquet, and the friendly bearing of the populace—occupies more than twenty pages of Dr. Russell's narrative.

The visit over, Meade again returned to Bombay, longing to resume the duties of his important charge—but again suffered for the crime of being indispensable; for, as will be explained in the next chapter, he was now destined for an appointment even more important than Mysore.

Meanwhile he had left Baroda free from all disturbance and rapidly recovering from the effects of long misrule. He had won the respect and gratitude of all classes, and his departure was regarded with deep regret.

The feelings of the community are expressed in the Minister's speech given in the appendix to this chapter, and six years afterwards when the young Gaekwar, on entering his nineteenth year, assumed the administration of his territories, Sir Mádhava Rao thus referred to the late Agent's services:—

"We in Baroda remember Sir Richard Meade as the founder of the existing new order of public affairs here. We have been moving on the broad lines laid down by him, and we feel we have been moving towards justice, security, prosperity and honour."

The Government of India made his services the subject of a special notification in the *Gazette of India* —an honour seldom accorded to any public servant, however distinguished, during his continuance in office; and, with the sanction of the Secretary of State for India, his term of service was extended for five years.

A copy of the *Gazette* notification will fittingly conclude the present chapter.

"FOREIGN DEPARTMENT,
"FORT WILLIAM, *2nd February*, 1876.

"The Governor-General in Council takes the occasion of the appointment of Colonel Sir Richard Meade, K.C.S.I., as Officiating Resident at Hyderabad, to place on record the high sense which the Government of India entertains of the services rendered by that officer during his recent employment as Agent to the Viceroy and Governor-General at Baroda.

"When Sir Richard Meade took charge of the Agency at Baroda from Sir Lewis Pelly, on the 10th April, 1875, there were many and most important matters on hand; the choice of a successor to Malhar Rao, and the adoption of suitable measures for giving the youthful Prince selected a sound and wholesome training; the re-establishment of the Native Government; revenue and fiscal reforms, particularly those relating to the incidence of the land revenue; the reorganisation of the regular troops of the State; the investigation into and adjustment of the long-standing claims of the Sirdárs and hereditary retainers of the Gaekwar; these are some of the most important subjects with which the Agent to the

Governor-General and Special Commissioner was called upon to deal, and with which, with the cordial co-operation of the able Minister, Sir Mádhava Rao, he has dealt to the complete satisfaction of His Excellency in Council.

"To the arrangements made by Sir Richard Meade, for the preservation of order, whether in the city of Baroda itself or in outlying districts, the Gaekwar's State is indebted for the peace and prosperity now reigning in those territories. The benefits to be expected from the measures of sound administration, which have been introduced into the State, in accordance with Sir Richard Meade's advice, are not less important, and, as the Government of India is deeply concerned in the welfare of the Baroda people, and of His Highness the Gaekwar, the cordial thanks and acknowledgments of His Excellency in Council are due to the Officer through whose successful exertions that welfare has been promoted.

"T. H. THORNTON,
"Offg. Secy. to the Govt. of India."

APPENDIX A.

Speeches of SIR RICHARD MEADE and SIR MÁDHAVA RAO on the occasion of laying the foundation stone of the college for the education of the Maháràja and the sons of the nobility on the 18th October, 1875.

SIR RICHARD MEADE said :—

"All present are doubtless aware of the circumstances under which the duty of providing for the installation of a new Chief on the Baroda *gadi* was forced on the British Government, and that after a patient and impartial inquiry into the claims advanced by his family to be regarded as lineal descendants of the founder of the Baroda State and dynasty, the young Prince Syají Rao, now before you, was selected for adoption by Her Highness the Maharání Jamna Bai, and was placed on the vacant throne with the usual ceremonies; while the task of organising an efficient native administration for the government of the country during the minority of the Chief was entrusted to Sir Mádhava Rao, an experienced and able statesman, who had already won for himself a high reputation as an administrator in Southern and Central India.

"Amongst the most important of the measures that had to be considered in connection with the new arrangements, was the question of the education and training of the young Prince who had thus been placed at the head of this large and important State, and the subject was one of much deep and anxious thought to Her Highness the Maharání, the Minister, and myself.

"In these days and still more in view of the future dawning on this great empire, it is essential that the native chiefs of India shall receive such an education and training as will fit them for their high destinies, and make them, so far as education can effect that object, good and just-minded men as well as competent and able rulers; and a truly weighty responsibility in this respect lies on all those to whose hands the control and management of minor princes are entrusted.

"Much is being done in many native States throughout India for the due training of these future Chiefs of the empire, on whose character and fitness to rule so much will hereafter depend; and the success of the Rajkúmar College, at Rájkot, is most encouraging to all who feel the importance of, and take an interest in, this great question.

"The Nizám of Hyderabad, the Mahárája of Mysore, and many other youthful Chiefs are being trained with the care suited to the requirements of their position, and after due consultation and consideration with Her Highness the Maharání, we have decided, with the approval of the Government of India, that similar measures shall be taken here without delay to secure for our young Prince Syají Rao the same advantages.

"The education of the Mahárája will be personally directed and superintended by an European gentleman who will be specially selected for the office, and who will be aided by a duly qualified native gentleman as his deputy.

"With His Highness will also be educated the sons of the sirdárs and principal personages of the State and of his own relatives, whom it is desirable to bring up with their future Ruler; and between whom and their Prince we may hope that the ties of school companionship will ripen into lasting feelings of loyal duty and affection on the one side and of kindly regard on the other.

"The measure that we are now inaugurating will thus provide for the education of those who will naturally hereafter form the Prince's companions and Court, as well as of the Prince himself, and we trust that full advantage will be taken by the sirdárs and others entitled to share therein of the privilege of having their children educated with their future Chief so offered to them.

"As I observe that several sirdárs are now present the

opportunity is perhaps a fitting one for my pointing out to them that the old channels to employment and distinction at the hands of the Prince are no longer open to their class. The days are passed for the acquirement of wealth and position by the leaders of bands of armed men, who, like their forefathers, aided in the establishment of the Gaekwar by their courage and hardihood. We trust that such days may never return, that the inhabitants of these fair provinces will be permitted to follow their avocations in peace, to enjoy the luxuriant fruits and harvests of their bounteous soil, and to live in full security of life and property.

"But the service of the State, in all its departments, will be open to the sons of the sirdárs equally with other classes, and it will be their own fault if they neglect the means now offered to them for qualifying for employment in it.

"I will now briefly describe the nature of the building whose foundation stone has been laid this morning. The plan which has been designed and prepared with much care by Mr. Hill, the State engineer, provides for everything that can be needed, and the accommodation will be ample and in all respects convenient.

"Sufficient land is attached to it to furnish a large playground for cricket and other sports, which will, we hope, receive every encouragement and form a marked feature of the institution. There will be a gymnasium for gymnastic exercises, and a separate roomy space for a ride, and horse-exercise and practice, in which I may remark the young Prince already promises to be an adept. Suitable buildings will also be provided for the Prince's horses and equipages and their attendants.

"The whole of the grounds, which cover about nineteen acres, will be surrounded by a wall, and the premises will be designated and known as the 'Mahárája's School'.

"I will now conclude with the expression of my hope that all present will join me in wishing success to this institution and the objects of its establishment.

"May our young Prince, in whose welfare and prosperity

I must ever take the deepest interest, be so trained up in it as to prove worthy of his destiny and a future blessing to his country and all classes of his subjects, and may those who are educated within its walls with him turn out, as we trust many of them will, valuable state officials, and loyal supporters of the Baroda throne."

SIR MÁDHAVA RAO said:—

"It is now my privilege to offer to you, Sir Richard Meade, the cordial acknowledgments of His Highness the Mahárája and of Her Highness the Mahárání for the prominent part you have kindly taken in this ceremony. That part, to a prosaic observer, may seem very simple and inelaborate though performed by you with such good-will and with so much technical precision. But reflecting minds will look beyond the meagre mechanical process. There is more in the bricks and mortar you have dealt with than meets the eye! What we have just witnessed is an unmistakable practical recognition on the part of the State of one of the most signal necessities of a progressive age—the necessity of combining wisdom with power. It is an unequivocal recognition of the capital fact that the right exercise of regal functions requires long previous preparation.

"The ceremony has a further significance of high political importance. It is the outcome of a genuine desire on the part of the British Government to preserve and perpetuate native principalities as useful members of the Imperial system. England repudiates ignorance as a basis of strength or stability. England is not the power that seeks security from darkness. England desires to be a great illuminating agent, and bids Princes and people alike be enlightened and happy.

"This bright and bracing morning is, I hope, typical of the new career, the foundation of which has been just laid. It is an auspicious circumstance that the foundation has been laid by the hand of ripe wisdom and enlarged experience—the hand that has done many a beneficent deed during thirty long years—the hand equally powerful to wield the sword of the soldier, the pen of the statesman, and, as now witnessed, the trowel of the mason!

"There is every reason to feel the sanguine hope that the young Mahárája, who has already given indications of uncommon capacity, will therein, under God's blessing, make acquisitions infinitely more precious than the gems shining resplendent on his breast—that he will realise the ideal of a wise and virtuous ruler of a regenerated kingdom. Permit me now to offer to all present the thanks of the Mahárája and the Mahárání for the friendly sympathy you have manifested by your participation in this ceremony.

"As for you, Sir Richard Meade, I have already thanked you; let me only reveal to you what you have not thought of. In laying the foundation of the Mahárája's school, you have, unconsciously, laid the foundation of a splendid monument of your own beneficent connection with this principality."

APPENDIX B.

Specimens of letters from the Gaekwar and the Maháráni Jamna Bai.

From the Gaekwar, *æt.* thirteen.

I.

"BARODA, *31st May*, 1876.

"MY DEAR SIR,—I was glad to get your letter. I hope you are very well and like Hyderabad. I wish I could write you a letter without help that you might be sure that I and my sister remember you, kind friend, very well.

"SYAJI RAO, GAEKWAR."

To Colonel Sir R. Meade from the Gaekwar, *æt.* eighteen.

II.

"BARODA, *20th February*, 1882.

"MY DEAR FRIEND,—I received your kind letter on Tuesday morning, the contents of which gave me a deal of pleasure. Before writing any further I should say that the happiness of my subjects will be the basis of my public career, in which I will try to fulfil the expectations of my well-wishers and valued friends, of whom certainly you are one. . . . Before ending this letter I must cordially thank you and Lady Meade for the interest you both take in my welfare. Both of their Highnesses and Tára Bai Sahib are quite well.

"Your sincere friend,

"SYAJI RAO, GAEKWAR."

To Colonel Sir R. Meade from the Mahárání.

I.

"BARODA, MOTI BÁGH, 30*th July*, 1878.

"DEAR SIR RICHARD MEADE,—I have to tell you that on Saturday, the 5th instant, at a Durbar in the Nazzar Bágh, Mr. Melvill invested me with the Insignia of the Imperial Order of the Crown of India, sent to me by Her Majesty the Empress of India. I feel this to be a great honour, and very truly do I appreciate all the gracious acts of kindness bestowed on me. Mr. Melvill was pleased to say, he was glad to be the person deputed to convey the honour to me, and from Mrs. Melvill who was present at the Ladies' private Durbar and assisted Mr. Melvill in pinning the decoration, I receive constant proofs of kindness and friendship. I know you will like to hear this, as you have ever sympathised with me. I also had the pleasure of seeing my good friends Col. and Mrs. Coles, who came to Baroda at my request to be present at the Investiture. I only wish I could also have had the great happiness of seeing you at the same time, but I sincerely trust this is only postponed, and that some day you will come to Baroda. You will not I think go to England without seeing us. Pray accept my best wishes for your health and happiness. May I ask you to express to Lady Meade, when you write, my best remembrances? and believe me,

"Ever your Friend,

"JAMNA BAI."

To Colonel Sir R. Meade from the Mahárání.

II.

"BARODA PALACE, 18*th February*, 1882.

"MY DEAR FRIEND,—Blessed was the day when your letter of the 22nd January reached my hands. It recalled to my mind the frequent visits you paid kindly to me while your stay at Baroda.

"The Indian Government had the pleasure to instal my son, Bála Sahib, formally as the Ruler of Baroda. This to my opinion was the only aim I had left to obtain. My son-in-law Sir Desai was present to witness the festivities celebrated in connection with the Installation. I am very glad to say that he has proved worthy of my daughter. During his long stay of about two months I found his disposition very affable and was much pleased with the mutual affection and love they bore towards each other. I now hear to my great satisfaction that he will be shortly invested with the full power of his State.

"Please pay my best compliments to Lady Meade and tell her that I am very anxious to know about her health.

"I am very glad to say that my dear Tárabai often recollects those days when she used to sit on your knees during your visits to me. She cordially and humbly joins with me in paying my best compliments to you and Lady Meade.

"The Mahárája, Tárabai and I are all in good health, the climate being very agreeable.

"Hoping you, Lady Meade and your children are all right,

"I remain,

"Your ever sincere friend,

"JAMNA BAI, GAEKWAR."

CHAPTER XVI.

HYDERABAD.

Sir Richard appointed Resident—Lord Northbrook's letter—Description of the State of Hyderabad: its area, climate, scenery, architectural remains, etc.—Its capital and surroundings—Wild and picturesque appearance of its armed population—Civilised bearing of the upper classes and their cordial friendship with Englishmen—Government of the Nizám—Powers and duties of the Resident—Special importance of the position at the time Sir R. Meade took office.

Sir Richard's arduous duties in Baroda having been at length satisfactorily completed, he prepared to return to his pleasant home at Bangalore, with fond hopes of being allowed a period of comparative rest, and time to devote his attention to the interesting administrative work of the Mysore Chief Commissionership and the training of the promising young Chief.

But it was not so to be. While at Bombay he was spoken to by the Viceroy, Lord Northbrook, as to his willingness to undertake an office—even more onerous than those he had already filled—the post of Resident at Hyderabad.

He was nearly fifty-five years of age, the time when, under the Rules of the Service, military officers are usually required to retire as *emeriti*; he had served in India for thirty-seven years with hardly any leave, and was anxious on many grounds to stay, for a time at least, at Bangalore. But he was in fairly good health, and, feeling it to be his duty, at once agreed to accept the post offered.

And on the 27th November, 1875, a few days after his return home, he received the following letter from Lord Northbrook :—

"OODEYPORE, *25th November*, 1875.

"MY DEAR SIR RICHARD,—I have taken you at your word, and as the circumstance which I had in my mind when I spoke to you at Bombay has arisen, I have appointed you to Hyderabad.

"In doing this you are as well aware as I am that the position is the most difficult and important there is in India at the present time. I will only add that it could not be put into better hands. . . .

"Believe me,

"Yours very sincerely,

"NORTHBROOK."

HYDERABAD in the Deccan,[1] the new scene of Sir Richard Meade's labours, is the most important of all the Muhammadan states under the protection and suzerainty of the British Government, and its ruler, the Nizám, is one of the few Princes entitled to a salute of twenty-one guns.[2]

Including the assigned districts of Berár (on the

[1] So called to distinguish it from Hyderabad in Sind. The word *Deccan* (properly *Dakhin*) is a corruption of a Sanscrit word signifying "South". The word means literally *right hand*, having the same root as the Latin *dextra ;* but as the Hindú worshipping towards the rising sun has on his right hand the *south*, *Dakhin* has come to mean the *south* as well as the *right hand.*

[2] In India the salute for the Queen-Empress is 101 guns; that for the Royal Flag and Viceroy and Governor-General of India is thirty-one guns. Next in rank come the ruling Chiefs of Baroda, Hyderabad and Mysore, who have salutes of twenty-one guns.

north), which, since 1853, have been administered by British officers, Hyderabad has an area considerably larger than Great Britain and a population (chiefly Hindú) of upwards of 12,000,000 souls. It is surrounded on all sides by British territory.

Omitting (for the present) the Berár districts, which are separated from Hyderabad proper by a chain of mountains, and drain westward through the Tapti valley into the Gulf of Cambay, the Nizám's territory may be described as a high-lying plateau, from 1000 to 2000 feet above the sea, between the Western and Eastern Gháts, intersected by the beds of numerous streams, affluents of two great rivers flowing from west to east,—the Godávari and the Kistna.

The Godávari, rising in the Bombay Presidency, within fifty-two miles of the Arabian Sea, winds through the northern portion of the Nizám's dominions; then in a mighty stream, combining the united waters of the Dudna, the Mánjira, the Pranhíta, and the Indrávati, flows to the south-east, forming, for nearly 200 miles, the boundary between Hyderabad and British territory; then, through a deep chasm in the Eastern Gháts, enters the Madras Presidency, near Rájahmandri; supplies silt-laden waters to a network of canals, irrigating the rich deltaic area between the mountains and the sea, and pours the surplus, through seven channels, into the Bay of Bengal,—after a course of nearly 900 miles.

The Kistna, rising near Mahábaleshwar in the Western Gháts, forms (with its principal affluent the Tungabhádra) for nearly 400 miles the southern boundary of Hyderabad, and, after a course of nearly 800 miles through a deep-set rocky channel, passes, like the first-named river, through a rift in the Eastern Ghâts, to the Madras littoral, and, after providing irrigation for more than 400,000 acres, flows into the Bay of Bengal,—at a point not far from the mouth of the Godávari.

The area drained by these two river-systems is climatically divided into two distinct regions—the dry and the comparatively moist.

The south-west monsoon, having drenched the Bombay littoral and the Western Ghâts, has little rain to spare for the Deccan ; its western highlands are bleak and cheerless ; its intersecting valleys, at first narrow and winding, gradually broaden into treeless plains ; the soil, save in the vicinity of rivers, is poor and shallow, and drought and famine are not infrequent visitors. Towards the east the rainfall gradually increases ; the country is more hilly and its climate and scenery show unmistakable signs of the influence of the north-east monsoon.

In both regions, with the help of irrigation, rich crops are grown of cotton, indigo and sugar-cane ; but while in the west the rain crop is precarious, in the east, thanks to a more copious rainfall and an ancient system of irrigation tanks, rice cultivation flourishes and drought and famine are unknown.

The mineral resources of the hills (but little exploited yet in the territories administered by the Nizám) are believed to be considerable ; coal is worked in paying quantities at Singareni, and under the direction of an English company, to which a concession has been granted, the resources are being gradually developed.

The climate, less genial than that of Bangalore, is, for India, salubrious and equable, exempt from the fierce heat and severe cold of the north and the depressing influences of the sea-coast. The scenery, as might be supposed, is very varied; the western uplands, strewn with boulders and bristling with granitic tors, have been described as a "magnified Dartmoor"; on the north volcanic ranges assume fantastic shapes; in the centre are dreary plateaus and stony water-courses; in the east primeval forests occupy the hill-sides, bordering a river broad and rapid as the Rhine; and lakes and streams and luxuriant vegetation take the place of treeless plains.

Ethnically, archæologically, historically, the region is full of interest. Traces of old-world occupation abound in the shape of megalithic monuments; and about twenty miles from Hyderabad is a prehistoric cemetery, the cairns and dolmens of which extend for miles; three Hindú races, widely differing in character and language—the Marátha, the Telinga and the Canarese—occupy respectively the north, south-eastern and south-western districts; the architectural remains of once-flourishing Hindú dynasties are still to be seen at Deogiri (Daulatábád), Gulbarga and Warangal, while at Gulbarga, Bídar and Golconda are the ruined mosques, palaces, tombs and gateways of three out of the five Muhammadan kingdoms, which flourished in the Deccan between the middle of the fourteenth and end of the seventeenth century, until destroyed, piecemeal, by Aurangzeb, who thus paved the way for the domination of the Maráthas and the ultimate destruction of the overgrown Mughal Empire.

But to the ordinary traveller the most interesting part of Hyderabad is, undoubtedly, the capital itself—"a survival of dominant Islamism, a mirror of the gorgeous East, a page out of the *Arabian Nights*".[1]

It has no claim to antiquity, for it was not founded till the close of the sixteenth century.[2] The main street is fine, but presents few features of architectural interest; for, with the exception of the principal mosque and tombs adjacent and the lofty structure called the Chár Minár, the city contains no striking buildings.[3] The palaces of the Nizám and his nobles are immured within high walls, which reveal nothing to the outer view and when seen are disappointing; and there are no grand gateways or elaborately carved house-fronts which form an attractive feature of many Oriental towns. But in a suburb on the north side of the river Músi (opposite the Nizám's palace) stands the British

[1] For the description of Hyderabad we are indebted to valuable notes by Colonel Trevor, C.S.I., formerly First Assistant to the Resident, and to the graphic pages of Mr. Caine's *Picturesque India*.

[2] By Kutb Shah Muhammad Kuli, fifth in descent from Sultán Kutb Shah, founder of the dynasty of Golconda.

[3] The mosque, a copy of that of Mecca, differs in style from the mosques of Patán or Mughal type ordinarily found in India, and is thus of special interest; in its broad enclosure are the marble tombs of former Nizáms. The Chár Minár is a deep gateway with four minarets, and four sides arched, standing at a *quadrivium* in the main street. The chambers in the upper storey were originally designed for students, but are now used as commercial store-houses.

Residency, one of the grandest modern buildings in India, outside the Presidency towns, in the midst of a beautifully wooded park enclosed by a crenellated wall with bastions.

The charm of Hyderabad consists partly in its position—amid wild and rocky scenery with isolated granite peaks; partly in the beauty and interest of its surroundings—its gardens, tanks and bridges; its charming drives—to the tombs and fortress of Golconda, the lakes of Husain Ságar and Mír Alam; the shrine of Mol Ali near Trimalgherry; or the broad cantonments of Secunderábád and Bolárum; but chiefly in the picturesque throngs of human beings which fill its main bazaars and the mediæval splendour of its palace retinues.

The Nizám, as the principal Mussulman potentate of India, has attracted to his service civil and military Muhammadans from almost every part of Asia and even from Africa, all of whom go about armed to the teeth with the quaint weapons of their country and wearing their distinctive costumes. Turks, Arabs, Moors, Afghans, Zanzibáris, Persians, Bokhariots, Rohillas, as well as Sikhs, Rájputs, Maráthas, Parsis, Madrassis and every variety of Hindú swarm in the great city of Hyderabad, which contains (including suburbs) a population of nearly 400,000 souls.

In marked contrast, however, with the armed crowds which throng the streets is the remarkably civilised bearing of the upper classes. Having had for generations to govern and conciliate a large and not unwarlike Hindú population, the ruling classes of Hyderabad are singularly free from religious bigotry; while, owing to frequent dealings in the past with representatives of European Powers, to the continued presence of British officers and troops and the civilising influence of the Resident and his staff, their ideas are, in many respects, more advanced and their relations with Europeans more unrestrained and cordial than in any other part of India. Balls, dinner-parties, race-meetings, hunts, polo contests, athletic games, and other gatherings, at which the English society meets and mixes with the local aristocracy on the most friendly terms, have long been the order of the day; so much so that a lady visitor once observed that she supposed that the chief business of the British Resident was "to entertain and be entertained".

As for the Government, the Nizám is nominally an absolute Ruler; but members of his family and Arab commanders of his body-guard and others hold the position of grandees,[1] with large revenue assignments and more or less influence in affairs; while, as often happens in an Indian native State, the ordinary business of the Government is in the hands of an official class of foreign extraction.

The powers of the British Resident (which will be described more fully later on) are great, but undefined; and his duties require at all times tact and judgment. Formerly the independent ally, the Nizám has gradu-

[1] Or *págadárs*. *Pága* is a Marátha term for "troop," and *págadár*, literally *troop-holder*, is applied to persons to whom the revenues of a tract have been assigned in consideration of their maintaining a troop of horse. The principal commandant of the body-guard is the head of the *Shams-ul-Umra* family, who has the title of the *Amír-i-Kabír*.

H.H. Mír Mahbúb Ali Khán,
Nizám and Súbahdár of Hyderabad and the Deccan
(*æt.* ten years).

ally become the *protégé* of the British Government; it is for the Resident, while firmly maintaining the latter's paramount position, to avoid wounding the former's susceptibilities—a task not always easy. As a rule he scrupulously abstains from all interference, or appearance of interference, with the internal administration, but has had, at times, to interpose to save the State from ruin. Meanwhile, his presence at the capital, supported by a division of the British army and a local force commanded by British officers, quietly but powerfully assists in maintaining order, and he and those associated with him are able by friendly counsel and, what is perhaps even more important, the "every-day acts of upright and earnest Englishmen," to exercise a beneficial influence upon affairs.

At the time Sir Richard Meade came upon the scene the position of Resident was of special importance and responsibility, for the Nizám was then a minor of nine years. The affairs of the State were ably conducted by a remarkable man, the late Minister, Sir Sálár Jang, who acted as Regent in conjunction with the premier noble, the Amír-i-Kabír, representing the dynastic interests. But there were difficulties ahead, and more than one "burning question" to be dealt with relating to the maintenance of the force known as the Hyderabad Contingent, the continuance of British administration of the Berár districts assigned for its support, and other matters affecting the Treaty relations between the British Government and the Nizám.

Such is a general description of the State of

Hyderabad and the position of affairs when Sir Richard Meade took office; but to enable the reader fully to understand the difficulties with which he had to contend it is necessary to describe in greater detail the political situation and the history of the relations of the British Government with that of Hyderabad. These will form the subject of the two following chapters.

The Residency, Hyderabad.

CHAPTER XVII.

HYDERABAD (*continued*).

Aurangzeb arranges for the administration of the Deccan—Chin Kalich Khan (Ásaf Jáh) appointed Viceroy—In the reign of Farokhsír heads a movement against the Sayyads and liberates the Emperor from their domination—Ásaf Jáh Minister at Dehli—Resigns and proceeds to Hyderabad—Defeats the Mughal Governor and becomes Nizám of the Deccan—Tries to protect the Emperor from the Maráthas, but is disastrously defeated at Bhopál—Joins his forces with the Emperor's in endeavouring to resist Nádir Shah's advance—Death of Ásaf Jáh in 1748—Struggle for succession——French and English take sides in the dispute—By treaty with the English in 1759 the French are excluded from Hyderabad—Series of treaties providing for the protection of Hyderabad by a British force in return for territorial cessions, etc.—A Resident appointed in 1788—Further cessions—Allotments of territory made to the Nizám on four occasions—Organisation of the Hyderabad Contingent—Owing to misrule in Hyderabad the pay of the Contingent falls into arrears—Lord Dalhousie—Treaty of 1853 by which Berár, Dharaseo and Raichúr are assigned to the British Government as security for cost of Contingent—Attitude of the Nizám's Government during the Mutiny of 1857—Honours conferred on Nizám and Minister by British Government—Dharaseo and Raichúr restored to the Nizám and new Treaty executed—Berár and its progress under British rule—Administration of Hyderabad proper—Its disordered condition under Nizám Sikandar Jáh—Súraj-ul-Mulk appointed Minister and is succeeded in 1853 by his nephew Sálár Jang.

HAVING subjugated the Deccan the Emperor Aurangzeb placed the conquered districts under the control of military Governors, who must have had an anxious time, for the country was desolated by long-continued war and overrun by Marátha freebooters and the disbanded soldiery of the annihilated Governments.

In A.D. 1696 he selected for the post of Governor of Bíjapúr[1] (the most important of his recent conquests) a Turki noble, by name Chin Kalich Khan, grandson of Ábid Kuli Khan, formerly *Kázi* (Chief Judge) of Bokhára, who came to Dehli in A.D. 1658 and was killed at the siege of Golconda in A.D. 1687.

Chin Kalich Khan, being a man of ability and prudence, acquired great influence in this part of the Deccan, and in 1713, six years after the death of Aurangzeb, was appointed by Farokhsír (the Emperor, who granted a charter to the East India Company) Súbadar or Viceroy of the Deccan, with the title of Nizám-ul-Mulk[2] Ásaf Jáh,[3] a title still retained by the Rulers of Hyderabad.

He was from time to time displaced by more favoured courtiers, but being, as his title implies, a

[1] Formerly seat of the *Ádil Sháhi* dynasty, the most powerful of the five Muhammadan kingdoms which flourished in the Deccan between the middle of the fifteenth and end of the seventeenth century. The walls of this deserted capital are six and a half miles round; and enclose in its area of two and a quarter square miles some of the grandest architectural remains in India. The mosques and tombs and gardens of the citadel are described in the *Official Gazetteer* of the Bombay Government as "gems of art"; while "palaces, arches, tombs and minarets, all carved from rich brown basalt, garlanded by creepers and broken and wrenched by *pipal* and *banyan* roots, furnish fresh interest even after days spent in the ruins".

[2] *I.e.*, "Administrator of the realm".

[3] *I.e.*, "the equal of *Ásaf*," Ásaf being the name of the traditional Grand Vizier of King Solomon.

man of great sagacity, he kept aloof from the dissensions of the Imperial Court and firmly established his power and influence in Hyderabad. On the accession of the Emperor Muhammad Shah he headed a movement against the Sayyads—two brothers, who had for years past practically ruled the Empire—and after twice defeating the forces sent against him, liberated the Emperor from their domination.

Ásaf Jáh was, soon afterwards, appointed Wazír, or Chief Minister, at Dehli; but the office was distasteful to him, and in A.D. 1723 he sent in his resignation and proceeded to Hyderabad to resume his old appointment of Viceroy of the Deccan. Under secret instructions from head-quarters the Mughal Governor of Hyderabad resisted his return; but at Shákar-Khelda in Berár Ásaf Jáh obtained a decisive victory over his opponent, who was slain in the conflict. Ásaf Jáh thereupon became Nizám of the Deccan, practically independent of Imperial control and founder of the present reigning dynasty.

In A.D. 1738 he was called upon to protect the Emperor from the Maráthas, and moved from Dehli with a large force in pursuit of the retiring army of the Peshwa. But at Bhopál he was surrounded and had to make a disastrous retreat and surrender all the country between the Narbadda and the Chambal. And in the following year he joined his forces with those of the Dehli Emperor in the attempt to stem the invasion of Nádir Shah. His troops took no part in the disastrous battle of Karnál, but he was present at the massacre at Dehli, and he is said to have prevailed upon Nádir Shah to stop it.

After the death of Ásaf Jáh in 1748 there was, as often happens in Muhammadan principalities, a struggle for the succession among the members of the family.

The Mughal Emperor, though nominally the Paramount Power, was too weak to interfere, so an opportunity was offered to the representatives of two rival European Powers having trade settlements on the coast—England and France—to take sides in the dispute. Heretofore, indeed, whatever was the position in Europe, peace prevailed between Europeans in the East. But all this was now to be changed. From henceforth French and English were constantly engaged in internecine conflicts between aspirants for power in Hyderabad or the Carnatic, and commercial rivalry between Madras and Pondicherry developed into a vital struggle for political ascendency in India.

It would be beyond the scope of the present Memoir to describe the history of that period: how the French, thanks to the genius of Dupleix and Bussy, taught us the value of the sepoy, and were on the eve of establishing an Empire in South India, but were checked in mid-career by orders from home; how the statesman Dupleix was succeeded by the brave but unfortunate Lally; how the genius of Lawrence, and Clive and Coote, aided by the mistakes of their opponents, destroyed the French supremacy, which finally perished at the battle of Wandiwásh and the fall of Pondicherry in A.D. 1761. Suffice it to say that by a treaty executed between the British Government and the Nizám (Salábat Jang) in A.D. 1759, the French were excluded from Hyderabad territory; and that by a series of treaties executed in 1766, 1768, 1789, 1790, 1798, 1800, and confirmed in 1803 and 1831, the Nizám became the perpetual ally of the British Government for defensive purposes, the British Government undertaking, in return for certain territorial cessions :—

(1) To locate at Hyderabad a Subsidiary Force of all arms, of a strength ultimately fixed at not less than "eight battalions of sepoys and two regiments of cavalry with the requisite complement of guns," or about 10,698 men (Treaty of 1800, art. 3);

(2) To protect the Nizám from external enemies and secure him in the sovereignty of his dominions.

While the Nizám undertook :—

(1) In time of war to co-operate immediately with a force of 6000 infantry, and 9000 cavalry and requisite train of artillery, "and use every effort to bring the whole force of his dominions into the field as speedily as possible" (Treaty of 1800, art. 12);

(2) To enter into no political negotiations with other States (Treaty of 1800, art. 15);

(3) To make the British Government arbiter in all disputes with other Powers (Treaty of 1800, art. 16), and

(4) Not to employ or retain any European in his service without its knowledge and consent (Treaty of 1798, art. 8).

By article 15 of the Treaty of 1800 it is declared that the Honourable Company's Government have "no manner of concern with any of His Highness's children, relations, subjects or servants, with respect to whom His Highness is absolute". But this provision, though still observed in spirit, has had, with the full consent of the Chiefs themselves, to be modified in practice; for its literal observance would have led to the Nizám's destruction. Moreover, the Treaties themselves contemplate the interference of the British Government in times of difficulty, for no British troops—whether belonging to the Subsidiary Force or the Contingent—are to be employed in coercing the Nizám's subjects until "the reality of the offence has been ascertained": the general result being this, that though the Nizám is nominally the Ally, he is in reality the protected Dependant or Vassal of the British Government.

To secure the execution of the Treaties a Resident was first appointed in 1788, and the office has been continued ever since and is still the blue ribbon of the political service in India;[1] and

To secure the payment of the enlarged Subsidiary Force, further permanent cessions of territory were made in A.D. 1800 and now form part of the Madras Presidency. The territory ceded consisted of the acquisitions made from Tippú Sultán and allotted to the Nizám after the destruction of the former's power. "Thus," says the historian of India, "the Nizám secured the future defence of his person and his State

[1] Among those who have filled the office may be mentioned the names of Sir Charles, afterwards Lord, Metcalfe, who acted subsequently for six months as Governor-General of India, and, after retirement, was successively Governor of Jamaica and of Canada; General Sir John Low, a soldier and statesman, father of Lieut.-General Sir Robert Low, of Malakand fame; and Sir Richard Temple, who, after governing successfully three provinces, retired from the Indian Civil Service with a baronetcy, and has recently, after a service of several years in Parliament, been created a Privy Councillor. Among the first Assistants to the Resident was Captain, afterwards the well-known Major-General Sir John Malcolm, great-uncle of the present Lady Meade, whose father, Colonel Duncan Malcolm, also held the same appointment for many years.

without any sacrifice of money or the loss of any portion of his original dominions."

These arrangements proved highly beneficial to the Nizám, for they not only secured him complete protection from external aggression, but were the means of procuring for him on four occasions considerable accessions of territory,—by allotments made—after the first and second war with Tippú Sultán; after the Marátha war of 1804; and after the overthrow of the Peshwa in 1822.

But complaints were made, especially after the first Marátha war, of the inefficiency of the troops furnished by the Nizám; and, with a view to remedying the evil, it was arranged in 1807 to have a portion of the Nizám's troops employed in Berár organised under British officers; and in 1813, during the Ministry of Chandú Lál (a Hindú official, who conducted the administration of the Nizám's territories for nearly five and thirty years), the system was extended to troops employed in Hyderabad.

These troops formed the nucleus of what was afterwards known as the Hyderabad Contingent, a force which has played an important part in preserving order in the Nizám's territories and done good service in campaigns—in the Mutiny, in Afghanistan, in Burmah. By the middle of the present century it had become unnecessarily large and very costly, and its pay, like that of the Subsidiary Force in former years, was allowed to fall into serious arrear and there were other causes of difficulty and friction.

"The eagle eye of Lord Dalhousie perceived the root

of the evil, and he determined to apply a complete and lasting remedy."[1] Accordingly by a Treaty executed in 1853 a new arrangement was effected; the Contingent was to be no longer controlled by the Nizám's Government but directly under the orders of the Government of India and constituted an auxiliary force maintained "for His Highness, his heirs and his successors". Its minimum numerical strength was considerably reduced. Instead of "6000 infantry and 9000 cavalry and the requisite train of artillery," it is to consist (art. 3) of

"Not less than 5000 infantry and 2000 cavalry and four field batteries of artillery . . . commanded by British officers and controlled by the British Government through its representative the Resident at Hyderabad".

It is to be always at the disposal of the Nizám for the maintenance of order in his territory. And with this view the force has been distributed into detachments located at suitable positions in the Nizám's territory.[2] But it is only to be employed to crush rebellion or resistance to authority "after the reality of the offence has been clearly ascertained".

In the time of war portions of both the Subsidiary Force and Contingent are to be available for service outside the Hyderabad frontier, but *per contra* the Nizám is relieved for ever from the onerous obligation of unlimited military co-operation in time of war in-

[1] Marshman.

[2] At *Ellichpur* in Berár, at *Aurangabád*, *Jálna* and *Hingoli* in the northern, *Mominábád* in the western, *Raichúr* on the southern frontier of Hyderabad, with headquarters at *Bolárum* near the capital.

curred under the treaty of 1800, for it was agreed that:—

"Excepting the said Subsidiary and Contingent Forces His Highness shall not, under any circumstances, be called upon to furnish any other troops".

To provide for the regular payment of the troops and debts due to the British Government, and to prevent "differences and dissensions," three out-lying tracts forming part of the Nizám's territories, with revenues estimated, at their then annual value, to yield the amount required, were assigned to the British Government in trust for the support of the force, namely:—

The districts north of Hyderabad between the Sátpúra and Ajanta ranges known as BERÁR or the BERÁRS; the Raichúr districts on the east; and Dharaseo on the west.

The districts were to be under the "exclusive management of the British Resident for the time being"; and it was provided that the balance of the receipts, if any, after deducting the cost of administration and the charges of the Contingent should be paid to the credit of the Nizám.

But seven years afterwards, in recognition of his services in 1857, two out of the three tracts above named (Raichúr and Dharaseo) were restored to the Nizám.

BERÁR still remains under British administration, but so great and so rapid has been the improvement of its revenues that, after defraying the cost of the Contingent and all administrative charges, it has provided for many years past a considerable surplus for the benefit of Hyderabad. In all—between 1833 and the present time—about 600 lakhs of rupees have been paid on this account into the Nizám's Treasury, after providing a reserve of about forty-six lakhs of rupees as a working balance.[1]

From the above statement it will be seen that the Resident at Hyderabad has a threefold duty to perform. Besides conducting the political relations between the British Government and the Nizám (a delicate and often an anxious task), he controls the Hyderabad Contingent, a force nearly as large as a division; and directs (as Chief Commissioner) the administration of a territory larger and more populous than Denmark. He, furthermore, under Treaties executed between 1870 and the present time, exercises administrative and judicial powers over all lines of railway passing through the Nizám's dominions.

BERÁR, the territory referred to in the last paragraph, is a broad valley running east and west, with a network of streams draining into the river Purna, an affluent of the Tapti. It was annexed to Hyderabad by Ásaf Jáh in A.D. 1724, but was soon overrun by Maráthas, and held by the Bhosla family till 1803, when it was restored to the Nizám as his share in the spoils of the first Marátha war.

The tract is not beautiful to behold but eminently productive; its rainfall regular and copious and its black cotton soil excellent. Under the administration

[1] Latterly the surplus has fallen off in consequence of drought and other causes; but the fluctuation is probably temporary only.

of successive Residents it has thriven greatly. The Nagpur branch of the G. I. P. Railway connects it with the seaboard, so its trade has enormously developed. Its population, chiefly Marátha, has doubled, and is now close upon 3,000,000; its cultivated area has nearly doubled, and amounts at the present time to nearly 7,500,000 acres.

Though many oppressive taxes have been abolished, its gross revenues have increased more than fivefold, and now reach the satisfactory figure of nearly 1,250,000 of tens of rupees. Courts of justice, on the model of those in British India, have been established, crime has been repressed, the cultivated and culturable area surveyed and mapped, sanitation and forest conservancy attended to, roads constructed through the length and breadth of the province, postal services organised, schools, hospitals and dispensaries opened in large numbers. It possesses some of the richest and most extensive cotton fields in the world; and good coal seams are being worked at Wurda.

Berár, in a word, from being the haunt of freebooters and well-nigh desolate from insecurity of life and property, has become a centre of trade, with ninety-seven factories where steam power is employed, and "one of the most promising regions to be seen in India".[1]

While the prosperity of Berár has been thus increasing by leaps and bounds, the administration of Hyderabad proper, under the direct control of the Nizám's Government—thanks to the exertions of an

[1] Hunter's *Imperial Gazetteer*.

able Minister, aided by the advice and influence of the Resident—has decidedly improved.

During the first half of the present century the condition of Hyderabad was far from satisfactory, and during the later years of Nizám Sikandar Jáh's rule had fallen into great disorder. There was much oppression; local rebellions were frequent, and the roads, such as they were, infested with robbers;[1] and it became necessary for the maintenance of order and the collection of the revenue to employ the assistance of British officers.

On his death and the succession of Násir-ud-Daulah, the British officers were, at the latter's request, removed, but disorder and mismanagement immediately recurred; the state of Hyderabad became a scandal and a disgrace, and ultimately affairs became so disorganised and the credit of the State so low that bankers refused to grant loans. At length the management of affairs was placed in the hands of Súraj-ul-Mulk, an honest and capable official, the son of a former Minister, and under his direction some improvement was effected. It was during his tenure of office that the Treaty of 1853 was executed,—a treaty which, like many good things Indian, has been the object of fierce attack, but has secured for Hyderabad several inestimable benefits; it removed what was once a perpetual cause of friction between the British Government and the Nizám; reduced the extravagant cost of the Contingent; provided for the internal tranquillity of the

[1] Strange to relate, Sir S. Jang's chief confectioner was a Thug robber who had been captured when a boy by Captain Malcolm, first Assistant to the Resident at Hyderabad, and father of Lady Meade.

Nizám's dominions, and lastly laid the foundations of the present splendid prosperity of the Assigned Districts.

Almost immediately after the execution of the Treaty Súraj-ul-Mulk died and was succeeded in office by his nephew Sálár Jang.

CHAPTER XVIII.

HYDERABAD (*continued*).

Sálár Jang—Early training—Family and antecedents—First efforts at reforming the Hyderabad Administration—Difficulties—Mutiny of 1857—Loyal attitude of the Nizám's Government—Death of Nizám, but same policy pursued by his successor—British Residency attacked by Rohillas, but insurgents beaten off and tranquillity maintained—Honours conferred upon Nizám and his Minister by British Government—Portions of the assigned districts restored to the Nizám's rule, a debt of Rsx. 500,000 due to the British Government cancelled and a new Treaty of friendship executed—Sálár Jang grateful but not satisfied, and hopes for ultimate restoration of Berár—Prosecutes his reforms with increased energy—Testimony of Sir R. Temple—Organisation of Reformed Troops with a view of supplanting the Contingent—Sálár Jang twice saved from dismissal from office by remonstrances of British Government—Made K.C.S.I. in 1867—Death of Nizám Afzal-ud-Daulah, leaving a son less than three years old—Sir Sálár Jang appointed co-Regent during minority and promoted to be G.C.S.I.—Policy becomes more advanced—Begins to question suzerainty of British Government—Has few followers among his own countrymen, but Englishmen of position sympathise with his aspirations—In 1874 demands restoration of Berár and disbandment of Contingent—Arguments of the Memorial—Answer of the Government of India—Lord Salisbury rejects the Memorial of the co-Regents—A fresh agitation thought probable—In these circumstances Sir Richard Meade selected by Lord Northbrook for the post of Resident—The two statesmen Sir Sálár Jang and Sir Richard Meade contrasted.

WHEN SÁLÁR JANG became Minister, he was only twenty-four years of age, but he had been long educated under European supervision, and specially trained for the office he was thus early to assume.

He was the nephew (as already mentioned) of Súraj-ul-Mulk, the Minister at the time of the assignment of Berár in A.D. 1853, and grandson, by the father's side, of Munír-ul-Mulk, who was appointed to the same office in A.D. 1808,[1] and Munír-ul-Mulk was son-in-law and successor of Mír-Álam, a sincere friend of the British Government, who held various high offices under the Nizám's Government between A.D. 1784 and A.D. 1808, the time of his death.

His father's family came originally from Medína, but had been settled in Hyderabad territory since the middle of the seventeenth century; his mother's family was of Persian origin.

Until the year 1870 Sálár Jang never left for a single day the capital of Hyderabad; yet his knowledge of men and affairs was remarkable, while his fine presence, refined manners, enlightened views and generous hospitality made him a great favourite with the English community. He discharged his duties as Minister (says Sir Richard Temple)[2] "with unwearying assiduity and an efficiency unprecedented in the Deccan". He had an earnest desire to improve the administration and develop the resources of his country, and his policy, so long, at any rate, as it was confined to measures of internal administration, secured the cordial sympathy

[1] He was appointed in opposition to the wishes of the British Government, and had as his Deputy one Chandú Lál, who held office for more than four and thirty years. The arrangement by which a Muhammadan was nominally at the head of the Administration, while the working man was a Hindú, was made expressly by the Nizám Sikandar Jáh, and is not an unusual one in Indian states, for a Hindú is generally a better man of business than a Mussulman, and acts as a check upon the ambition of his immediate superior.

[2] *Men and Events of my Time in India*, p. 288.

and support of the British Government and its representatives.

But from the first he had great difficulties to encounter from his own countrymen.

In the first place his master, the Nizám Násir-ud-Daulah, though loyal to the British Government, was naturally distressed at the assignment of Berár;[1] hated innovation, and regarded with some jealousy the growing power and influence of his Minister. The Nizám's successor, Afzal-ud-Daulah, was even more apprehensive of innovation, and kept his Minister "in such a state of thraldom that he was almost a prisoner in his house and never allowed to leave Hyderabad or even have an interview with the British Resident without special permission". On one occasion, indeed (in 1861), the Minister was on the point of being dismissed, and was only retained in office under remonstrances of the British Resident; and on another occasion (in 1867) matters came to such a pass that Sálár Jang sent in his resignation; but by the good offices of the British Government a reconciliation was effected and the Minister was invested by the Nizám with the order of K.C.S.I., which had just been conferred upon him by Her Majesty.

Then in religion Sálár Jang was a Muhammadan of the Shiah sect, whereas the Nizám and the members of his family were Sunnis; and the sectarian ani-

[1] Though he deliberately accepted the arrangement in preference to the disbandment of the Contingent, which was offered as an alternative. His Minister (Sir Sálár's uncle) and the premier noble (the Shams-ul-Umra) were strongly in favour of the Treaty, and when the Nizám signed it he was in "unusually good spirits".

mosities between the Sunni and the Shiah in the East are even more pronounced than those between Protestants and Roman Catholics in Western countries. And though the Minister was personally free from all religious bigotry the fact that he belonged to a hated sect was a good weapon of attack.

Again, by the customs of the realm the royal domains (known as *Sarf-i-khás* lands), including tracts and villages scattered throughout the territory, as well as the military fiefs of *págadárs*[1]—generally connections of the reigning Chief or the leaders of Arab mercenaries—were excluded from the jurisdiction of the civil administration, an arrangement which made efficient police control impossible, and in Berár had to be got rid of by special treaty.

Then there were the inevitable vested interests to deal with, and especially those of the Arab mercenaries, whose chiefs had in many cases become mortgagees of the land assigned for their support, and objected to be paid off and turned adrift; and would never have been got rid of but for the presence in the vicinity of a British military force.

Again, the vast "swashbuckler" element at the capital, composed partly of armed retainers of the Chief and the *noblesse* and partly of loafers of various nationalities who flocked from all parts to Hyderabad, as an Alsatia for ruffianism, was a source of danger most difficult to control.

Lastly, like all reformers, and especially those in Eastern lands, he was the victim of constant jealousy and court intrigues; but, notwithstanding all the diffi-

[1] See note in preceding chapter.

culties of his position, he was able (as we shall hereafter show) to achieve wonders.

Before, however, he had made much progress in his reforms, when he had been only four years in office, his powers of statesmanship were severely tested. In 1857 came the great Mutiny, in its inception (as already explained) a sudden outburst of long-smouldering disaffection in the native army; but though the revolt was primarily a military one it was utilised by persons who had political or other grievances against the British Government, and at Meerut, where the first outbreak occurred, it had for its immediate object the destruction of British power and the resuscitation of the Mughal Empire. In these circumstances the attitude of Hyderabad at this juncture was a matter of grave importance and great anxiety.

Fortunately the re-establishment of the Empire of Dehli had no great attraction for the Hyderabad Chief, so the Nizám, advised by Sálár Jang, at once decided to throw in his lot with the British Government.

But a new difficulty arose. On the 18th May, eight days after the Meerut outbreak, the Nizám Násir-ud-Daulah died, and for a time the situation of Hyderabad was very critical.

However, on his deathbed, the late Nizám enjoined his son and successor Afzal-ud-Daulah to remain faithful to the British Government, and, thanks to this injunction, and the earnest advice and influence of the Minister, the young Nizám promptly adopted the same policy as his predecessor. Fanatical Mullahs preached sedition in the Mecca Mosque and tried to rouse the population to extirpate the infidel, but, with the help of Arab guards over whom Sálár Jang had influence, an outbreak was prevented.

At length, however, on the 17th July, a band of fanatical Rohillas, accompanied by some 4000 of the townspeople, made an attack upon the Residency. But having received timely information from the Minister, the Resident (Major Cuthbert Davidson) was prepared; the attack was beaten off by artillery, and a charge by the Hyderabad Contingent Cavalry dispersed the rioters. Thenceforth, till the taking of Dehli, Hyderabad remained tranquil; and for those three months the unswerving loyalty of the Nizám and Sálár Jang was of inestimable benefit.

Berár from first to last was free from all disturbance.

The services of the Nizám and his Minister and the latter's enlightened administration were duly recognised by Lord Canning's Government and obtained well-merited applause in England.

The Nizám received the honour of K.C.S.I., the fertile districts of Dharaseo and Raichúr, which formed part of the assignment made for the support of the Hyderabad Contingent, were restored to him, together with Shorapor, the confiscated territory of a rebel chief; and the debt of Rsx. 500,000 due to the British Government by the Nizám was cancelled.

Sálár Jang received the thanks of the Government of India and a valuable present, and, with his concurrence, a new Treaty, embodying these arrangements and confirming all previous treaties and engagements, was executed in 1860.

In acknowledging the receipt of the copy of the

Treaty duly ratified by Lord Canning the Minister observed that, "Under the new arrangement the foundations of the ancient friendship and firm fidelity mutually existing between the two Governments had acquired more than their former strength".

But though officially grateful for the honours and substantial gifts conferred upon his master and the recognition of his own services, Sálár Jang was, we are informed, really far from satisfied; and, in particular, the restoration of Dharaseo and Raichúr was regarded rather as an instalment of favour than a final and adequate reward. From this time, we are told, "the hope was ever before him that, by justifying the confidence and earning the respect of the English, he would ultimately succeed in crowning his tenure of office by placing at the foot of his Prince the restituted province of Berár".

With this view he pressed on his improvements with increased energy. He strove manfully to reform every part of the administration, the land revenue, the dispensing of justice, the police, the finances. "His official assiduity," says Sir Richard Temple, "and mastery of details left nothing to be desired . . . he was an excellent imitator; whatever improvements the British Government introduced he would sooner or later adopt, *longo intervallo*, perhaps, but still with some effect. Thus roads, caravanserais, medical schools, drains and conservancy, besides many miscellaneous improvements, all had a share of his attention. He exercised his vast patronage well, appointing competent and respectable men to civil offices, and endeavouring to infuse an honest fidelity into the whole service of the State. That he fully succeeded in these efforts is more than we can affirm . . . but, upon a retrospect of the circumstances under which he had to act, it seems wonderful that so much was accomplished by him."

In the capital, indeed, the improvement was immense, but outside the capital, owing to the Minister's inability to leave it and see with his own eyes, many of his reforms were imperfectly carried out. In the collection of the revenue there were still cases of oppression, and of the sums collected a good deal never reached the coffers of the State. Primary education made little progress, and outrages and disorder in outlying villages remained in some cases unchecked because the Minister objected, on political grounds, to call in the aid of the Contingent.

Another part of his policy was open to criticism, at least from a British point of view. He commenced the formation of a force called the "Reformed Troops," organised on the model of the Contingent, but not under the control of the Resident. The force was officered by Europeans of different nationalities, and the Commandant, in virtue of his office, wore the sword of Raymond, a Frenchman who was in the Nizám's service towards the end of the eighteenth century, and whose memory was so much revered by native soldiers that lights were (and possibly are still) kept burning at his tomb.

These Reformed Troops were intended ultimately to do the work of the Contingent, and by proving its existence to be unnecessary, to strengthen the Nizám's claim for the disbandment of the force and the restoration of the territory assigned for its support. But the measure was obviously open to objection as an unnecessary drain upon the finances of the State, besides being unfriendly to the protecting Power, and an evasion of the spirit, if not of the letter, of the Treaty of 1853.

In A.D. 1869 Nizám Afzal-ud-Daulah died, leaving a son, Mír Mahbúb Ali Khán (the present Nizám), less than three years old.

During the minority, the administration was entrusted by the Government of India to Sir Sálár Jang in conjunction with the premier noble of the State, known as the Amír-i-Kabír. The latter was the head of the Shams-ul-Umra family—a family connected with that of the Nizám—was Commandant of the body-guard, and is described by Sir Richard Temple as "a high-born Muhammadan of the old school, refined, dignified and judicious, though somewhat enfeebled by age". It was thought that by this arrangement the interests of the reigning family and the nobility would be properly secured, while those of the administration and the people would be safe in the hands of the Minister.

Sir Sálár Jang had now a freer hand and continued his reforms—at any rate on paper—with greater vigour; and in recognition of his conduct and services was in 1871 promoted to the rank of G.C.S.I. At the same time his policy became more advanced. He was now anxious not only for the abolition of the Contingent and the restoration of Berár, but to bring back the Nizám's status to that which he possessed at the time of the

Yours very Sincerely
Salar Jung

earliest treaties. In other words, he began to question the validity of those rights of suzerainty which had been exercised by the British Government, more or less, since the commencement of the present century; the result partly of the growth of British power and partly of gross and long-continued misrule and anarchy in Hyderabad.

It was, probably, for the same reason that he objected to the young Nizám visiting British territory, or even leaving his capital for a tour through his own territories, and regarded with jealousy all educational arrangements calculated to bring the Prince under the influence of English officers.

It was urged, indeed, by the Minister's opponents that personal ambition was the mainspring of his acts; that he hoped that his efforts on behalf of the Nizám would secure for him a position like that of the "Mayor of the Palace" of the Franks, or the "Peshwa" of the Maráthas, with possible succession to his son. The imputation may or may not have been true, but if true, the object was not, from his point of view at any rate, an unworthy one.

However this may be, in 1874 Sir Sálár Jang, with the reluctant assent, it is said, of his colleague the Amír-i-Kabír, presented to the Government of India a demand for the disbandment of the Hyderabad Contingent and the restoration of Berár to the direct administration of the Nizám.

The memorial was ably drawn up with the help of English friends. It was far from friendly in tone; it was, in fact, an indictment of the policy pursued by the British Government towards Hyderabad since the commencement of the present century, and questioned, *inter alia*, the validity of the treaties of 1853 and 1860; the latter of which had been arranged and executed while Sir S. Jang himself was Minister.

Notwithstanding the unfriendly imputations it contained the memorial was dispassionately considered by the Government of India, during the Viceroyship of Lord Northbrook, and was transmitted to the Secretary of State for India with an elaborate despatch drafted by the Foreign Secretary, the late Sir Charles Aitchison.

The Government of India had no difficulty in showing that the statements in the memorial were historically inaccurate, while the interpretation placed upon the treaties was inadmissible, but it was further pointed out that, irrespective of the treaty rights claimable by the British Government, it was no light matter to transfer a populous and wealthy province which had enjoyed for more than twenty years the benefits of British rule to the administration of a native State, however well conducted;

That though, thanks to Sir Sálár Jang's enlightened policy, there had been a marked improvement in the administration of the Nizám's dominions, it could not be admitted for a moment that it approached the administrative standard of Berár;

That assuming the present administration of Hyderabad to be all that could be desired, there was no security for its continuance—at any rate beyond the lifetime of the present Minister;

That no such security could be obtained without a comprehensive revision of the treaty relations between the British Government and the Nizám; including arrangements as to the military force to be maintained by the British Government and the Nizám's Government respectively.

To the memorial the Secretary of State for India, the Marquis of Salisbury, gave the only possible reply—courteously but firmly declining to question the validity of the treaties of 1853 and 1860, and declaring that the administration of Berár must remain, as now, in the hands of British officers acting on the Nizám's behalf, and subject to the payment of all surplus revenues into the Nizám's treasury.

But there was reason for believing that the Minister of Hyderabad would not be prepared to accept the negative as final and that fresh agitation and difficulties might be expected.

And so it proved. In Hyderabad itself, indeed, there was little to fear, for Sir Sálár Jang had few followers amongst his own countrymen, by whom, *Asiatico more*, he was regarded with suspicion ; but not a few Englishmen of position sympathised with his aspirations, and, in particular, the late Duke of Sutherland, who had made Sir Sálár's acquaintance during his brief visit to India, Lord Napier of Ettrick, late Governor of Madras, the late Sir George Yule, formerly Resident of Hyderabad, and Sir Bartle Frere, late Governor of Bombay, were his outspoken supporters.

Their grounds of support, however, were diverse and conflicting, and their opinions, based on imperfect information of existing facts, were, however well meant, of little practical value—but their publication added greatly to the difficulties of the situation and the responsibilities of the Resident.

Under all the circumstances it was felt by Lord Northbrook's Government that the presence at Hyderabad of a British Resident of exceptional ability, who combined kindliness and matured experience with force of character and sound judgment, was all-important, and there was a consensus of opinion that the man for the hour was—Sir Richard Meade.

And thus two high officials, differing in character and nationality, but both eminent and patriotic, were brought into contact at an important crisis. On the one hand was an Oriental statesman of European reputation, fascinating in manner, plausible in argument, and described by the journals of the day as the "Talleyrand of India"; on the other, a British military officer, little known in England, but with wide political experience in India, courteous and kindly and singularly modest, but clear-headed, straightforward and firm as a rock, a faithful servant of the State and implicitly trusted by all who knew him.

CHAPTER XIX.

HYDERABAD (*continued*).

Arrival of Sir R. Meade—Letter from Lord Northbrook—Sir R. Meade's friendly relations with Sir Sálár Jang maintained throughout his career at Hyderabad—Lord Northbrook succeeded, as Viceroy, by Lord Lytton—Question of the Nizám's education—Difficulties raised by the Minister—Policy of the Government of India—Beneficial results of Sir R. Meade's insistence.

SIR RICHARD MEADE proceeded to Hyderabad early in December, 1875, and took charge from his predecessor, Mr. C. B. Saunders, at a railway station in Hyderabad territory, where their trains crossed. Soon after his arrival he received the following letter from the Viceroy:—

"GOVERNMENT HOUSE,
"CALCUTTA, *December* 30, 1875.

"MY DEAR SIR RICHARD,—When Sir Sálár Jang visited me to-day I took occasion to mention to him that I had received from Lord Salisbury a despatch conveying the decision of Her Majesty's Government against reopening the treaties under which we administer Berár. I said that the despatch would be communicated to him in due course. If you come to Calcutta I propose to defer sending you the despatch until I have had an opportunity of conversing with you on the subject.

"I then said that I wished to have no reticence with him

on the matter, speaking not as Viceroy but as a friend. I said I had studied the question carefully—that I could not accept the accuracy of the historical review of the relations between the Nizám and the British Government which he had sent in; on the contrary, that my reading of the history led me to the conclusion that, without the support of the British Government, the State of Hyderabad would not now exist.

"I said that I would not touch upon the negotiations which preceded the existing treaties. No permanence, I observed, could attach to any treaty engagements if the plain language of treaties was to be modified by reference to preliminary negotiations.

"The question therefore was to be considered in reference to the treaties only, that is to say, while the Nizám's Government might propose to reconsider the treaties, it rested with the British Government to agree or to disagree with the proposal.

"I could not believe that any Viceroy, or any Government at home, would consent to reopen the Berár treaties by themselves alone. Any negotiation of the kind must embrace the former treaties and the whole military status of the Hyderabad State, and that such a negotiation must be on the understanding that the protection of Hyderabad must rest with the British Government, and that no larger force than was necessary for the support of the dignity of the Nizám should be maintained by Hyderabad.

"I said that this view of mine was not taken in consequence of any doubt of the loyalty of Sir Sálár Jang, but that he knew from experience the danger of military forces in times of difficulty, whatever the sentiments of the Rulers might be.

"I repeated that these were my individual sentiments, such as I should express in the House of Lords if I was at home, and not the official views of the Government. Such matters were settled by the Home Government.

"I said that our wish was to support Sir Sálár Jang in all

his reforms, but that he must accept the decision of the Government when it was conveyed to him.

"Whether this conversation will be of any use or not I cannot pretend to say. At any rate I have opened my mind to him freely; and as I honestly believe the position I have taken in this case to be sound and right, I do not think any harm can come of my talk.

"No one was present at the time, and I have written down what took place immediately after while the matter was fresh in my memory.

"Yours very truly,

"NORTHBROOK."

Thus informed of the Viceroy's views respecting the most important of the questions with which he had to deal, Sir Richard Meade took measures to acquire a full and accurate knowledge of the state of affairs at Hyderabad, and made it his first duty to cultivate good and friendly relations with Sir Sálár Jang and to endeavour to obtain his confidence. And here it may be stated that, in spite of all that subsequently happened, Sir Richard Meade's relations with the Minister were always of a most friendly character. At times when the political relations between the two Governments were strained friendly social intercourse was always maintained between them, and even when differences threatened to be critical, the two statesmen would often enjoy a game of billiards together as if nothing had happened.

After a short interval, when Sir Richard was beginning to feel a firm footing in his new office, he received the unwelcome intelligence that Lord Northbrook had resigned the Viceroyship and that one of those changes so disastrous to the successful conduct of political affairs in India was about to take place.

A Viceroy thoroughly acquainted with the affairs of Hyderabad, who knew and had confidence in Sir Richard Meade, was to be succeeded by another, appointed by a different party in the State, and, though of acknowledged ability and diplomatic training, necessarily little conversant with Indian affairs. The circumstance added to the difficulty of Sir Richard Meade's position, but it did not in the slightest degree affect him in the discharge of his duties. However, he had no reason to complain of the change.

One of the first matters of importance which attracted the attention of the new Resident was the arrangement in force for the education and training of the young Nizám. The matter, obviously one of supreme interest, had received the attention of the Government of India immediately after the decease of the late Nizám in 1869.

The Government of India had, of course, no desire whatever to interfere with the religion of the young Chief, nor did it propose to exercise minute interference with his moral and intellectual training; but, as Paramount Power, it was deeply interested in seeing that the general scheme of his education was satisfactory, and properly carried out. For on the personal training of the young Nizám depended not only the cordiality of future relations between Hyderabad and the British Government, but, what was more important, the happiness of some 10,000,000 of people.

Many objections, some of them of the most puerile character, were raised by the Minister to the plan suggested by the Government of India, but it was ultimately arranged that when the young Prince attained the age of seven years his education should be placed under the supervision of an English gentleman, with whom also was to rest the selection of subordinate teachers. The "English gentleman" was to be appointed by the Minister, subject to the approval of the Government of India; and while offering to his pupil all the advantages of an English education, was not to neglect those studies which are specially necessary for an Indian Prince. With the religious training of his pupil he was to have no concern.

Accordingly, in 1873, at the suggestion of the Secretary of State for India, the matter was again pressed on the attention of Sir Sálár Jang. The Minister demurred and prayed for postponement on the ground that the young Nizám was physically unfit for sustained mental exertion, etc., etc., but at length, under pressure from the Government of India, he yielded, and on the suggestion of the Resident nominated the following officers: Sir George Yule, formerly Resident at Hyderabad; Colonel A. Thornhill, formerly Assistant Resident; Mr. J. G. Cordery, formerly Assistant Resident; Colonel Oliphant, and Colonel Meadows-Taylor, C.S.I., to be a committee for the purpose of selecting a suitable preceptor.

These gentlemen selected for the office Captain John Clerk, a son of the Rt. Hon. Sir George Clerk, formerly Governor of Bombay. He was thereupon appointed on a salary of £2400 per annum, and proceeded to Hyderabad at the end of January, 1875.

But, as pointed out by the Resident at the time, little good could be expected from tutors and teachers unless the young Nizám could be gradually transplanted into some more wholesome atmosphere than that which surrounded him, or, at any rate, be allowed free access to the Residency, to see something of the territories he was to govern and escape the life of morose and sensuous seclusion which had characterised the Nizáms of Hyderabad since the days of Sikandar Jáh. But this, unfortunately, could never be effected, and truth compels us to state that, in the matter of the Nizám of Hyderabad's education, the British Government did not receive that support and assistance from the Minister which his antecedents had led them to anticipate.

There was doubtless much to be said in explanation of his attitude. He naturally feared to excite the opposition of the Zenána, and it was perhaps too much to expect a Minister, who had been for years the virtual Ruler of the State, to exhibit much zeal in training his future Chief to take an independent and active share in the administration.

But early in 1876 Captain Clerk, having unfortunately lost his wife by cholera, had to proceed to England, and Sir Richard Meade was called upon to suggest arrangements for the future. He was constrained to report that the Prince's education up to the present time had been a mere farce. Not only was the access of the tutor so restricted that it was impossible for him to educate in the narrowest sense, much less to exercise any moral influence over his charge, but the Resident was practically excluded from all power of supervision; while even the Nizám's uncle and brothers-in-law and other near relatives were only allowed occasional and ceremonial intercourse with him.

In these circumstances, soon after the advent of Lord Lytton as Viceroy, Sir Richard addressed a letter to the Calcutta Foreign Office upon the subject, to which the following reply was received :—

"FOREIGN OFFICE, SIMLA, *May 5th*, 1876.

"MY DEAR SIR RICHARD MEADE,—The change of Viceroys and the journey to Simla have caused some delay in replying to your confidential letter of April 3rd regarding the education of the young Nizám ; I am now desired to forward for your information a *précis* of the correspondence which has taken place upon the subject. From this you will perceive that in the matter of the education of the young Nizám the policy of the Government has hitherto been not to interfere directly with his education, but to exercise a general supervision, and see that the arrangements made for the selection of an English gentleman as tutor and as to the scheme of education are on the whole satisfactory.

"In your letter under acknowledgment you desire that the scope of the Government's interference should be enlarged. You recommend, His Excellency understands :—

"(1) That the Resident be allowed free and unrestrained access to the Prince with a view to your exercising moral influence over him.

"(2) That the Resident be associated with the arrangements made for the Prince's education with a view to his supporting the authority of the tutor in exacting obedience from his pupil, and

"(3) That the Government should have a voice in the appointment of Captain Clerk's successor.

"With regard to these recommendations Lord Lytton concurs with you as respects the first, and he authorises your continuing to insist courteously, but firmly, upon having free and unrestrained access to the Nizám.

"With regard to the second recommendation, His Excellency desires me to say that if you will submit officially a practical scheme for giving effect to your proposal he will take it into careful consideration.

"With regard to the last recommendation, namely that the Government should have a voice in the selection and appointment of Captain Clerk's successor, hitherto all that the Government of India has insisted upon has been that the mode of selection shall be good and that the appointment shall be subject to the approval of the Government. With these safeguards against an injudicious choice the selection and appointment of a tutor have been left to the Ministers of the State. Having regard to this and looking to the whole history of the case, Lord Lytton does not think that the marked departure from previous policy in claiming for the British Government a voice in the appointment of Captain Clerk's successor would be expedient at the present time.

"I am,

"Dear Sir Richard Meade,

"Yours sincerely,

"T. H. THORNTON."

This letter is quoted *in extenso*, as evidence of the extreme anxiety of the Government of India to spare the feelings of the Minister and abstain so far as possible from all direct interference with his proceedings.

But in acknowledging the receipt of these instructions, and promising the submission hereafter of the scheme asked for by the Government of India, Sir Richard Meade observed :—

"I would rather withdraw altogether from any concern in the arrangements connected with the Nizám's education than be a party to a continuance of a system which will certainly bring most serious reproach hereafter on all who have had a voice in it".

Meanwhile, Sir Sálár Jang (as will be narrated in the next chapter) proceeded to England, and after his return other more absorbing matters occupied attention. The Resident, however, continued to press his point and was well supported by his superiors and by some of the Nizám's relatives. But great is the power of obstruction. Every movement in advance was resisted, and up to the time of Sir Richard's departure in 1881, no thoroughly satisfactory arrangements had been made for the training of the Hyderabad Prince. Still, though no drastic measures were adopted much good was done by the Resident's action in the matter. The training of the Nizám, though not all that could have been desired, was infinitely better than that of his predecessors and of many Indian Princes. For this however His Highness has to thank, not his late Minister, but the British Government and especially the kindly but firm insistence of its representative, Sir Richard Meade.

CHAPTER XX.

HYDERABAD (*continued*).

Sir Sálár Jang's visit to England—His courteous reception—Letters to Sir Richard Meade—Hopes and aspirations on returning.

EARLY in 1876 Sir Sálár Jang intimated to the Resident his intention of proceeding to England, in compliance, he said, with an express and urgent invitation from His Royal Highness the Prince of Wales, and added that he proposed, after spending a few weeks in England, to return by way of St. Petersburg, Berlin and Constantinople.

Sir Richard Meade had no desire to thwart Sir Sálár's wishes, but he felt it his duty to point out to the Minister that, as he was acting as co-Regent of Hyderabad, under the authority of the Government of India, it was incumbent upon him to obtain the approval of that authority before leaving his post, and its sanction to the arrangements proposed for carrying on the administration during his absence. He added, that as Sir Sálár Jang's colleague was old and infirm, while there were no officials of experience who could be trusted should times of difficulty arise, the present time, when both the Viceroy and his representative had but recently assumed office, was not very convenient for the visit.

Sir Sálár Jang, however, was persistent, partly from

a natural desire to visit England under favourable conditions, but mainly, no doubt, because he thought that his presence in England would secure the sympathy and influence of persons in position and possibly of the Press, in the prosecution of his claims for the restoration of Berár. Ultimately the Government of India consented; fairly satisfactory arrangements were made for the conduct of affairs during the Minister's absence, and, early in March, Sir Sálár Jang started, with a suite of fifty-two persons, and accompanied by Captain G. H. Trevor, second Assistant to the Resident, as political officer in attendance.

He was present at Bombay when the new Viceroy, Lord Lytton, landed, and their meeting was of a most friendly character.[1]

On the 8th of April Sir Sálár Jang sailed for Europe. He reached Rome on the 5th of May and was most graciously received by the King and Queen of Italy; he

[1] When at Paris, on his way to India, Lord Lytton was surprised to receive from Sir Sálár Jang a memorandum of confidential conversations and correspondence with the late Resident respecting Berár and other matters, together with copies of secret official documents, accompanied by comments of a most unfriendly character—a paper printed for circulation in England, apparently without the consent or knowledge of the person with whom the conversations had been held, or of the office to which the documents belonged. This was a breach of diplomatic propriety which could not be allowed to pass unnoticed. When, therefore, it came to the knowledge of Sir R. Meade, he courteously pointed out to the Minister that the proceeding (though, doubtless, due to ignorance) was a breach of confidence and would, if it was to be repeated, render all friendly discussion of pending questions difficult or impossible. Sir Sálár Jang was understood to promise that what had been complained of would never be repeated. But see footnote to page 303.

had an interview with the Pope, who thanked him for the friendly treatment accorded in the Nizám's territories to Roman Catholics, and on the 13th of May arrived at Paris. Here he met with a severe accident (by slipping on the stairs of his hotel) which resulted in a fractured thigh-bone and prevented the continuance of his journey until the end of May. His sufferings, as may be supposed, were intense, but he bore them with the greatest fortitude and, though terribly crippled, determined to proceed.

At Calais he was met by the political A.D.C. of the Secretary of State for India, and arrived in London in time to attend a grand reception given at the Foreign Office by the Prime Minister to the Prince and Princess of Wales.

As might have been expected, Sir Sálár was most courteously received. He was called upon by the Prince and other members of the royal family, by Lord Salisbury, Lord Northbrook, and many distinguished persons of all ranks; the Prince of Wales gave a banquet in his honour; he was presented to the Queen at Windsor, where he dined and slept; he was the guest of the Duke of Sutherland at Dunrobin; Oxford University conferred upon him the honorary degree of D.C.L., and on the 25th of July the freedom of the City of London was presented to him. Most persons regarded him as an Indian Prince, duchesses curtsied to the ground before him, and when he returned to India on the 24th of August, the crew of his steamer manned the yards and cheered.

The following letters from Sir Sálár Jang to Sir Richard Meade during the period of his visit, will perhaps be of interest partly as conveying the Minister's impression of what he saw in Europe and partly as showing how cordial were the relations between the Minister and the Resident at the time.

"ROME, *5th May*, 1876.

"MY DEAR SIR RICHARD MEADE,—I have great pleasure in telling you that I have made a very prosperous journey since I arrived at Naples, and I have been very much pleased with all I have seen. The Italian authorities gave me a most complimentary reception on landing at Naples, and during my stay there they showed me every possible courtesy; such kindness was very gratifying, more especially when it was quite unexpected.

"I was fortunate during my stay at Naples to meet the great General, Count von Moltke, and I felt it was a great privilege to meet and converse with him. At Naples I visited most of the places of interest, and saw a great deal of the beautiful surrounding country.

"I arrived here yesterday, and am very much struck with the beauties of this city—but my time is far too short to see a tenth of the beautiful buildings and interesting objects with which the place abounds. I was very much struck with the grandeur of St. Peter's.

"This morning I had the honour of being invited to a private audience with the King of Italy, and His Majesty was exceedingly courteous. To-morrow I am to have the privilege of meeting the Crown Prince and his beautiful Princess, and I have seen and received great kindness from H.M.'s Ambassador, Sir Augustus Paget, and I hope to see His Holiness the Pope before I leave. I intend staying at Florence, Venice, Milan and Turin *en route* to Paris and I hope to reach London about the 20th of this month. I am very much interested in all the novelties which daily come before me and I am very glad to have undertaken the journey. I am enjoying excellent health and not one of my suite has been sick.

"Trusting that you and Lady Meade are very well, and with my very kind regards,

"I am,

"Dear Sir Richard Meade,

"Yours very sincerely,

"SÁLÁR JANG."

"140 PICCADILLY, LONDON,
"*9th June*, 1876.

"MY DEAR SIR RICHARD MEADE,—I was very much pleased to receive your telegram soon after my arrival in London, and I am glad now to be able to confirm my reply which I sent you last week.

"Sir James Paget and Mr. Prescott Hewett come to see me every day, and consider that I am making very good progress, but they think that I shall be unable to walk for another fortnight. It is very disappointing to be so laid aside when there is so much going on in which I want to take a part; but I cannot help feeling that things are best as they are and there is nothing for me to do at present but practise patience. I was very glad to get to London, and away from the Paris hotel.

"I am sure you will be pleased to hear that the arrangements made by the Secretary of State for bringing me over from Boulogne was most convenient, and I travelled with the least possible fatigue.

"At Boulogne a very fine steamer, the *Alexandra*, was placed at my disposal by the British Government, and I was met there and conducted on board by Mr. FitzGerald of the India Office and by Mr. Shaw the manager of the S.E. Railway Company. A pavilion had been erected on deck for my special use, and I was able to enjoy the crossing. The Channel was very smooth, and we reached Folkestone under two hours. At Folkestone I was received in a way I did not at all expect. The Mayor and Corporation and crowds of well-dressed people came down to the landing-place, and I was carried on shore amidst shouts and hurrahs and firing salutes. Of course it was rather mortifying that I could not walk, but I made the best of things. The Town Clerk read an address from the Mayor, Aldermen and Burgesses, welcoming me to England, and I read my reply. Immediately after this I was introduced to the old Marquis of Tweeddale, and then accompanied by the Duke of Sutherland, and attended by all my suite and several friends who had come to meet me, I started in a special train, provided by Government, for London. At Charing Cross several of my old friends met me, and here again I was lifted out of the train into the Duke's carriage, and His Grace very kindly brought me to my house. You will understand how glad I was to get into my own house and to be at rest after a very tiring day. I like my house very much, the situation is excellent—so cheerful—and in fact everything is full of interest and delight and there is only one drawback to everything—my leg!

"Since my arrival here I have received a great deal of kindness and attention. Her Majesty, the Prince of Wales, and several people among the nobility and gentry have been most kind in their inquiries, and I have had over 100 visitors. No one could have been kinder and more attentive than Lord Northbrook. He lives nearly opposite to me, and has been in two or three times and comes again to-morrow. This attention on the part of Lord Northbrook is very gratifying to me.

"You will be pleased to hear that I have seen your old friend Sir William Hill—Lady Hill also kindly came to see me. They are both very well.

"I am engaged to dine with the Prince of Wales on the 20th, with the Duke of Sutherland on the 22nd and Mr. Disraeli on the 24th, and on the 21st the Hebdomadal Council of the University of Oxford have invited me to Oxford to receive the Honorary Degree of D.C.L. I have accepted with real feelings of pride (but at the same time with sincere misgivings as to my fitness) such a high distinction, but I am not quite sure yet that I shall be able to be present at Oxford on the Commemoration Day.

"The Athenæum and the Travellers' Clubs have made me an honorary member, and every one appears to be anxious to help in making my stay in England agreeable. I have had invitations to visit several of the provincial and manufacturing towns, but I am not able at present to make any engagements to pay visits. I must first get well, and then see how my time goes—for agreeable as everything is, I feel that I have duties at Hyderabad which must receive my first consideration.

"Mr. FitzGerald of the India Office, appointed by the Secretary of State to show me civility, is most kind and obliging, and I have received an exceedingly kind note from Lord Salisbury, who has been out of town since my arrival.

"With my kindest regards to Lady Meade and yourself,

"Yours, etc.,

"SÁLÁR JANG."

"140 PICCADILLY,
"*23rd June*, 1876.

"MY DEAR SIR RICHARD MEADE,—I have to thank you for a very kind letter dated 26th May, and which I received on the 19th instant. I am very much obliged for your kind inquiries and expressions of regret at my unfortunate accident, and I am glad to be able to tell you that I am now making good progress.

"I have been enjoying several entertainments lately. Firstly, the dinner given to me by Their Royal Highnesses the Prince and Princess of Wales,—here I had a most pleasant evening, and I was especially struck with the beauty of the Princess and her exceeding charm of grace and dignity of manner.

"Yesterday I dined with the Duke and Duchess of Sutherland at their magnificent mansion. At dinner I met many of the leading men of the day, and in the evening the Duchess received some 400 of the nobility and gentry. I was present too yesterday at the Horse Show, which I enjoyed.

"I shall have a great deal to tell you on my return, and meanwhile with my kindest regards to Lady Meade and yourself and hoping you are both quite well,

"I am, etc.,

"SÁLÁR JANG."

"140 PICCADILLY,
"*7th July*, 1876.

"MY DEAR SIR RICHARD MEADE,—I am happy to inform you that I am sufficiently recovered now to be able to go about in a carriage, although I am not yet able to get on my legs and walk.

"You will no doubt be glad to hear that I have had the honour of being presented to the Queen at Windsor. Her Majesty was extremely kind and gracious to me. I had the honour of dining with her by command and of sitting next to her at table. The Park at Windsor, which, by Her Majesty's gracious kindness, I was able to drive through, is the best I have ever seen.

"I have been to several parties here, and His Royal Highness the Prince of Wales did me the honour of dining with me on Thursday evening.

"I have been to Woolwich and to Greenwich. The Arsenal at Woolwich is I think one of the greatest wonders of Europe. It is astonishing what enormous power of destruction the inventive genius of Englishmen has imparted to their weapons of offence.

"At Greenwich I had the honour of entertaining the Duke of Sutherland and other gentlemen to a fish dinner. The Trafalgar I think fully bears out its reputation for choice cookery.

"I have also had the opportunity of seeing some of the finest mansions in London—I mean Stafford House, and a mansion belonging to Mr. Halford and known as Dorchester House. Both are magnificent in their way, and full of rare gems of Art. There is nothing in the East, certainly nothing in India, to compare with these. I have also been to see Sir Patrick Grant at Chelsea.

"I am leaving London now for Trentham, whence I proceed to Dunrobin, Edinburgh and a few other places in the North. I shall return to town by the 20th.

"With kind regards to yourself and Lady Meade,

"I am, etc.,

"SÁLÁR JANG."

"140 PICCADILLY, LONDON,
"*21st July*, 1876.

"MY DEAR SIR RICHARD MEADE,—I am much obliged to you for your kind letter of the 14th June, and thank you for all your good wishes, and beg you will convey to Lady Meade my kind regards and best thanks for her good wishes.

"I am very pleased to hear the good account you give of the Nizám, and thank you for your kind mention of my sons, —but your allusion to my nephew and your remarks about his conduct are most especially gratifying to me. I am happy to tell you that on more than two or three occasions my nephew has written to me at great length about your very kind behaviour towards him—your kindliness of manners and anxious desire to assist him and your admirable advice to him altogether create such a debt of gratitude on my part to you that I feel I shall never be able to repay it. The fact of your kindness having been so marked during my absence from my post, and the knowledge that you entertain towards myself no ordinary feelings of friendship, lead me to believe that on my return you will continue towards me your very valuable friendship and kindly advice, and I feel convinced that the Nizám's State will greatly benefit by your counsel and by the way in which you discharge the duties of your high office; and I pray that you may long be spared to fill such an important post.

"I returned from Scotland on the 18th, having very much enjoyed my visit to Trentham and Dunrobin. I must leave until we meet giving you details of all that I have seen and done. For the next few days I have made engagements for almost every hour of every day—on Monday I go to Oxford, on Tuesday to the City, on Wednesday I receive deputations from Manchester, on Thursday I go to Goodwood Races, on Friday I have a party at Richmond, and I intend leaving London on the 31st, Paris on the 3rd, Milan on the 5th and Brindisi on the 7th, and I trust to be with you at Hyderabad on or about the 26th of August.

"With my very kind regards to Lady Meade and yourself, and hoping that I shall find you both in good health on my return,

"I am, etc.,

"SÁLÁR JANG."

"140 PICCADILLY, W.,
"*27th July*, 1876.

"MY DEAR SIR RICHARD MEADE,—I was very glad to receive your kind letter of 28th June, and I just write these few lines to tell you that I hope to have the pleasure of seeing you in a few days after you receive this letter.

"I am very much gratified to hear your reiterated expressions of approval of my nephew's management of affairs, and I am exceedingly thankful that he should have such an adviser as yourself to consult with.

"I have been doing a great deal this last week, but I am not at all knocked up.

"I shall have a great deal to tell you on my arrival, and I look forward with real pleasure to seeing you again.

"With my kindest regards to Lady Meade and yourself,

"I am,
"Dear Sir Richard Meade,
"Yours sincerely,

"SÁLÁR JANG."

"*P.S.*—I am very glad to tell Lady Meade that I have had the pleasure of seeing her uncle, Sir G. Malcolm, and Colonel Malcolm, and they were most kind and agreeable; and I am sure you will be glad to hear that I have had the honour of private interviews with several of the Cabinet Ministers this last week: with Lord Salisbury, Lord Derby and Mr. Disraeli. It is most interesting to have had the opportunity of talking to such leading men. To-morrow I am going to Osborne by Her Majesty's command to pay my respects on leaving England. Everybody has been most kind in their endeavours to make my visit agreeable, and no one more so than Her Majesty, the Prince of Wales and the Duke of Sutherland and Lord Elcho.

"I must close this now, as I have a good many things to do so near my departure; and again sending you my best regards,

"I am, etc.,

"SÁLÁR JANG."

Though Sir Sálár Jang had received no official encouragement in England, yet his reception had been so friendly that he returned more than ever intent upon the great object of his life and full of hope of ultimate success.

In a letter to Lord Northbrook, he says :—

"It appears to me that there are three courses before me : either I must recover Berár, or I must be convinced of the justice of the reasons for withholding it, or—I must die".

And, owing, probably, to the injudicious advice of English friends, he was more than ever determined to assert, on behalf of the Nizám, the independence of Hyderabad and question the suzerainty of the British Government.

Lord Lytton considered—and justly considered—the proceeding to be unfriendly and inopportune. Correspondence followed, in the course of which it was intimated that the presence of the Hyderabad Minister at the Imperial Assemblage could not be permitted, except on the understanding that the suzerainty of the Queen-Empress was unquestioned.

The Minister and his charge proceeded to Dehli.

After their arrival frank and friendly discussions took place between the Resident, acting under the immediate instructions of the Viceroy, and Sir Sálár Jang; discussions conducted on both sides with perfect courtesy,[1] and ultimately, through the influence and good offices of Sir Richard Meade, it was arranged that the Minister, on his part, should unreservedly withdraw the imputations on the good faith of the British Government contained in the first memorial, and that on this understanding a second memorial on the Berár question, if couched in temperate and friendly language, would be received and considered by the Government of India, *after* the conclusion of the Imperial Assemblage.

And thus—through the tact and judgment of the subject of this memoir—a regrettable incident, which seemed likely at one time to mar the success of the

[1] Without Meade's consent or knowledge Sir Sálár Jang sent printed copies of his version of these confidential discussions—a version inaccurate on material points—together with copies of demi-official notes which had passed between himself and Sir R. Meade, to friends in London, by whom they were shown to influential persons. This second breach of diplomatic confidence by the Hyderabad Minister is referred to not *per invidiam*, but to show the difficulties of Meade's position.

Assemblage, was, for the time being, satisfactorily closed.

Meanwhile the politico-social work of the Imperial Assemblage fortnight went on apace, to the great delight of the young Nizám.

He was present at the reception of the Viceroy at the railway station; and the next day paid a state visit to His Excellency and was formally presented by him with a silken banner and invested with the gold commemorative medal. The ceremony was as follows:—

The banner, richly blazoned with the armorial bearings of the Nizám and surmounted with the imperial crown, was brought in by Highland soldiers and planted in front of the throne. The Viceroy descended from the daïs and advancing with the young Chief towards the banner said:—

"I present Your Highness with this banner, on which are blazoned the armorial bearings of your family, as a personal gift from Her Majesty the Queen in commemoration of her assumption of the title of Empress of India.

"Her Majesty trusts that it may never be unfurled without reminding you, not only of the close union between the throne of England and your loyal and princely house, but also of the earnest desire of the Paramount Power to see your dynasty strong, prosperous, and permanent."

His Lordship then placed round the Chief's neck a crimson ribbon, from which was suspended the gold medal bearing a portrait of Her Majesty, and addressed the Chief with these words:—

"I further decorate you, by command of the Queen and Empress, with this medal. May it be long worn by yourself and long kept as an heirloom by your family, in remembrance of the auspicious date it bears."

The visit was returned in due course and all went off well.[1]

During the time devoted to receiving and returning the visits of the Chiefs—a function which occupied the Viceroy nine hours daily for upwards of a week—there were banquets and receptions and entertainments of every kind, and for those who had leisure there was the great city of Dehli itself, a place of special interest to the Nizám. He was the first of his dynasty who had visited Dehli since the invasion of Nádir Shah, when Ásaf Jáh, the founder of his house, witnessed the great massacre and is said to have prevailed upon the conqueror to stop the carnage.

[1] Including visits and return visits of Chiefs and receptions of distinguished persons and deputations, the Viceroy had to give more than 120 audiences. As every word falling from the lips of a Viceroy on these occasions is of political importance, it was necessary to consider beforehand carefully the topics of every official conversation and the language to be used at them.

It thus fell to the lot of the present writer to draft the heads of upwards of seventy of these conversations. These drafts were printed on slips of paper and prefixed with a brief account of the Chief to whom they referred. During the interval elapsing between the exit of one Prince and the arrival of another, the slip relating to the new-comer was handed to Lord Lytton, who mastered its contents with marvellous rapidity; and, on the new arrival taking his seat, was prepared with appropriate subjects of remark. Each Chief went away full of wonder at the Viceroy, who seemed to know everything of everybody and take the deepest interest in the affairs of every State, regarding each of which he made the most pertinent inquiries.

Then came the great day of the proclamation, a day never to be forgotten by those present and especially by those privileged to view the scene from the Viceregal daïs.

Ranged in a vast semicircle in front of the throne —blazing with jewellery and clad in the colours of the rainbow—were all the principal Ruling Chiefs and the flower of the nobility of India, interspersed with the Governors, Lieutenant-Governors and Chief Commissioners of provinces and other high officials, in diplomatic or military garb; in front of each Ruling Chief and Governor was the Imperial Banner, and in rear of each Chief a brilliant suite.

Of the Ruling Chiefs no less than sixty-three were present. Besides the three great Feudatories of the Crown—that is to say, the Nizám of Hyderabad, the Mahárája of Mysore and the Gaekwar of Baroda— there were the Mahárája of Jammú and Kashmir (Warden of the Northern Marches), and the Chiefs of the Punjab—Sikh, Rájput and Mussulman; the Mahárána of Udaipur (of celestial origin), the Mahárájas of Jeypore and Jodhpur, and all the best blood of Rájputána; the Marátha Princes of Gwalior and Indore, the Afghán Queen of Bhopál, and other Chiefs (Marátha and Rájput) of Central India, and a train of minor chiefs from Kathiawár, the Bombay littoral and Sindh; from the region of the Upper Ganges—miscalled the North-West Provinces—the Central Provinces and Bengal.

The aggregate populations under the direct rule of the Chiefs present at Dehli approached 40,000,000; while their united territories exceeded the combined areas of England, Italy and France. And, it may be added, of the Chiefs who attended a considerable number—including five of the most powerful among them—had been, at some time or other, under the official control and influence of Meade.

The titular Chiefs and native gentlemen attending (exclusive of members of the suites of Ruling Chiefs) were nearly 300 in number, comprising the flower of the Indian nobility and persons of distinction from almost every province of the Empire. Among them were the Prince of Arcot and the Princess of Tanjore, from the Madras Presidency; the Mahárája Sir Jai Mangal Singh, and some of the principal landowners and citizens of Bengal; the Mahárája of Balrampur and the principal Talúkdárs of Oudh; forty representatives of the most distinguished families of the North-Western Provinces; scions of the ex-royal family of Dehli; descendants of the Saddozais of Kábul, and the Alora Chiefs of Sindh; Sikh Sardárs from Amritsar and Lahore; Rájputs from the Kangra Hills; the semi-independent Chief of Amb on the Hazára border; envoys from Chitrál and Yassín, who attended in the train of the Mahárája of Jammú and Kashmír; Arbábs from Peshawur; Patán Chiefs from Kohát and the Deráját; Bilúch Tomandárs from Dera Gházi Khan; leading citizens from Bombay; Gond and Marátha nobles from the Central Provinces; Rájputs from Ajmere; and natives of Burmah, Central India, Mysore and Baroda.

In addition to the Feudatories and nobles of the Empire, His Excellency the Governor-General of the Portuguese Settlements in India; the Khan of Khelát; a deputation from the Sultán of Muscát; ambassadors from His Majesty the King of Siam; and the Mahárája Adhiráj of Nepál; the envoy from the Amír of Káshgar; the Foreign Consular Body; and a large concourse of English and Indian officials and visitors—were present as spectators. "No Empire but that of England," says an officer who was present, "could have drawn together such an assemblage, no country but India could have produced such a scene."[1]

In the centre of the vast semicircle—extending from end to end about 800 feet—sat the young Nizám and by his side Sir Richard Meade. Close by, but slightly in the rear, sat the faithful Minister, supported by the nobles and high officials of the State in brilliant costumes. In rear of the semicircle were lines of elephants with gold trappings, state carriages and throngs of liveried retainers, and beyond them a vast cordon of British troops supported by the troops of Feudatories.

At noon a flourish of trumpets from six heralds announced the arrival of the Viceroy.

Then the Queen's proclamation was read in sonorous tones by the Chief Herald and thereafter a translation in the Úrdú language was read out to the assembled Chiefs by the Foreign Secretary.

At its conclusion the Royal Standard was hoisted in honour of Her Majesty the Empress, and a grand salute of 101 salvoes of artillery was fired, interspersed at intervals with *feux-de-joie* from the combined lines of British and Native infantry; while massed bands played the National Anthem, followed by the stirring strains of the March in "Tannhäuser".

"The scene at this moment," wrote an eye-witness, "was very unique. The splendid semicircle of Princes,

[1] Sir Owen Burne, *Asiatic Quarterly Review* for January, 1887.

the vast expanse of troops, brilliant retinues, state elephants and crowds on crowds of human beings shading off into the distance; the strains of music sounding above the roar of the artillery and the reverberations of the *feux-de-joie*, combined to produce an effect never to be forgotten by those present."

As the end of the last salvo died away the Viceroy delivered an address, explaining the intentions of Her Gracious Majesty in assuming the new title :—

The Queen, regarding India as a glorious inheritance, recognised in its possession a solemn obligation to use her vast power for the welfare of its people with "scrupulous regard for the rights of her Feudatory Princes".

And he claimed as a distinctive feature of the present, as contrasted with past *régimes*, the maintenance of order, justice and perfect religious toleration.

In this connection he paid tribute to the work of the "Administrators and faithful servants of the Crown"; to the co-operation of non-official European subjects; to the services of officers and men of the British Army, European and native, and of the Volunteers.

He gave a hearty greeting to the "Princes and Chiefs of the Empire" and the "Allies and Feudatories of the British Government".

As for the native subjects of the Empress, he recognised their claim to share largely in the administration of their country.

" It is on the gradual and enlightened participation of her Indian subjects in the undisturbed exercise of mild and just authority, and not upon the conquest of weaker States or the annexation of neighbouring territories, that Her Majesty relies for the development of her Indian Empire."

His Excellency concluded by reading a telegraphic message of greeting received that morning from the Queen, which ran as follows :—

"WE, VICTORIA BY THE GRACE OF GOD, of the United Kingdom, Queen, Empress of India, send through our Viceroy, to all our Officers, Civil and Military, and to all Princes, Chiefs and Peoples now at Delhi assembled, our Royal and Imperial Greeting, and assure them of the deep interest and earnest affection with which we regard the people of the Indian Empire. We witnessed with heartfelt satisfaction the reception which they have accorded to our beloved son, and have been touched by the evidence of their loyalty and attachment to our House and Throne. We trust that the present occasion may tend to unite in bonds of yet closer affection ourselves and our subjects; that from the highest to the humblest all may feel that under our Rule the great principles of liberty, equity and justice are secured to them; and that to promote their happiness, and to add to their prosperity, and advance their welfare, are the ever present aims and objects of our Empire."

At the conclusion of the message all present spontaneously rose and joined the troops in hearty cheers.

Then Sindhia the Marátha rose and said :—

"Shah-in-Shah, Pádshah,—may God bless you! The Princes of India bless you and pray that your sovereignty (hukúmat)[1] and power may remain steadfast for ever."

Then in a transport of delight, the Afghán Lady of Bhopál — breaking for a moment the bonds of

[1] This word implies the power of giving absolute orders which must be obeyed.

Eastern etiquette—uttered a few words of hearty response to the royal greeting.

The Mahárájas of Udaipur and Jaipur desired, in the name of the United Chiefs in Rájputána, that a telegram might be sent to the Queen offering their dutiful and loyal congratulations to Her Majesty on her assumption of the Imperial Title.

The Mahárája of Kashmír expressed to the Lieutenant-Governor of the Punjab, who was sitting near him, his great satisfaction at the tenor of the Viceroy's speech, adding, that the day would never be forgotten by him or his children; that it would ever be regarded as an auspicious one, and that "the shadow of Her Majesty's great Empire would be for ever his great protection".

A slight pause followed, in expectation of some words from the principal Muhammadan Potentate present, the Nizám of Hyderabad, or his Representative. For a moment there was ominous silence, but, at length, under pressure from the nobles and ultimately from the young Nizám himself, Sir Sálár Jang rose and spoke as follows:—

"I am desired by the Nizám to request Your Excellency to convey to Her Majesty, on the part of himself and the Chiefs of India, the expression of their hearty congratulations upon her assumption of the title of Empress of India, and to assure her that they pray for her long life and for the enduring prosperity of her Empire both in India and England".

At the conclusion of Sir Sálár Jang's speech, the Viceroy bowed and left the daïs, with the same ceremonies as were observed on his arrival.

A state banquet and brilliant reception afterwards concluded the day's proceedings.

The three days succeeding the day of the proclamation were occupied by the Viceroy in receiving and replying to loyal addresses from municipal committees and other public bodies; in receiving farewell visits of ceremony from the Chiefs, ambassadors and noblemen present in camp and in the transaction of important official business.

But the round of entertainments still went on; there were polo matches, athletic contests, native dances, and one evening a grand display of fireworks under the direction of the master of pyrotechny, Mr. Brock, of Crystal Palace fame, who came out expressly from England for the purpose.

But perhaps the most interesting of the minor spectacles was that of the races—when all the chivalry of India were assembled on the platform of the grand stand to witness the contest for the Imperial *grand prix*.

On a settee in the centre of the stand sat the three boy Chiefs, in the middle the young Nizám and on either side the Chief of Mysore and the newly appointed Gaekwar of Baroda, all of them *protégés* of Sir Richard Meade. Holkar was there, with a good word and an embrace for every one;[1] and Sindhia, looking stern and

[1] With a sly reference to the Berár question Holkar observed to the present writer: "There are some matters open to dispute, but there is one on which no dispute is possible, namely, that the Foreign Secretary must have a *lohá ka mizáj* (an iron constitution)".

weary—he was suffering from a mortal illness—but true as steel. And the Rájput Chiefs were in great force; and there too was the Mahárája of Kashmír with fine lineaments betokening a Rájput origin, and a plume of black heron's feathers in his turban. The Sikh Chiefs of Jhind and Nabha were well in evidence, and Náhun from the Simla hills and Bháwalpur with an ancestral headgear of immense proportions. And Sir Sálár Jang, of course, was present, intently watching each gesture of his charge. He complained that the young Nizám was being crowded, but as the crowd consisted of Princes of the highest rank, and the Nizám himself was supremely happy, it was difficult to see what could be done.

But meanwhile the great event commenced; a good start was effected and after an exciting race the Imperial Cup was won brilliantly by the horse of the Prince of Jodhpur, close pressed by that of Lord William Beresford, amid the enthusiastic plaudits of the crowd. The news was received by the owner with true Rájput nonchalance, but, no doubt, with intense pleasure.

But all good things must have an end, and on the 5th of January the proceedings of the Imperial Assemblage were terminated by a grand military display, when 14,000 of the troops of the three Presidencies, under the Commander-in-Chief in India, passed in review order before the Viceroy, followed by the troops and retinues of the native Ruling Chiefs. At sunset a salute of 101 guns from the Flag Staff Tower in the vicinity of the Viceregal camp, formally closed the proceedings, and at 11 P.M. the Viceroy, having bade a hearty farewell to all the Chiefs, left by train for Patiála, the capital of the most important of the Sikh States, to place on the throne the young son and successor of the late Chief; and meanwhile the Chiefs and Governors and high officials and visitors departed by rail or road to the four corners of the Empire.

And in the course of a few hours all was changed.

The great canvas city overlooking the broad plains of the Jamna (westward of the "Ridge,") with its waving standard, wide avenues, and pacing sentries; the groups of encampments, large and small, stretching as far as the eye could reach to the west and north and south; the lines on lines of picketed horses, and rows on rows of crouching camels—had disappeared as if by magic; the troops had marched; the elephants with their coloured trunks, burnished headpieces and gold and silver trappings, the state carriages, the gay throngs of retainers had gone. The sound of the great gong, which proclaimed the hour and half-hour in the Viceregal Camp and was heard around for miles, had ceased; the everlasting fanfare of trumpets, and neighing of steeds, and recurring boom of artillery salutes were no longer heard, and an array of empty pavilions, a dismantled race-course, a débris of innumerable biscuit-tins and provision-cases, and a few gurgling camels receiving the last loads were all that physically remained of the Great Imperial Assemblage of 1877.

But it was immediately followed by a great physical blessing—a deluge of rain; which completed the desolation of the scene, but saved the spring crops of Upper India for the benefit of the famine-stricken peasants of the South.

And its political results have been important.

Our Feudatories have been led to feel that they are no longer isolated communities, but part of a great Empire.

Many of them have established Imperial Service Corps, some of which have already done brilliant service in campaigns; others have constructed railway feeders connecting their territories with the imperial system; others (notably Hyderabad) have expended large sums in the advancement of scientific research.

While throughout the length and breadth of India the "Empress Day" is regarded as the great day of the year, ushered in by a shower of honours for services to the State, to Science, or Humanity, and enlivened by salutes, parades of troops, durbars and other appropriate festivities.

APPENDIX TO CHAPTER XXI.

NOTE ON THE ARRANGEMENT OF THE IMPERIAL ASSEMBLAGE.

THE organisation and arrangement of the Assemblage was a work involving not only much thought and labour, but very delicate handling; for the gathering together at one place of Feudatories and Chiefs from all parts of the Indian Peninsula was a proceeding as novel as it was important, and promised to be full of difficulties.

In India most of the political experts were opposed to the idea, and predicted that questions of precedence and slumbering claims of various kinds would infallibly arise, and heart-burnings and umbrage and even more serious difficulties ensue.

But it was decided by the Government that these difficulties must be faced, and the Foreign Office was called upon to do its best to meet them.

And to assist the Foreign Department in its task, and in making the necessary military and administrative arrangements, a consultative Committee of the following officers was appointed by Lord Lytton:—

Major-General (now F. M. Lord) Roberts, Q.M.G. of the Army;

Colonel (now Major-General Sir Owen) Burne, Private Secretary to the Viceroy;

Colonel (afterwards Sir George) Colley, Military Secretary to the Viceroy;

Major (now Colonel Sir Edward) Bradford of the Political Department,

with the present writer, then Acting Foreign Secretary, as President.

The Committee sat constantly for weeks, and were assisted by several experts, and amongst them Sir L. Pelly, Mr. F. Henvey of the Foreign Office, and SIR RICHARD MEADE, whose advice was of the greatest value; and the proceedings and orders passed filled a large volume.

The great precedence question was settled in a very simple and effectual manner. It was decided to have the Chiefs arranged, so far as possible, geographically, and in a vast semicircle, so as to be all equidistant from the throne. On the geographical principle, the Mahárája of Kashmír and the Punjab Chiefs (the most northern of our Feudatories) had their place on the extreme left of the semicircle (looking from the daïs), the Nizám was in the centre, and the Mysore Chief (the most southern) on the extreme right. This arrangement was quite in accordance with Indian ideas, for in almost every Indian language the word for "south" has also the meaning of "right-hand". These points having been settled, the remaining Chiefs were arranged in groups to the right or left of the Nizám with reference to the geographical position of the Province or Agency to which they were attached.

This solution of the difficulty gave complete satisfaction. There were other difficulties—one, in the case of Hyderabad, of a very grave nature—but none on the score of disputed precedence or position. And the other difficulties were, by tact and firmness, overcome, and at length all the great Feudatories and Chiefs of India agreed to attend, and were present on the appointed day.

But there were innumerable minor questions to be settled; indeed, from the time the invitations were issued until the day of Proclamation, there was a stream of references from all parts of India, which had to be dealt with promptly and judiciously.

Then the arrangements for the journeys of the Chiefs and their retinues, the allotment of their respective camping-grounds, supplying good food, maintaining order and enforcing sanitary arrangements in the vast concourse brought together, were a task which involved much forethought and correspondence; and the Committee had further to arrange for the reception of the Khan of Khelát, a quasi-independent Prince, the Portuguese Governor of Goa and his suite, and a large number of Foreign Consuls—and to keep them all in good-humour—a task not always easy.

But, thanks to the hearty co-operation of the political and administrative officers throughout India, all ended well.

The Committee, however, did not confine their action to organising the Assemblage. They made a series of recommendations for giving *éclat* and practical value to the great event, many of which were embodied in a despatch to the Secretary of State for India and for the most part approved of by Her Majesty's Government.

Inter alia the Committee recommended—(1) The establishment of a consultative "Council of the Empire," composed of selected Feudatories of the Crown, for discussion of questions of Imperial concern, such as coinage, postal arrangements, customs, and arrangements for Imperial defence.

This was approved and certain distinguished Princes were appointed "Councillors of the Empress," but, owing to vastness of distances in India and the unwillingness of chiefs to dispense with retinues and ceremonial and various other causes, the Council has never met.

(2) The grant of honorary rank in the British Army to chiefs whose military position or achievements entitle them to the distinction. This has been carried into effect.

(3) The preparation of a *libro d'oro*, or official register of titles, with a view of enhancing the value of existing titles and checking their unauthorised assumption—a proceeding which is going on, at a rapid pace, throughout India. This was not approved of, but is more than ever needed.

(4) The institution of the Order of the Indian Empire, as a means of recognising more fully and freely than heretofore services of every description rendered in the public interest to the Empress and peoples of India. The Order has been instituted; and that its institution has been considered beneficial may be inferred from the fact that it has since been greatly developed and enlarged.

CHAPTER XXII.

HYDERABAD (*continued*).

Second memorial for restoration of Berár—Railway loan—Minister's attempt to raise it secretly and on improvident terms prevented by Sir Richard Meade—Secret manufacture of arms of precision and reorganisation of the troops brought to notice by Resident and put a stop to—The co-Regent question—Sir Sálár Jang on death of Amír-i-Kabír determines to have no colleague—Government of India insist upon appointing a co-administrator—Difficulties regarding choice of a successor, as the person with best claims was disliked by Sir Sálár Jang—Views of Sir Richard Meade and Lord Lytton—Government of India after full consideration decide to appoint the Vikar-ul-Umra, brother of the late co-Regent—Sir Sálár Jang protests—Threatened resignation—Makes overtures—Declines to accept Nawáb as colleague and refuses to resign—Decided action of the Viceroy—Sir Sálár Jang yields—Instalment of the new co-administrator in special Durbar described—Despatch of the Government of India—Thanks and congratulations conveyed to Sir Richard Meade—Letter from Lord Northbrook—Working of the new arrangement—Attacks by the press upon the Nawáb—His death—His son, Ikbál-ud-Daulah, now Prime Minister in Hyderabad—Final decision of the Berár Question—Accepted by Sir Sálár Jang and colleague—Congratulations from the Viceroy and Lord Northbrook—Result beneficial both to the British Government and to the Hyderabad State.

THE second memorial regarding the restoration of Berár to the direct administration of the Nizám's Government was duly presented in May, 1877.

It contained the same arguments as that first presented, but all expressions imputing bad faith and other inappropriate observations were carefully eliminated;

and the contentions were further supported by a large number of quotations from the utterances and writings of ex-Residents and other persons of position and experience.

Like the memorial originally presented, it was dispassionately considered by the Government of India and transmitted to the Secretary of State for final orders.

But, meanwhile, other events occurred which required serious attention and energetic treatment :—

RAILWAY LOAN.

So far back as April, 1876, it came to the knowledge of the Resident that Sir Sálár Jang, before leaving Bombay for England, had entered into secret negotiations with a view of raising in London a loan of £1,000,000 sterling. The loan was nominally for the extension of railway communication in Hyderabad, and, to evade the provisions of the Acts of the British Legislature which prohibit the loan of money by British subjects to Indian Princes without the sanction of the Secretary of State in Council, or the Government of India, it was arranged that the loan was to be raised in the name of a firm of bankers in Hyderabad, to whom Sir Sálár Jang proposed to give a guarantee.

The raising of money in England for railway extension in Hyderabad, if done in accordance with statutory requirements, is, of course, a perfectly legitimate operation ; the object was good, and Sir Richard Meade was the last person in the world to place unnecessary obstacles in the way of its attainment ; but the manner in which it was proposed to raise the loan was irregular ; the terms extravagant, and there was no guarantee that the money, when received, would be spent upon the object for which it was nominally borrowed.

He at once, at a personal interview, explained to Sir Sálár Jang the objections to the proceeding, and at length obtained an assurance from the latter that he would make no further attempt to raise money in England for State purposes without the knowledge and approval of the British Government.

On the Minister's return from England he pressed for sanction to his proceeding with the loan project. The Government of India, though favourable to railway extension in Hyderabad, did not see their way at the time to recommend the particular proposal to the Secretary of State; but they offered to advance funds for the construction of the line on terms more favourable than it would have been possible for Hyderabad to obtain in London; or themselves to construct the line for the Hyderabad State, the latter paying interest, at a low rate, on the amount expended—the line when constructed to be the property of Hyderabad.

These offers did not satisfy Sir Sálár Jang and were declined. Ultimately, with the sanction of the Secretary of State, the capital was obtained in England through a company (the Nizám's State Railway Company) on terms and conditions less favourable indeed than those offered by the Government of India, but far more favourable to Hyderabad than those obtainable in Sir Sálár Jang's first scheme.

For this beneficial result Hyderabad has to thank the vigilance and wisdom of Sir Richard Meade. For there can be no doubt that, if left to himself, the Minister (whatever may have been his real object in the matter) would have entered, directly or indirectly, into transactions with London financiers without the salutary supervision of the India Office. These transactions, conducted, as they would have been, secretly and without sound advice, besides being pecuniarily disastrous to the State, would have been a source of endless embarrassment and difficulty to the Government of the Nizám.

Years afterwards—such is the irony of fate—at the special request of the Nizám's Government, Sir Richard Meade himself was invited to become chairman of the company, and held that office until death.

SECRET MANUFACTURE OF ARMS.

Another matter of importance dealt with during the same summer was the discovery of the secret manufacture in Hyderabad of large quantities of arms, of preparations for the manufacture of breech-loading guns and the unauthorised reorganisation of the Nizám's army, including the Arab levies. That the proceedings were discovered and quietly checked before harm had been done and efficient measures taken to prevent their repetition is another debt due to the vigilance and practical statesmanship of Sir Richard Meade. But the details are of too confidential a character for publication, so we proceed to another matter of importance which caused Sir Richard Meade and the Government of India much trouble and anxiety, and no small public stir at the time.

THE CO-REGENT QUESTION.

At the beginning of April, 1877, Sir Sálár Jang's colleague in the administration—the Amír-i-Kabír—died. He had long been ailing, and, though a loyal representative of the interests of the Nizám as well as a friend to the British Government, he had latterly been more or less a nonentity in matters of policy and practical government.

On his decease, Sir Sálár Jang intimated to the Resident that there was no necessity to appoint a successor, as he (Sir Sálár Jang) had "determined to have no colleague".

This was an assumption of supreme power in Hyderabad which could not, of course, be acquiesced in; so it became Sir Richard Meade's duty to remind Sir Sálár Jang (in the most friendly terms) that the appointment or non-appointment of a successor to the late co-administrator was a matter for the decision of the British Government as Paramount Power in India. And the Government of India, on being referred to, declined to ratify Sir Sálár Jang's determination, but intimated the intention of filling the vacancy caused by the Amír-i-Kabír's death, and associating with the Minister a representative of the interests of the Nizám and the nobility.

But then a difficulty arose—who was to be nominated?

The person admitted even by Sir Sálár Jang himself to be best fitted for the post—by position, and intelligence—was the Amír-i-Kabír's brother, the Nawáb Vikar-ul-Umra. He was not only first of all the nobles of Hyderabad, but was closely connected by marriage with the ruling family; for his wife was a sister of the late Nizám, while his two sons[1] had married sisters of the present Chief.

[1] One of those two sons is the present Prime Minister of Hyderabad.

Practically the only reason against his appointment was the fact that he was a *persona ingratissima* to Sir Sálár Jang. And the reason for the Minister's dislike was the fact that the Nawáb had strongly opposed the Minister's recent proceedings in the Berár question, as likely to imperil the friendly relations between the British Government and Hyderabad.

The ill-feeling between Sir Sálár Jang and the Nawáb was further accentuated by the action of the Minister. Taking advantage of an expression of confidence in his sense of justice contained in a letter from Sir Richard Meade—an expression which Sir Sálár Jang construed as giving him a free hand in the matter, but was never intended to have such meaning—Sir Sálár Jang decided (during the Resident's absence on short leave) upon a step of considerable importance. He resolved to break up the titles and dignities held by the late Amír-i-Kabír; and, while bestowing the empty title of Amír-i-Kabír Shams-ul-Umra upon the Nawáb as head of the house, conferred the more lucrative and influential appointments (including the command of the body-guard) upon his nephews, the sons of another brother; his object being to lower the position and influence of his great opponent and secure the suffrages of his late colleague's representatives.

It now became the duty of the Resident to advise the Government of India as to the course to be pursued. He was personally much annoyed at the Minister's late proceedings, which had been carried out with unnecessary haste under cover of the Resident's presumed approval; but for that very reason he was particularly careful to deal with the question before him on broad grounds of policy, irrespective of the episode which has just been described.

The case was full of difficulty.

On the one hand, there were obviously grave objections, in the interests of the Hyderabad State as well as of the British Government, to allowing Sir Sálár Jang to remain in sole charge of the administration with full power over its resources.

It was clear also that the Nawáb had the strongest possible claims to the vacant post of co-administrator and there was no one else to take his place.

But on the other hand, there was the probability that the appointment of the Vikar-ul-Umra would lead to the resignation of Sir Sálár Jang.

The retirement of Sir Sálár Jang (for a time at any rate) would not, indeed, in Sir Richard Meade's opinion have been an unmitigated evil, for the Minister's system of "underground" communication with influential partisans in England greatly hampered the Resident in the conduct of affairs, but, as usual, he regarded the question, not from a personal, but a public point of view; and from this point of view he feared the Minister's resignation would be entirely misunderstood in England. The English public were necessarily ignorant of Hyderabad affairs and the political requirements of Indian administration; but in Sir Sálár Jang they recognised an Indian statesman of enlightened views, who had done good service to England in 1857, while English society had been recently fascinated by his charming manners and splendid hospitality.

In these circumstances Sir Richard Meade was, in the first instance, disposed—as a choice of evils—to allow matters to slide, and abstain from filling up the vacant post.

But in considering the question Lord Lytton's knowledge of the state of parties in England led him to have greater faith than Sir Richard Meade in the good sense of Parliament in regard to Hyderabad affairs; and, on the other hand, he attached very great importance to the effect which would inevitably be produced on the Indian friends of the British Government by the rejection of the Vikar-ul-Umra; a nobleman who was entitled from his position and relationship to the Nizám to expect the post, whose appointment (irrespective of his quarrel with Sir Sálár) was desirable in the public interests, and whose only disqualification for the office was the fact that he had strenuously opposed the Minister's recent proceedings as at once ill-timed and unfriendly to the British Government.

The question was, therefore, referred back to Sir Richard Meade for further consideration, and, on the 23rd June, 1877, he addressed the Foreign Secretary as follows:—

"After fairly looking at all the weighty points involved in or bearing on this very important question, I am of opinion that it is essential that Sir Sálár Jang should *not* be suffered to mature his undoubted views and policy; and that it is better, with this object, to risk present inconvenience and trouble than future complications which may prove of the gravest character.

"In opposition, therefore, to the views I have already laid before the Government (though excepting on this one point my opinions are unchanged), I think there are good grounds for appointing the Vikar-ul-Umra to his brother's place as co-regent. And if the measure is decided upon I will do all in my power to give effect to it."

On the 12th of July, 1877, the matter was fully discussed by the Viceroy in Council and it was unanimously agreed that the appointment of the Vikar-ul-Umra as co-administrator in the place of the late Amír-i-Kabír was the only just and proper course.

The decision of the Government of India was not officially communicated to the Resident until after the departure of the Viceroy from Simla on his way, through Hyderabad territory, to Mysore to superintend the famine operations in those territories; but, in communicating its purport semi-officially to the Resident, Lord Lytton intimated some doubt whether Sir Sálár Jang had any real intention of resigning.

The receipt of the directions of the Government of India was followed, as was expected, by protests and threats of resignation on the part of Sir Sálár Jang. These were carefully considered and deliberately replied to; and those who wish for details will find a copy of the despatch in the appendix to this chapter (app. A).

The Minister then made overtures to the Nawáb Vikar-ul-Umra, agreeing to accept him as colleague if he would aid him in raising a loan of fifty lakhs of rupees to replenish the depleted Treasury; but the Nawáb declined to make any promise.

He then addressed a letter to the Resident declining to accept the Nawáb as colleague, and refusing also to resign. This being practically a defiance of the Government of India, decisive action became necessary.

Accordingly on the morning of 23rd September the Resident was instructed by telegram to proclaim the appointment of the Nawáb as co-administrator of Hyderabad. If Sir Sálár Jang accepted him as colleague, well and good; if not, the Minister would not be permitted to retain office, but the appointment might be offered to his nephew. All possible courtesy and consideration were to be shown to Sir Sálár Jang.

On the evening of the 23rd all was over; Sir Sálár Jang announced that "he accepted the Viceroy's decision".

On the 24th the appointment of the Nawáb Vikar-ul-Umra, now the Shams-ul-Umra Amír-i-Kabír, as co-administrator was notified in the State *Gazette*.

And on the 29th of September he was formally installed at a special Durbar held in the Nizám's palace.

The proceedings on this memorable occasion are thus described in the Resident's report:—

"The assembly of the Durbar was fixed for half-past seven A.M. this morning, and at that hour I entered the great Durbar Hall, which has not been before used since my advent here, accompanied by Major-General Macintire, C.B., commanding the Subsidiary Force; Brigadier-General Wright, C.B., commanding Hyderabad Contingent, and between thirty and forty British officers, including the Residency staff—all in full dress—and was met by His Highness the Nizám in the usual manner.

"The Durbar Hall was filled with people and all the principal nobles and officials were present.

"After some few remarks, in the course of which I conveyed to His Highness a message which the Viceroy had given me when I met His Excellency at Shahábád for delivery to him, I stated the object of the Durbar and requested the Nizám's permission for my notification of the 24th instant (of the Persian version of which I had brought a copy) to be read in the Durbar.

"This was done accordingly amidst the deep attention of all present. When it was concluded I rose and crossed to where Nawáb Shams-ul-Umra was sitting, and taking him by the hand I led him before the Nizám, to whom I presented him as the Minister's colleague henceforth in the administration during His Highness's minority; at the same time briefly explaining the grounds upon which the Viceroy in Council had selected the Nawáb for this purpose.

"I then offered Shams-ul-Umra my congratulations on his appointment, and addressed to him a few earnest words expressive of the Governor-General's hope and expectation that he and the Minister would sink all personal feelings and work together loyally for the good of the State and the maintenance of the best possible relations with the British Government.

"The Minister had by this time joined the group, and both he and Shams-ul-Umra declared their determination to work harmoniously together, and to avoid all causes for strife or difference. The Nawáb added a brief and warm expression of his gratitude for the favour that had been shown him, which he said would never be forgotten by him or his family.

"When they had resumed their places I addressed His Highness and all present, stating that it had been represented to me that reports had been circulated that the Nawáb's appointment was a precursor to an intended interference by the British Government in the internal administration of the State, and that I was glad of the opportunity to assure His Highness and all the assembled nobles and officials that there was no such intention on the part of the Government. I went on to say that the British Government, as the ostensible guardian of the State, was entitled to be consulted and informed on any important changes that might be contemplated in the State institutions and establishments, as well as on other matters of importance, in respect of which His Highness's Government should be guided by its advice; but that interference of the nature which had been spoken of had never been thought of and that I trusted no sensible person would credit such reports.

"I concluded these remarks, which were listened to with deep attention, with an assurance to all present that the British Government had but one object in view as regards the State of Hyderabad, *viz.*, its good government and the prosperity of its people, so that, when the time arrived for His Highness's assumption of the direction of affairs, he might enter upon the responsible position of the Ruler of his country with every possible advantage in these respects.

"After some further conversation on general subjects the Durbar broke up in the usual manner.

"His Highness the Nizám behaved with perfect self-possession and propriety.

"As regards Sir Sálár Jang the occasion must no doubt have been a very trying one to him, but he was quite collected and self-possessed and performed his part in the Durbar ceremony with his usual grace and care.

"I may add that there was not the very slightest expression of disapproval at the measure of Nawáb Shams-ul-Umra's appointment that I or the officers with me could observe, either amongst those assembled at the Durbar or the soldiery or the populace in the streets of the city through which the procession passed on elephants, as usual, going to or returning from the palace; and that I have every reason to believe that, with the exception of the persons immediately dependent upon the Minister, that measure is generally approved and popular among all classes in Hyderabad and may indeed be described as being received with a general feeling of gratitude towards the British Government."

The report was acknowledged by the Government of India in an important despatch from which extracts are given in an appendix to this chapter (app. B). After reviewing the situation and expressing emphatic approval of the "tact, conciliation, firmness and foresight" evinced by Sir Richard Meade, it explains the aim and object of the policy pursued, and, while cordially recognising the merits and abilities of Sir Sálár Jang, affirms in language friendly but unmistakable the Suzerain Power of the British Government in respect to Hyderabad affairs.

A great crisis had been firmly and successfully dealt with and hearty congratulations reached Sir Richard from all quarters.

"From first to last," wrote the Viceroy in a private letter, "I think that you have, throughout all the circumstances recorded in your recent correspondence, official and private, acted with great judgment and admirable temper. Your conduct has been far-seeing and energetic, whilst, at the same time, it has been courteous and singularly conciliatory under no slight provocation."

The Foreign Secretary, Mr. (afterwards Sir Charles) Aitchison, who had just resumed office, wrote: "The crisis at Hyderabad has been coming any time this last five years. I entirely agree with the line you have taken in the present controversies. . . . I am sure the course you felt it your duty to take must have been very painful to you, but am glad you took it and adhered to it firmly."

And from England Lord Northbrook addressed him the following letter:—

"STRATTON, *November 1st, 1877.*

"MY DEAR SIR RICHARD,—I am exceedingly obliged to you for having written to me so full an account of the proceedings which led to the appointment of the Nawáb Vikar-ul-Omra as a colleague to Sir Sálár Jang. It seems to me that the resolve of Lord Lytton not to allow Sir Sálár Jang to be the sole Minister was right, and I congratulate you upon the success which has attended your action in the matter. . . .

"Pray remember me kindly to Lady Meade. I am afraid she doesn't forgive me for sending you to Hyderabad. But what has occurred makes me more than ever certain that it was necessary in the public interest for you to be there.

"Yours very sincerely,

"NORTHBROOK."

The new arrangement, so long at least as Lord Lytton was in power, worked well. Sir Sálár Jang, upon the whole, carried out his part in the transaction loyally; and though there was a certain amount of healthy friction at times, yet, thanks to the tact of Sir Richard Meade, who was on the most friendly terms with both parties, there was no serious disagreement.

"The appointment of the Nawáb Amír-i-Kabír," wrote Mr. (now Sir Alfred) Lyall, who succeeded Mr. Aitchison as Foreign Secretary in 1878, "has, under your management, proved a most successful measure." And in a letter to Sir Richard Meade dated the 6th of

June, 1880, the private secretary to the Viceroy writes: "His Excellency has no doubt that the Nawáb's appointment has proved to be of substantial benefit to the administration".

Attempts were, however, persistently made by a London journal,[1] a supporter of Sir Sálár Jang, to vilify and discredit the Nawáb with the view of bringing about, if possible, his dismissal from the office of co-Regent; and after the departure of Lord Lytton its articles became so violent that the Nawáb determined to appeal to law; accordingly he brought an indictment for libel, against the proprietor and editor of the journal; but the proceedings were stayed by a writ of *nolle prosequi*, issued by the Attorney-General, and the co-Regent was referred to a civil suit for redress. Before, however, civil proceedings could be launched he died.

But time has its vicissitudes. By the lamented death of Sir Sálár Jang in 1883, and of his two sons, a few years afterwards, the once all-powerful family, which for more than thirty years commanded the resources and directed the policy of Hyderabad, has well-nigh disappeared; and the present Prime Minister of the Nizám—the Nawáb Ikbál-ud-Daulah—is the son of the late co-Regent.

FINAL DECISION OF THE BERÁR QUESTION.

Soon after the air had been cleared by the several important measures described in the preceding paragraphs, the reply of the Secretary of State to the

[1] The *Statesman*.

second memorial for the restoration of Berár was received.

It was similar in tenor to the reply given to the first memorial.

The decision was communicated to the co-administrators and carefully and anxiously considered; and on the 12th June, 1878, Sir Sálár Jang and his colleague formally intimated that:—

"They fully accepted the decision of the Secretary of State on the Berár question".

Sir Sálár Jang added, during an interview with Sir Richard Meade:—

"That as the decision of Her Majesty's Government had intimated that the reopening of the Berár question, if it were ever permitted, must form part of a general revision of the existing Treaty arrangements between the two Governments, he could not advise the Nizám to move further in the matter. For regarding, as he did, the old Treaties as the most precious gems in the Nizám's possession, he would not on any account have them touched or revised."

Thus ended, for the time being at any rate—to the great relief of all parties—the great Berár question.

The Viceroy telegraphed to the Resident his congratulations. "The Foreign Department," wrote Sir Alfred Lyall, "is very grateful to you for this entirely advantageous termination of an important question and an embarrassing controversy." "You have indeed won a great victory," wrote Sir Edward Bradford from Ajmir in Rájputána; and General Sir E.

Johnson (a late member of the Viceroy's Council) wrote in the same strain from England.

"I think," said Lord Northbrook, in a letter dated 18th September, "the decision about Berár is based on the proper foundation, *viz.*, that the treaties referring to the Berárs cannot be treated by themselves, but that if they are to be revised the whole must be considered. This, as you know, was always my view, and I thought the position a fair and sound one. If the Nizám cannot accept it, we are content to let matters remain as they are. I congratulate you on the result of your work at Hyderabad."

In thus concluding a necessarily imperfect description of the transactions at Hyderabad during the years 1876 and 1877, the writer of these pages deeply regrets to have been constrained, in the course of his narrative, to mention facts and proceedings in derogation of the many merits and services of the late SIR SÁLÁR JANG, a statesman for whom he had the highest admiration and with whom his personal relations were of the most friendly character; but he has felt it due to the memory of one of the best Political Officers of India, whose action has been strangely misrepresented, to explain how the case stands; and it is also due to the memory of the Viceroy, on whom devolved the thankless task of checking the unwise and ambitious projects of a justly influential Minister, to let the public know how much they owe to LORD LYTTON's just and fearless action in Hyderabad affairs.

And now that nearly twenty years have elapsed since the transactions of these eventful years it is possible to speak with some confidence as to the result. It may safely be affirmed that the result has been immensely beneficial, not only to the British Government, but also to the Hyderabad State.

For while our political position in Hyderabad is stronger, our relations with the Nizám are not less, but, on the contrary, far more friendly. In States as well as individuals nothing is more conducive to friendliness than a clear understanding of relative positions; and this is what has been achieved by the discussions and proceedings of 1875, 1876 and 1877, in which Sir Richard Meade took so important and honourable a part.

APPENDIX TO CHAPTER XXII.

A.

From the Officiating Secretary to the Government of India to the Resident at Hyderabad.

"CAMP, OOTACAMUND,
"15th September, 1877.

"SIR,—I have laid before the Viceroy and Governor-General your letter, No. 66, dated 29th August, transmitting for the consideration and orders of His Excellency copy of a letter from Sir Sálár Jung, remonstrating against the appointment of the Nawáb Vikar-ul-Omrah, Amír-i-Kabír, as his colleague in the administration of the Hyderabad State in the room of the Nawáb's deceased brother.

"The Governor-General has attentively considered the Minister's representation, but he can discover no sufficient reason for withdrawing or modifying the orders contained in my despatch of the 19th August.

"The ground on which the Minister demurs to the Nawáb's appointment is a personal objection to act as colleague of that nobleman; the existence of this objection was, however, known to the Government of India, and the circumstance was carefully considered before a decision was arrived at; but, after full deliberation, the reason was not deemed sufficient for excluding from office the only person in Hyderabad qualified by rank, influence and position to fill the post of co-administrator.

"The greatest weight and consideration are due, and have been given, to the personal views and wishes of Sir Sálár Jung in this important matter, but they cannot be regarded as the sole ground for the action of Government, or as precluding the paramount and guardian Power from adopting an arrangement otherwise deemed best for the interests of the Hyderabad State.

"With reference to the suggestion of Sir Sálár Jung that he should be permitted to submit for the acceptance of the British Government the name of another nobleman as his colleague, I am to observe that the proposal does not commend itself to the Governor-General's approval; for, apart from the fact that a nominee of the present Minister would necessarily be wanting in independence and in the representative character essential to the office of co-administrator, the Government of India has already received the expression of the Minister's opinion that no one save his own son-in-law and nephew is competent to fill the post.

"Under the above circumstances, I am to request that you will courteously but clearly inform Sir Sálár Jung of the Governor-General's inability to reconsider his determination, and that you will arrange that the orders directing the notification of the appointment of the Vikar-ul-Omrah as colleague in the administration be carried out without further delay.

"I have, etc.,

"T. H. THORNTON."

B.

From the Acting Foreign Secretary to the Government of India to the Resident at Hyderabad.

"SIMLA, *October 23rd*, 1877.

"SIR,—I have received and laid before the Governor-General in Council your confidential letters of the 23rd September and 29th September, 1877, with their enclosures, reporting your proceedings subsequent to my letter of the 22nd September, and to your interview with His Excellency the Viceroy upon that date.

"From these documents it appears that His Excellency

Sir Sálár Jung has at length accepted the arrangement whereby, in accordance with the settlement of 1869, the Nawáb Shams-ul-Omrah, Amír-i-Kabír, chief noble of Hyderabad, is appointed his colleague in the administration of the Nizám's Territories during His Highness' minority.

"You further report that the installation of the Nawáb as co-administrator took place on the morning of the 29th September at a special Durbar held at the palace and presided over by His Highness the Nizám, at which yourself, the Minister and all the chief nobles and officials in Hyderabad were present: and you express your confident belief that the measure is generally popular among all classes, and regarded with feelings of gratitude towards the British Government.

"The Governor-General in Council has received this information with sincere satisfaction. In the first place, His Excellency is glad to be informed of the satisfactory termination of a crisis, unprovoked by the British Government, which might otherwise have deprived the Hyderabad State of the services of an able Minister; he also rejoices to receive Sir Sálár Jung's assurance that the personal ill-feeling he was said to entertain towards his new colleague has really no existence —an assurance corroborated by the overtures reported in paragraph seven of your letter of the 29th September to have been made to the Nawáb by the Minister's confidential secretary; but His Excellency is chiefly gratified at the cordial approval with which almost all classes in Hyderabad have regarded the action of the Government of India in withstanding the assumption by a single Minister of supreme power in the Nizám's dominions. The Governor-General in Council is convinced that such assumption would have been most inexpedient, and that a firm adherence to the administrative arrangement sanctioned by the Government of India in 1869 (which is all that has been insisted upon) is best for the interests of the Nizám's Government and people, as well as for the preservation of cordial relations between Hyderabad and the Suzerain Power.

"These fortunate results, I am desired to observe, are mainly to be attributed to the able manner in which you have dealt with the important and difficult questions which have arisen during the late discussions; and His Excellency in Council cannot too emphatically express his appreciation of the tact, conciliation, firmness and foresight which you have evinced throughout the conduct of these arrangements. The services of your first assistant Captain Euan Smith, C.S.I., also merit the special acknowledgments of the Government of India.

"The treaties with Hyderabad constitute the British Government supreme protector of the State from external and internal enemies. In the exercise of this protective power the British Government has for more than three quarters of a century preserved the peace and the dynasty of Hyderabad. In the exercise of this power it has frequently remonstrated against acts of maladministration and oppression. In the exercise of this power it on two occasions interfered to prevent the dismissal of His Excellency Sir Sálár Jung from office by the late Nizám. In the exercise of this power it assumed in 1869 and still holds the guardianship of the young Nizám, and has arranged and will continue to arrange for the proper administration of His Highness' Territories until he comes of age.

"Few, it will be observed, have experienced the benefits of this protecting power more fully than Sir Sálár Jung himself; through the influence of the British Government (as already noticed) the Minister was twice maintained in office in opposition to the wishes of the Ruling Chief, and on the demise of the late Ruler it was not the authority of the deceased, for such authority was never given, and, had it been given, would have been of no effect—nor the desire of the chiefs and people, but the power of the British Government which secured him the high position of co-administrator during the minority of the present Nizám. . . .

"I have, etc.,

"T. H. THORNTON."

CHAPTER XXIII.

HYDERABAD (*continued*).

Meade asks permission to resign—Reply of the Viceroy—Letter to Lord Cranbrook—Owing to financial losses Meade constrained to delay retirement—Gratifying letter from Lord Lytton—Afghan War—Loyal conduct of Sir Sálár Jang and the Hyderabad Chiefs—Anxiety in Hyderabad, but dangerous movements effectually checked—Administrative improvement—Striking change in attitude and conduct of Minister—Lord Lytton resigns office and is succeeded by the Marquis of Ripon—No material change of policy in Hyderabad—Affairs being tranquil, Meade gratefully declines prolongation of office and retires in March, 1881—Letter from Foreign Secretary—Public banquet in honour of departing Resident—Farewell letter from Sir Sálár Jang—His death and character.

THE BERÁR QUESTION having been set at rest, Sir R. Meade, who was approaching sixty years of age, thought the time had come when he might, in accordance with the earnest wishes of his family, think about retiring; and accordingly he broached the subject in a letter to the Viceroy's private secretary, in which he proposed to leave for England early in 1879.

His letter was thus answered by Lord Lytton:—

"SIMLA, 29*th July*, 1878.

"MY DEAR MEADE,—It was with the most sincere and unqualified regret that I learned some weeks ago, through Colonel Colley, your decision to retire from the service early next year.

"Your retirement on any other grounds than failure of health and strength would, at any time, and in any circumstances, be a serious loss to the service, and one which I should greatly regret.

"But the loss is rendered specially serious, and the regret with which I contemplate it is largely augmented, by the peculiar circumstances of our present relations with Hyderabad. The remarkable ability with which you have conducted those relations has, no doubt, enabled me to place them on a far more satisfactory and promising footing than that which previously existed for many years past, and you have so worthily won the rest you now claim that I cannot justifiably ask you to postpone it.

"But the sound basis on which our position at Hyderabad is now happily re-established, will for some years to come require vigilant watching, and delicate handling; and, on behalf of the important public interests which may be grievously compromised by any disturbance of it, I sincerely regret the necessity of so early a change in the Residentship at Hyderabad.

"Pray believe me, with the warmest appreciation, and the truest good-will,

"Yours faithfully,

"LYTTON."

At the same time his Lordship addressed the Secretary of State for India as follows:—

"SIMLA, *15th July*, 1878.

"To the Right Hon. Viscount Cranbrook.

"MY DEAR LORD CRANBROOK,—I venture to send you, privately, for your early information, the enclosed copy of a letter from Sir Richard Meade which I have just received with unqualified regret. You will see by it that for family reasons, which of course I cannot combat, Sir Richard has made up his mind to retire early next year from his service in India, although he is still anxious to obtain, if possible, in England some employment connected with India.

"Sir Richard Meade's retirement will be a very serious, and, in some respects, an irreparable loss to our Political Service, of which, during my own tenure of office, he has certainly been *facile princeps*. I should have been very glad to retain him in it at least a few years longer, had this been possible, for it will not be easy to replace him at Hyderabad, without risk to the maintenance of the good work he has done there, and I look upon the unexpected prospect of an early change in the Hyderabad Residency as a deplorable necessity in the present condition of our relations with the Nizám's Government. It is true that, owing mainly to the remarkable tact, temper, firmness, and general diplomatic ability of Sir Richard Meade himself, those relations are now more satisfactory and less anxious than they have been for many years previous to his present appointment, which is of recent date. But the smallest indiscretion or oversight on the part of his successor might seriously jeopardise all that has now been secured.

"Sir Richard Meade retires in the full force of his faculties and with unimpaired health, so that his experience and ability may still perhaps prove useful to India in some other form of employment at home. But in any case I feel that it would be discreditable to the Government of India, and to myself personally, were he finally to quit India without some special recognition by the Crown of the very important and brilliantly successful work he has accomplished within the last two years. The complete details of this long story will never appear upon official record. The manner in which, inch by inch, and step by step, we have without violence recovered lost ground in Hyderabad was settled mostly in personal and very confidential communication between Sir Richard and myself.

"As Meade is already a K.C.S.I. the only promotion that can be given him in the Order of the Star of India is the G.C.S.I., and for this I would ask now to recommend him. But I know not whether any G.C.S.I. is likely to be vacant at the time of his retirement, and for the Bath I am not entitled to make any recommendations. Should it be impossible to give Sir Richard the G.C.S.I. on his retirement, would you be indisposed to consider the possibility of recommending him to Her Majesty for a Baronetcy?

"Yours, etc.,

"LYTTON."

It would have been well if Sir Richard Meade had been able to carry out his plan; for, when he did retire, there was a new Viceroy and a new Secretary of State, neither of whom had cognizance of Lord Lytton's recommendation, or had the same opportunity of judging of the value of Meade's services. But unfortunately, before the close of 1878, his pecuniary resources had been so reduced by a bank failure, and a general depreciation of securities, that he was obliged to ask that his proposal to retire be kept in abeyance for the present. To his request he received from Lord Lytton the following gratifying reply:—

"BARRACKPORE, 21st *January*, 1879.

"MY DEAR SIR RICHARD,—I am more grieved than I can say to learn by your letter that you are among the victims of the recent bank failure. I sincerely trust your losses are not serious, that the welcome decision you have come to will enable you to repair them, and that they will not permanently cost you any greater sacrifice or inconvenience than a few years' further devotion to a service in which you have achieved distinction and which you would have quitted prematurely, to my great personal regret, had you quitted it now.

"The proverb says that 'it is an ill wind that blows nobody any good'. A change in the important post you now hold would have been to me just at the present moment rather embarrassing. The longer you hold it, the better pleased I shall be; and I beg you to regard your continued tenure of it as an addition to the services warmly appreciated by

"Your sincere friend and well-wisher,

"LYTTON."

So he remained at work. Meanwhile the outbreak of the Afghan war had made his presence at Hyderabad particularly desirable. The conduct of the Hyderabad Chiefs was indeed all that could be wished. Sir Sálár Jang and his colleague promptly offered military assistance to the Government of India, and proposed that one of the two Ministers should accompany the troops. Several of the Hyderabad nobles volunteered for the front, and the services of two of them—Mokarram-ud-Daulah, nephew of Sir Sálár Jang, and Khurshed Jah, son of the Amír-i-Kabír—were accepted, but owing to changes in the plan of campaign, were ultimately not availed of. But the offer was gratefully acknowledged, and a year afterwards, after the massacre at Kábul, a portion of the Contingent cavalry was employed and distinguished itself in the campaign.

Still there were elements of danger in Hyderabad, which could not be ignored, and one of the first effects of the outbreak of hostilities was to cause a stream of Patán desperadoes to flow towards the Nizám's capital —a significant indication of the character of the locality as a rendezvous for disaffection; and this was followed by an influx of Arab adventurers from Hadramát in South Arabia. But, thanks to measures taken by the Minister in conjunction with the Resident, these movements were effectually checked, as was a recrudescence of dacoity which took place about the same time; and all burning questions having been got rid of, Sir Richard Meade's remaining career in Hyderabad was comparatively "plain sailing".

Instead of painful correspondence and disagreeable interviews, he had the pleasure of frequently conveying to the Minister the thanks of the Government of India for services rendered, of congratulating him on administrative improvements effected in Aurangábad and helping him to arrange for a scientific exploitation of the Nizám's forests; and he had now more leisure to devote to the supervision of the administration of Berár and the development of its material resources, thus increasing the surplus payable to the Hyderabad treasury. There was still difficulty in connection with the Nizám's education, and occasional breezes between the co-administrators required some tact and friendly intervention to allay, and a violent quarrel between the Amír-i-Kabír and his nephews threatened at one time to end in bloodshed. But, on the whole, matters proceeded smoothly and satisfactorily, and more than once in his letters to the Viceroy the Resident remarks upon the striking change which had taken place in the attitude and conduct of the Minister.

But in 1881 a change of Government occurred in England; Lord Lytton resigned his office, and was succeeded by a new Viceroy, who was, of course, quite unacquainted with Hyderabad affairs.

In regard to those affairs there was, indeed, no reversal of past policy (the presence of Sir Alfred Lyall as Foreign Secretary and of most of the members of Lord Lytton's Council prevented such a catastrophe), but the new Viceroy had little personal knowledge of Meade, while the confidential relations which had been established, in consequence of frequent communications in critical times, between the Resident and the two preceding Viceroys, could hardly remain the same.

In these circumstances, and having regard to the fact that his extended term of office had nearly expired, while there was no "burning question" to be dealt with, Sir Richard Meade felt that he might, without inconvenience to public interests, make way for a successor. Accordingly—though his finances had far from recovered the shock of 1878—he made preparations for departure. A prolongation of his term of office for a few months was offered, but gratefully declined, and he left Hyderabad for the last time in March, 1881.

The Foreign Secretary, Sir Alfred Lyall, wrote: "I am sure that the Viceroy is fully sensible that public acknowledgments are due to you for the long and important services rendered by you at Hyderabad; and you must permit me, on the part of the Foreign Department, to say that I believe the Government of India has been greatly indebted to you for the unvarying judgment and ability with which you have discharged the duties of the highest political office in India".

The Hyderabad Club gave a public banquet in his honour; the members of the Bar expressed their admiration and good wishes, and the press was full of appreciative notices of his career and character. Many of his subordinates wrote grateful letters of farewell, and many friends, including Sir Sálár Jang and the Nawáb Amír-i-Kabír, witnessed his departure from the scene of his labours, some accompanying him to Bombay, where a number of friends from Berár had assembled to wish him God-speed.

So he bade adieu to India for ever, after a service of forty-three years, during twenty-one of which he had filled some of the highest and most responsible appointments in the political service of the Crown.

And shortly after arriving in England he was gratified by the receipt of multitudes of letters from the Princes and Chiefs of territories in which he had served, and, in particular, by the following letter from the Hyderabad Minister :—

"HYDERABAD, DECCAN,
"*27th March*, 1881.

"MY DEAR SIR RICHARD MEADE,—I write a few lines to wish you good-bye and God-speed home, which the sudden movement of the train and the hurried manner in which you were obliged to take your place prevented my doing at the station on Wednesday.

"As you said in your speech at the dinner given by the Hyderabad Club we have had many official differences during your career as Resident of Hyderabad, but I am sure our private relations have always been and will continue to be friendly as long as we are spared.

"On hearing from you of your safe arrival in England I hope to have the pleasure of writing to you, and I hope our correspondence will never be interrupted.

"I remain, etc.,
"SÁLÁR JANG."

And the correspondence continued until the close of 1882. On the 8th February, 1883, Sir Sálár Jang died of cholera at the early age of forty-nine.

He was undoubtedly one of the greatest Indian statesmen of modern times, and a most fascinating personality.

Born and brought up in an atmosphere of intrigue his methods were not always to be approved, but personally he was as uncorrupt as he was broad-minded and unsectarian; and as the man who, above all others, kept Hyderabad straight in 1857, as the introducer of comparatively civilised administration into what was one of the worst-governed States in India, and as one who did much to bring together the European and the Oriental in friendly social intercourse—he deserves to be gratefully remembered.

But in matters of *la haute politique*—affecting the relations between the British Government and the Nizám—Sir Sálár Jang was a dreamer, not a statesman; deserving—not, indeed, harsh judgment—but a place, with Rienzi, in the category of those "qui ont pris les souvenirs pour les espérances".

He dreamed of Hyderabad in the last century, when the Mughal Empire was dying and the power of England represented by a trading company. He forgot that the power, so represented then, was now successor to the throne of the Mughals—from which the Nizám derived his title and jurisdiction, and to which he remained, in name at least, subordinate. That Power was constituted by treaty supreme protector of Hyderabad from external and internal foes; but, irrespective of treaty rights, it could not, as Suzerain, acting in the interests of peace, allow the existence of an independent principality in the heart of India. So the Minister's aspirations had to be opposed, and the brunt of the opposition fell on Meade.

But let us remember the former's merits, not his dreams. And now that both Resident and Minister have passed away, and all questioning of British Suzerainty in India is buried (we hope for ever) in Sir Sálár's grave, we can look back on the events of 1877 with feelings, chiefly of admiration, for the perfect courtesy and friendliness maintained to the last by the two chief actors in the drama.[1]

[1] The following "true story" will show with what rare good humour Sir Sálár Jang accepted political defeat. One day soon after the co-regent crisis he took Lady Meade over his palace and showed her, amongst other things, the private room in which his important interviews with the Resident had taken place and where the ultimatum regarding the manufacture of arms and the appointment of a co-regent had been conveyed to him. Lady Meade having admired the room, Sir Sálár Jang observed with mock solemnity: "I don't like that room. That is the dentist's room, where all my teeth have been pulled out!" It might have been replied with truth: "If Sir Richard Meade was operator they must have been, at any rate, 'painlessly extracted'"

CHAPTER XXIV.

CALUMNIOUS ATTACKS.

Calumnious attacks in the *Statesman*—Position of a retired Anglo-Indian in such cases—Meade seeks to proceed against his traducer in a court of law—The Government of India recommends that he should be allowed to do so at public expense and to produce official papers—The Home Government considers proceedings unnecessary and inexpedient—Refuses Meade permission to publish vindicatory despatches, but Lord Hartington makes a statement in the House of Commons—Letters of sympathy from Lord Northbrook, Lord Lytton and other English friends and from Sir Sálár Jang—Observations of the *Pioneer* newspaper—Attacks renewed in 1883—Questions, based on the attacks, asked in the House of Lords, but the House refuses to hear them—An official letter sent to Meade expressing the Government's sense of the utter groundlessness of the attacks—Attacks repeated in India in an aggravated form—Meade protests and again receives handsome letters from the Government, but their publication still disallowed—Lord Lytton strongly of opinion that Meade should receive some public proof of confidence—But nothing further done during Meade's lifetime—Extracts from the despatches now published for the first time.

SIR RICHARD MEADE returned to England from India in April, 1881, hoping to enjoy a little well-earned repose, but he was not long allowed to rest in peace.

In July, 1881, within a few months of his return, he was made the object of a most virulent attack in the pages of a periodical then published in London and Calcutta—the same which had vilified the character of the Nawáb Amír-i-Kabír.

Of the author of this and subsequent attacks (who has been dead some years) we desire to say nothing harsh. He was a prolific writer of some ability, especially on economical subjects, and may be credited with a certain amount of genuine sympathy with the Princes and peoples of India; but he was the ready dupe of slanderers and not very scrupulous in his methods.

Many may be of opinion that the libellous productions of the *Statesman* might well have been left in the oblivion to which they have been long consigned so far as the general public is concerned,—but the members of Sir Richard Meade's family feel it due to his memory to place on record the complete official vindication of his character and conduct which, for the convenience of the Government, he was prohibited from publishing during his lifetime.

The article referred to denounced the policy of the British Government towards Hyderabad and in particular the action of Sir Richard Meade in connection with the Berár memorials, the co-Regent and other questions, and even held him responsible for a decision of Sir Sálár Jang in a dispute between members of the co-Regent's family—a decision to which the co-Regent's nephews took exception. It was full of outrageous misstatements; charging the late Resident, *inter alia*, with having treated Sir Sálár Jang with studied discourtesy and coerced him into submission by threats of forcible deportation, etc., and abounded in disgraceful innuendoes and other productions of malevolent bazaar gossip.

Attacks upon policy and proceedings, if fairly conducted, are of course perfectly legitimate, and Sir Richard Meade would have been the last person in the world to have complained of them. But the attacks in question far transcended the bounds of legitimate criticism and were nothing more nor less than atrocious libels, so vague in terms that it was difficult to meet them, and so worded as to leave the author, if brought to book, a loophole for escape.

By a high English official they would probably have been passed by as unworthy of notice, but a retired Anglo-Indian is in a somewhat different position. Among official circles in India where the late Resident and his traducer were both well known, the libels would be harmless, but translations of them were sure to be circulated far and wide by the vernacular press; while in England, where the name of Sir Richard Meade was little known, much harm might be done. Under such circumstances an officer in his position may be pardoned for being somewhat sensitive.

When the first libellous article appeared he was on the Continent, and was first apprised of the attack made upon him by a telegram from the India Office, asking for an immediate reply to it in view of a question of which notice had been given in the House of Commons. He sent a reply forthwith and at the same time took measures to call his traducer to account in a court of law.

But to do so effectually it was necessary to obtain the sanction of the Government of India and Secretary of State to the production and publication of confidential documents. He therefore addressed a letter to the Government of India containing a complete answer to the charges made against him and claiming its support in the proceedings he proposed to take.

His request was acceded to and the Governor-General in Council addressed the Secretary of State intimating that it appeared "incumbent upon the Government of India to give its full and hearty support to Sir Richard Meade in the painful position in which he had been placed" and recommending that proceedings for libel against the editor of the *Statesman* be instituted at the cost of the Indian revenues, and that "every facility be given to Sir Richard Meade by the production of official papers to establish the purity of his character and the rectitude of his conduct". The despatch further requested that Sir Richard Meade might be assured that "the Government of India had not permitted their high estimate of his character and services to be in the smallest degree affected by the charges brought against him".

But the Secretary of State, whilst cordially concurring in the high testimony borne by the Government of India to Sir Richard Meade's personal character as a zealous and upright public servant, was of opinion that the prosecution suggested by Lord Ripon's Government was unnecessary for his vindication as well as inexpedient in the public interest.

Sir Richard Meade asked permission to make public use of these vindicatory despatches, but this was not permitted at the time. Lord Hartington, however, undertook to make a public statement in the House of Commons, which was done on the 22nd February, 1882, and is thus reported in the *Times* :—

"SIR RICHARD MEADE.

"VISCOUNT BARING asked the Secretary of State for India, with reference to his answer in the House of Commons on 11th August last, whether he had been placed in possession of the views of the Government of India in regard to certain allegations made last year in the *Statesman* magazine derogatory to the character of Sir Richard Meade, late Resident at Hyderabad; and, if so, what action he had taken in the matter.

"The MARQUIS OF HARTINGTON—A report on this matter was received from the Government of India in October last to the effect that, in their opinion, it was conclusively proved by papers in their possession that in the transactions called in question in the *Statesman* articles, Sir Richard Meade had acted under the orders and in entire accordance with the wishes of the Government of India, and that throughout a long and difficult period that officer had been animated with a single desire to discharge his duty zealously and faithfully. The Government of India stated that Sir Richard Meade's career in India had been that of a zealous and upright public servant, that they retained an entire and unshaken confidence in his integrity and honour, and considered the imputations of corrupt conduct brought against him in the articles in question to be without foundation. I desire to add that Sir Richard Meade was personally anxious that legal proceedings should be instituted in order to give him the opportunity of denying on oath in the witness-box the charges made against him, and the Government of India supported this wish. I, however, considered that this course would be attended with no advantage, unless I was prepared to produce in court the confidential papers connected with the transactions called in question; and, as I have stated on former occasions, I do not think that this would, at the present time, be for the benefit of the public service. I also considered that this course was wholly unnecessary for the vindication of Sir Richard Meade's character, and I caused an intimation to that effect to be sent to that officer, with an expression of my entire concurrence in the opinion recorded by the Government of India as to his public services and personal integrity. I have reason to believe that Sir Richard Meade is quite satisfied with the action thus taken, but I am glad to have the opportunity of making this statement.

"MR. ONSLOW asked whether the report of the Indian Government could not be published in the Calcutta *Gazette.*

"The MARQUIS OF HARTINGTON—No, sir, that course would be inconvenient, as the report that was sent home contained confidential papers which it is not desirable to publish."

For a time the libels ceased and Sir Richard Meade had the satisfaction of receiving from multitudes of friends, including the Earl of Northbrook (a member of the Government), the Earl of Lytton, Sir Richard Temple, Sir Charles Aitchison, Sir George Campbell, Sir Alfred Lyall, Sir Stewart Bayley, Sir Michael Westropp (Chief Justice of Bombay), Sir R. Sankey, R.E., General Alexander, and other distinguished men, letters expressing indignation at these attacks. "I need hardly say," wrote Lord Northbrook, "that I do not attach the smallest importance to the base insinuations vented against you. I am very sorry indeed you should be subjected to such scandalous attacks, but you can well afford to treat them with contempt." "Your character and career," said Lord Lytton, "and your calumniator's character and career are so well known that I feel quite sure that any lies told by him in reference to yourself must be as innocuous as they are malignant and impudent." "Anything," wrote Sir Charles Aitchison, "more scandalous and atrocious in the way of journalism I never read in all my life," and the rest in similar strain. What the present writer thought of them will be seen from the subjoined letter :—

"*October 16th*, 1882.

"MY DEAR MEADE,—I have just returned from the Continent—hence the delay in returning the *Statesman* and your commentary.

"The former I read with indignation but not with surprise, for experience has made me well acquainted with the character of your accuser.

"With your friends, who know you to be the soul of courtesy and honour, the imputations will be valued as they deserve; but I am glad, nevertheless, to have seen your answer, as it will enable me all the more effectually to defend you, should your conduct as Resident of Hyderabad be ever assailed in my presence.

"I would add that my recollection of the events of 1876-7 entirely accords with your statement of them.

"Believe me, my dear Meade,

"Yours very sincerely,

"THOMAS H. THORNTON."

The opinion of Sir Sálár Jang (in whose interest the libellous article professed to have been written) was thus expressed:—

"HYDERABAD, DECCAN,
"*21st August*, 1881.

"MY DEAR SIR RICHARD MEADE,—I cannot allow this mail to go without sending you a few lines to say how grieved I am about the attacks which have been made on your character in the *Statesman*.

"The way in which certain allegations are made would lead people who do not know you to suppose that I had inspired them, or that I was prepared to corroborate them.

"I allude especially to the statement that I was intimidated into compliance with the appointment of the Nawáb Amír-i-Kabír by a threat from the Resident that I should otherwise be deported by rail to Madras.

"I hope I need not tell you that I have no knowledge of the manner in which an allegation so little in accordance with my knowledge of the facts came to be published, or who the author of it is. I deprecated such attacks when the subject of them was the Nawáb Amír-i-Kabír and I deprecate them still more in the present instance.

"Although we had our differences on some subjects I can certainly say that I never had any reason to complain of any want of courtesy or consideration from you on any occasion, and nothing ever occurred to lead me to harbour any ill-will against you or to wish to injure you in any way; on the contrary, I shall always hope to hear from you of your happiness and prosperity. . . .

"With kind regards, believe me,

"Yours very sincerely,

"SÁLÁR JANG."

And one of the leading newspapers in India (the *Pioneer*) thus commented upon the occurrence. After reciting the signal services of Sir Richard Meade it proceeds :—

"This is not the time or place to dilate on the many difficulties against which Sir Richard had to contend at the Court of the Nizám. Hyderabad has been for years a hot-bed of intrigue, and amid the struggles for power and influence between different parties the position of the British Resident is a most delicate one, and it is next to impossible for him to avoid making enemies. On the departure then of a Resident from Hyderabad it would not be surprising if malicious and disappointed persons should set damaging rumours on foot, though it would indeed be surprising to find any intelligent European of experience who would put any faith in such idle tales. The closest inquiry has however failed to discover that even such intangible rumours regarding the late Resident ever existed at Hyderabad, and the author of the libel must therefore have evolved the whole story out of his inner consciousness or must have been wilfully misinformed by some interested party anxious to do the late Resident an injury."

But though the attacks ceased for a time they were not over. On the death of Sir Sálár Jang in 1883, they were renewed, and an earnest-minded but somewhat credulous nobleman was induced to give notice in the House of Lords of a series of questions based upon these further calumnious statements. But the House, on the advice of Lord Kimberley, Secretary of State for India, in which Lord Salisbury, the leader of the Opposition, fully concurred—refused to allow the questions to be put or to be recorded in the Minutes; Lord Salisbury observing that: "If anybody ought to be gibbeted for what took place in Hyderabad it was himself, and not Sir Richard Meade, who had simply carried out the orders he had received". And in an official letter, dated 11th April, 1883, the Parliamentary Under-Secretary of State for India informed Sir Richard Meade that: "His Lordship in Council was completely satisfied that there was no ground whatever for any imputation against him in connection with the matters referred to in the questions".

Unabashed by this discomfiture the enemy returned to the attack in 1884 and the libels were even more unscrupulous, asserting *inter alia* that they had the support and sympathy of high officials of the India Office. But this time they were published in Calcutta and not in London, and thus had a full month's run before they were brought to the notice of the person against whom they were directed.

On his attention being called to them Sir Richard Meade again appealed to the Government of India, in a letter in which he exposed the utter baselessness of the accusations made against him, and indignantly protested against their repetition; and he received a reply to the effect that "the explanations contained in his letter were supported by the official records of the Foreign Office, and that, in the opinion of the Government of India, the vindication of his action was unanswerable". "I am at the same time to observe," continues the despatch, "that the confidence reposed in your ability and integrity as a public servant by successive Governors-General in Council has not in any way been shaken by the statements to which you refer, and, in the opinion of the Governor-General in Council, it is unnecessary to take further notice of them."

And the Under-Secretary of State added in a letter dated 28th August: "Lord Kimberley agrees with the Government of India in thinking that any further notice of these allegations is unnecessary, and His Lordship in Council is glad to have this opportunity of assuring you of his entire concurrence in the high opinion formed by that Government of your ability and integrity".

So far as words go the vindication was complete, but, though the libel was greatly aggravated by its being made to appear that it had the support of "high officials at the India Office," the vindication was not, on this occasion, repeated in Parliament, nor otherwise made publicly known, but was conveyed to Meade in "confidential" despatches, of which he was not permitted to make public use. The vindication thus failed to reach the persons, in England and India, among whom the libels (in their aggravated form) had been widely circulated, and who were not in a position to value them as they deserved.

Meade felt the embargo thus placed upon the vindication of his character very keenly, and his feelings were fully shared by his old chief, Lord Lytton, who thus expressed them (soon after the Conservatives had returned to power) in a letter from which we extract the following paragraphs:—

"My dear Sir Richard,— . . . The intrigues of Sir Sálár Jang were regarded by me as the greatest danger to which the British power in India was exposed during my own Viceroyalty,—a danger far greater than any which was involved in war or famine.

"That danger was imminent, and if the gravity of it remained unknown to the public and to Parliament it is because it was unostentatiously but effectually averted and its recurrence rendered impossible by the skill and courage with which you most ably carried out your onerous instructions in dealing with it.

"But your own services exposed you—after I had ceased to have any connection with the Government of India—to an infamous public attack upon your character, which it was the public duty of your official employers to punish if they could—and if not, to counteract by the most public demonstration of their respect for your character and their approval of your conduct.

"I understand from your letter that the public prosecution in England of your assailant was officially recommended to the Government at home by the Government of India, but that the Secretary of State deemed this course inexpedient for reasons which had reference exclusively to the convenience of the Government.

"The strongest expressions of confidence and approval were conveyed to you in official communications, which, for the same reason, you were not permitted to publish; and thus it appears that the State you served so well has been content to leave unredressed up to the present moment a public outrage suffered by one of its servants in the discharge of his public duties, and only provoked by the conscientiousness and ability with which he performed them.

"Justice, generosity, and courage may not be the virtues of any Parliamentary Government, but the Government which is now in office has the opportunity of repairing this neglect of them if it chooses to do so.

"You are quite at liberty to make any use you please of this letter from

"Yours,

"With much sympathy,

"LYTTON."

It is believed that Sir Richard Meade, to whom anything in the shape of pushing personal claims or ventilating personal wrongs was most distasteful, made no use, certainly no public use, of the above letter. It is now published as containing, not only a generous expression of the writer's sympathy, but, what is more important, a deliberate opinion of the value of Meade's work in Hyderabad recorded by the Viceroy under whose immediate orders he was serving.

But whether the letter was used or not—nothing was done. Times were changed. There was a new Viceroy and a new Secretary of State,—neither of whom had any personal knowledge of Meade and could hardly be expected to take much interest in his past services or present feelings; while the maxim *quieta non movere* is a favourite one with both parties in the State.

It thus happened that, up to the date of Sir Richard Meade's death, the last and worst outrage upon his character for the conscientious performance of his public duties was never publicly redressed.

In these circumstances the widow and the family are most grateful to the present Secretary of State for India for having, at length, allowed the publication of extracts from the vindicatory despatches—which the deceased desired (but vainly) to have published during his lifetime.

But, whatever were his feelings, Meade made no complaint and continued to work earnestly for India until the last. His last letter, written a few days before his death, was a long one addressed to the present Prime Minister of the Nizám.

CHAPTER XXV.

LAST YEARS.

Remaining years in England—Meade's busy and useful life—Health begins to fail—Proceeds to Hyères in February, 1894, and dies—The closing scene described by Mrs. Caine—Memorial window and inscription in the church at Innishannon—Concluding remarks on Meade's character and services.

LIFE AND WORK IN ENGLAND.

THE history of MEADE's remaining life, although a busy one, was uneventful and is soon told.

He at first resided on the Continent, but after a short interval took up his abode in London or its vicinity. For a few years he rented Hookwood, the charming estate of Mr. Leveson Gower at Limpsfield in Surrey, the home in former days of the great Mountstuart Elphinstone, the well-known diplomatist, statesman, and historian of India, and afterwards of his nephew, Lord Elphinstone, successively Governor of Madras and Bombay.

Eventually he bought a house in London (No. 65 Queen's Gate), where he resided for the last five years of his life. He soon became immersed in affairs, was for some years Chairman of the Nizám State Railway and Director or Chairman of several other companies, and was at the same time member of many charitable and philanthropic institutions. He was Chairman of the East Indian Association, formed for the independent discussion of subjects relating to India, Vice-Chairman of the Council of his old school (the Royal Naval School), a member of the Council of the National Indian Association, and connected with many similar societies, in all of which he took a keen and active interest, and was for some time a diligent worker among the poor in the East End.

The constant attention and labour these self-imposed duties entailed upon him probably shortened his useful life; but he loved work and always hoped to die in harness.

An unfortunate accident in October, 1893, severely shook his constitution and there were signs that his health was beginning to fail. In these circumstances a visit to the South of France was arranged with the object of giving him rest, but there was no serious apprehension that the end was near.

Early in February, 1894, he proceeded with Lady Meade to Costabelle, and after arrival wrote cheerfully of the place and its surroundings. But soon afterwards he became seriously ill and by his doctor's advice was removed to Hyères and such members of his family as could attend were summoned. His brother General J. de C. Meade and his eldest daughter Mrs. Caine and her husband General W. H. Caine hastened to Hyères and were present at the closing scene.

THE END.

The following account has been kindly furnished by Mrs. Caine:—

"We reached Hyères on Wednesday, 14th March, and found my dear father in a most critical state, but quite conscious and calm.

"The serious nature of his illness had, at my mother's wish, been broken to him that morning. He learnt it with perfect fortitude and resignation, and from what passed in the few intervals of consciousness which he had during the five sad days I was with him, and still more from his unconscious words, it was evident that his strong child-like faith in his Heavenly Father never failed him, but was his support through the dark valley.

"The last time his mind was clear he begged the nurse to read prayers, saying, 'We must not forget our duty to God and all His mercies to us, in our great affliction,' and some hours later, when he was evidently quite unconscious to the things of earth, he repeated in very broken accents detached sentences from the General Thanksgiving, the prayer of St. Chrysostom and finally the opening words of the blessing, 'The peace of God which passeth all understanding . . . and the blessing of God Almighty'—after which he scarcely spoke again.

"His gentleness and patience, even when his mind was clouded, much impressed the two Sisters who nursed him, and they both assured us that they felt it had been a privilege to attend the last hours of such a good old man.

"All the last day of his life, Monday (in Passion week), the 19th of March, he seemed to be sleeping with a smile on his face, and so, just after midnight, he passed peacefully and painlessly into the Life Eternal.

"On the 22nd of March, Holy Thursday, in 'the sure and certain hope' of the joyful dawn of the great Last Easter morning, his body was laid to rest, far from his own country and from the lovely valley where his parents and kindred sleep in the shadow of the picturesque ivied ruins of the old church by the Bandon River. He lies, amid the eucalyptus trees and a wilderness of flowers, in the portion reserved for Protestants of the pretty cemetery near Hyères; a spot which, though in a foreign country, seemed strangely familiar to us, for there are perhaps few places in Europe which more vividly recall the East than Hyères.

"And as my mother and I watched the sad little procession—the coffin covered with the Union Jack and wreaths of flowers—pass down the long avenue of date-palms, the sight carried our thoughts back to that distant land where the best years of his life had been passed, and in the welfare of whose people he was to the last deeply interested.

"A white marble cross has been placed over the grave by my mother, and a beautiful stained glass window and marble tablet have been erected to his memory by his family and many friends in the parish church of Innishannon, his birthplace.

"On the tablet is the following inscription:—

In loving memory of
GENERAL SIR RICHARD JOHN MEADE, K.C.S.I., C.I.E.,
Eldest son of Captain John Meade, R.N.,
This Window and Tablet
are placed in the Parish Church of Innishannon, his birthplace,
by relatives and friends who mourn his loss.
Born on the 25th September, 1821,
He entered into Eternal Life on the 20th March, 1894, at Hyères
in the South of France,
where his mortal remains have been laid.

"A gallant soldier and wise administrator, he served his country in many and varied capacities; taking part in the Burmese campaign of 1853-4 and in the Indian Mutiny, when he raised a Regiment of Cavalry, 'Meade's Horse,' afterwards merged in the well-known 'Central India Horse,' with which he was engaged in the actions about Gwalior in June, 1858, and captured the notorious rebel leader, Tantia Topee, the perpetrator of the massacre at Cawnpore. Subsequently he held several high offices as the Representative of the British Government at the Native Courts of Gwalior, Indore, Mysore and Baroda, being specially selected for the important post of Resident at Hyderabad, where, under trying and critical circumstances, he fully maintained the high reputation he had already acquired in other places. His name will ever stand high and be remembered among those who have won and maintained our Empire in the East.

"'Heaven's Light our Guide.'"

CONCLUSION.

We add a few words—to sum up the leading characteristics of the man:—

Of his merits as a military officer it is not for civilians to speak, but his admirable services during the Mutiny, his organisation of "Meade's Horse," his brilliant success and dash in circumventing and capturing Tantia Topi, the most resourceful and ubiquitous, if not the most daring, of all the rebel leaders: his boldness in entering the Gwalior Palace, then in possession of the rebels, at the risk of almost certain death, and inducing them to surrender it to our army without bloodshed or bombardment—are facts which speak for themselves.

As to his character as political officer and administrator, the writer of these pages has some claim to speak, for during the most important period of Sir R. Meade's career, he was, as Foreign Secretary, in constant communication with him, and had access to the official records of his past services.

In these capacities one dominant characteristic of the late Resident at Hyderabad was his reverence for legality.

Some have deservedly won their way to fame by triumphs achieved in spite of rules, or in audacious disregard of orders—a disregard ultimately justified by success.

But Sir Richard Meade was not of this kind. On the contrary he may be described as "splendidly methodical". With every incentive—from position and circumstances and the nature of his work—to irregular methods of procedure, he was methodical and business-like and punctual in everything—except meals!

Not that he was a red-tapist or *routinier;* far from it; he had much of the imagination and genius of a true statesman; but he firmly stood by "rules and regulations" notwithstanding.

Another dominant characteristic was caution. He was deliberate—not slow—in forming an opinion; and was careful to regard the matter from all points of view, except as to its effect upon himself, which was never included in his calculations. But once formed, his opinion was clear and decisive and difficult to shake.

But whatever were his own views he never questioned the deliberate decision of his superiors; though, on one or two occasions, he asked to be relieved of the duty of carrying out a policy which he regarded as disastrous. But this was done from no feeling of personal pique, but solely in the public interests; and, save in these exceptional cases, he thoroughly and carefully carried out orders, even though opposed to his own views.

In a word, he had the rare merit of combining great independence of judgment and originality of view with a scrupulous regard for the instructions he received.

Another characteristic quality of Sir Richard Meade was self-reliance. He never had a "right-hand man," but acted, in all important matters, as his own secretary. At the same time he never committed the mistake of interfering with details properly left to subordinates; but he never appropriated their brains without acknowledgment.

Then his patience was unbounded, not only in dealing with men, but (what is equally important) in carrying out and developing a policy; and he was, further, blest with a serenity of temper most unusual in an Irishman.

Turning, for a moment, to the intellectual side of his character, his despatches, without being laboured or pretentious, were models of clearness, well reasoned and admirably expressed; his official memory (an important item of efficiency) retentive and singularly accurate, and his industry unceasing.

Above all he was the soul of honour, of good sense, courtesy and straightforwardness; and though ready enough to say what was pleasant at the proper time, and full of "benevolence in little things," he had not a trace of *humbug* in his composition.

And it was the rare combination of these moral and mental qualities,—and not any special superiority of attainment, or astuteness, or plausibility, which gave

Meade his strength,—which earned for him the confidence of his superiors and of the chiefs to whom he was accredited, and enabled him to deal successfully with the "Talleyrand of the East".

It would not, indeed, be difficult, in the multitude of distinguished servants of the Crown in India, to point to men of abilities more brilliant and administrators more highly trained; but in the particular branch of the service to which he was attached he was considered by Lord Lytton (no mean judge of diplomatic talent) to be *facile princeps* of the officials of his time.

As for the opinion of his contemporaries and of those under whom he served—that of Lord Lytton is given above.

Lord Canning eulogises his "patience, energy, and tact," and the spirit of "an English gentleman" which marked his conduct of affairs.

Lord Lawrence valued greatly his services in Gwalior and testified to his firm but conciliatory treatment of its Chief.

Lord Mayo spoke of him as a political and administrative officer of the first rank.

Lord Northbrook officially describes him as an officer "whose character for calmness of judgment is well known".

Sindhia regarded him as the saviour of his palace.

Holkar (whose aggressiveness he often had to curb) as "one of his most intimate friends".

Sir Sálár Jang, whose political pretensions it was Meade's duty firmly to oppose, acknowledged his unvarying courtesy, and doubtless appreciated his firmness too.

Sir Mádhava Rao, in a speech from which we have already quoted—a speech delivered in 1881, on the occasion of the enthronement of the Gaekwar (long after Meade had left Baroda)—dwells upon his varied knowledge and vigorous intellect; his indomitable industry; his conscientiousness; calmness of judgment; sincerity; courtesy; absence of ostentation. "He always did," said the speaker, "more than met the eye."

At his farewell dinner at Berlin Sir Edward Malet, our late ambassador, observed that the "best diplomat is the diplomat who is least heard about". Judged by this test Sir Richard must have been a diplomat of the first rank. Few Indian "politicals" have been more trusted by the Government they served or by the Chiefs in whose territories they have represented the Suzerain Power; but until the close of his twenty-two years of political service few were less known to the general public than Sir Richard Meade, yet his work was none the less important or worthy of remembrance; while the map of India, prefixed to this volume, will show at a glance how vast were the territories which came under his control.

Indeed, it may safely be affirmed that, in the long roll of able and upright officers who have, from time to time, represented the justice, the honour, and the civilising influence of England in the Feudatory States of India—officers whose work, though little seen and known, has done more to consolidate the Empire than many battles—few can claim a higher place than the subject of this memoir; for few had such wide experience, few such length of service: none had a higher sense of duty; none discharged it more conscientiously, few so ably, so quietly and so successfully as RICHARD MEADE.

Socially he was among the most courteous and genial of men, and a true friend. His domestic life was singularly happy, and the intense devotion of the members of the family to the memory of him they have lost is touching evidence of his loving and lovable nature.

INDEX.

Note.—M. stands for Sir Richard Meade.

A.

B.

C.

D.

E.

L.

M.

N.

O.

P.

Q.

R.

S.

T.

U, V.

W.

Y.